Expository Thoughts on
The Gospel of Mark

Register This New Book

Benefits of Registering*

- ✓ FREE **replacements** of lost or damaged books
- ✓ FREE **audiobook** – *Pilgrim's Progress,* audiobook edition
- ✓ FREE information about new titles and other **freebies**

www.anekopress.com/new-book-registration

*See our website for requirements and limitations.

Expository Thoughts on
The Gospel of Mark

J. C. Ryle

We love hearing from our readers. Please contact us
at www.anekopress.com/questions-comments with
any questions, comments, or suggestions.

Expository Thoughts on the Gospel of Mark – J. C. Ryle
Revised Edition Copyright © 2020
First edition published 1856

Unless otherwise indicated, scripture quotations are taken from the New American
Standard Bible® (NASB), copyright © 1960, 1962, 1963, 1968, 1971, 1972, 1973, 1975,
1977, 1995 by The Lockman Foundation. Used by permission. www.Lockman.org.

Cover Design: J. Martin
Cover Background: ilolab/Shutterstock
Editors: Sheila Wilkinson; Ruth Clark; Jeremiah Zeiset

Printed in the United States of America
Aneko Press
www.anekopress.com
Aneko Press, Life Sentence Publishing, and our logos are trademarks of
Life Sentence Publishing, Inc.
203 E. Birch Street
P.O. Box 652
Abbotsford, WI 54405

RELIGION / Biblical Commentary / New Testament / Jesus, the Gospels & Acts

Paperback ISBN: 978-1-62245-686-4
eBook ISBN: 978-1-62245-687-1
10 9 8 7 6 5 4 3 2 1
Available where books are sold

Contents

Preface ix	Mark 6:1-6 79
Mark 1:1-8 1	Mark 6:7-13 82
Mark 1:9-20 4	Mark 6:14-29 85
Mark 1:21-34 8	Mark 6:30-34 90
Mark 1:35-39 12	Mark 6:35-46 93
Mark 1:40-45 15	Mark 6:47-56 95
Mark 2:1-12 19	Mark 7:1-13 99
Mark 2:13-22 23	Mark 7:14-23 103
Mark 2:23-28 27	Mark 7:24-30 106
Mark 3:1-12 33	Mark 7:31-37 109
Mark 3:13-21 37	Mark 8:1-13 113
Mark 3:22-30 40	Mark 8:14-21 116
Mark 3:31-35 44	Mark 8:22-26 119
Mark 4:1-20 47	Mark 8:27-33 121
Mark 4:21-25 51	Mark 8:34-38 125
Mark 4:26-29 54	Mark 9:1-13 129
Mark 4:30-34 57	Mark 9:14-29 133
Mark 4:35-41 60	Mark 9:30-37 137
Mark 5:1-17 65	Mark 9:38-50 140
Mark 5:18-20 69	Mark 10:1-12 145
Mark 5:21-34 72	Mark 10:13-16 148
Mark 5:35-43 76	Mark 10:17-27 150

Mark 10:28-34 153

Mark 10:35-45 157

Mark 10:46-52 160

Mark 11:1-11 165

Mark 11:12-21 168

Mark 11:22-26 172

Mark 11:27-33 175

Mark 12:1-12 179

Mark 12:13-17 183

Mark 12:18-27 186

Mark 12:28-34 189

Mark 12:35-44 193

Mark 13:1-8 197

Mark 13:9-13 201

Mark 13:14-23 204

Mark 13:24-31 207

Mark 13:32-37 211

Mark 14:1-9 215

Mark 14:10-16 219

Mark 14:17-25 222

Mark 14:26-31 226

Mark 14:32-42 229

Mark 14:43-52 233

Mark 14:53-65 236

Mark 14:66-72 239

Mark 15:1-15 243

Mark 15:16-32 247

Mark 15:33-38 250

Mark 15:39-47 254

Mark 16:1-8 259

Mark 16:9-14 262

Mark 16:15-18 266

Mark 16:19-20 269

J. C. Ryle – A Brief Biography 273

Other Similar Titles 277

Preface

THE VOLUME NOW IN THE READER'S HANDS is a continuation of a work already commenced by *Expository Thoughts on Matthew*.

The nature of the work has been so fully explained in the preface to the volume on Matthew that it seems unnecessary to say anything on the subject. It may be sufficient to repeat that the reader must not expect to find in these *Expository Thoughts* a learned critical commentary on the Gospels. If he expects this, he will be disappointed. The work before him makes no pretense to being anything more than a continuous series of short, practical expositions. I cannot pretend to say that I have thrown any new light on the difficulties in Mark. But I can honestly say that I have endeavored to put the reader in possession of all that can be said on each difficulty.

In composing these expositions on Mark, I have tried to keep continually before me the threefold objective which I had in view when I first commenced writing on the Gospels. I have endeavored to produce something which may be useful to heads of families in the conduct of family devotions – something which may assist those who visit the poor and desire to read to them – and something which may aid all readers of the Bible in the private study of God's Word. In pursuance of this threefold objective, I have adhered steadily to the leading principles with which I began. I have dwelt principally on the things needful to salvation. I have purposely avoided all topics of minor importance. I have spoken plainly on all subjects and have striven to say nothing which all may not understand.

I cannot expect that the work will satisfy all who want some book to read at family devotions. In fact, I know from communications which I have received that some think the expositions too long. The views of the heads of families as to the length of their family devotions are so exceedingly various that it would be impossible to please one class without displeasing others. In some households the family devotions are so short and hurried that I should despair of writing anything suitable to the master's desires. In such households a few verses of Scripture, read slowly and reverently, would probably be more useful than any commentary at all. As for those who find four pages too much to read at one time and yet desire to read my *Expository Thoughts*, I can only suggest that they have an easy remedy in their own hands. They have only to leave out one or two divisions in each exposition, and they will find it as short as they please.

In preparing for publication of this volume on Mark, I have looked through all those commentaries mentioned in my preface to the volume on Matthew which throw any light on Mark. After careful examination, I feel obliged to say that in my humble judgment very few commentators, whether ancient or modern, seem to give this Gospel the attention it deserves. It has been too often treated as a mere abridgment of Matthew. This view of it I believe to be an entire mistake.

I now send forth these *Expository Thoughts on Mark* with an earnest prayer that it may please God to use the volume for His glory. It has been written under the pressure of many public duties and amid many interruptions. No one is more conscious of its defects than myself. But I can honestly say that my chief desire, if I know anything of my heart, in this and all my writings is to lead my readers to Christ and faith in Him, to repentance and holiness, to the Bible and to prayer.

If these are the results of this volume in any one case, the labor I have bestowed upon it will be more than repaid.

Mark Chapter 1

Mark 1:1-8

The beginning of the gospel of Jesus Christ, the Son of God. As it is written in Isaiah the prophet: "Behold, I send My messenger ahead of You, who will prepare Your way; the voice of one crying in the wilderness, 'Make ready the way of the Lord, make His paths straight.'" John the Baptist appeared in the wilderness preaching a baptism of repentance for the forgiveness of sins. And all the country of Judea was going out to him, and all the people of Jerusalem; and they were being baptized by him in the Jordan River, confessing their sins. John was clothed with camel's hair and wore a leather belt around his waist, and his diet was locusts and wild honey. And he was preaching, and saying, "After me One is coming who is mightier than I, and I am not fit to stoop down and untie the thong of His sandals. I baptized you with water; but He will baptize you with the Holy Spirit."

THE GOSPEL OF MARK, which we now begin, is in some respects unlike the other three Gospels. It tells us nothing about the birth and early life of our Lord Jesus Christ. It contains comparatively few of His sayings and discourses. Of all the four inspired histories of our Lord's earthly ministry, this is by far the shortest.

But we must not allow these peculiarities to make us undervalue Mark's Gospel. It is a Gospel singularly full of precious facts about the Lord Jesus, narrated in a simple, terse, and condensed style. If it tells us few of our Lord's sayings, it is eminently rich in its catalogue of His doings. It often contains minute historical details of deep interest which are wholly omitted in Matthew, Luke, and John. In short, it is no mere abridged copy of Matthew, as some have rashly asserted, but the independent narrative of an independent witness who was inspired to write a history of our Lord's works rather than of His words. Let us read it with holy reverence. Like all the rest of Scripture, every word of Mark is *inspired by God*, and every word is *profitable*.

Let us observe in these verses *what a full declaration we have of the dignity of our Lord Jesus Christ's person*. The very first sentence speaks of Him as *the Son of God*.

These words, *the Son of God*, conveyed far more to Jewish minds than they do to ours. They were nothing less than an assertion of our Lord's divinity. They were a declaration that Jesus was Himself very God and *equal with God* (John 5:18).

There is a beautiful fitness in placing this truth in the very beginning of a Gospel. The divinity of Christ is the citadel and preservation of Christianity. Here lies the infinite value of the atoning sacrifice He made upon the cross. Here lies the peculiar merit of His atoning death for sinners. That death was not the death of a mere man like ourselves, but of one who is *over all, God blessed forever* (Romans 9:5). We need not wonder that the sufferings of one person were a sufficient propitiation for the sin of the world when we remember that He who suffered was *the Son of God*.

Let believers cling to this doctrine with jealous watchfulness. With it, they stand upon a rock. Without it, they have nothing solid beneath their feet. Our hearts are weak. Our sins are many. We need a Redeemer who is able to save to the uttermost and deliver from the wrath to come. We have such a Redeemer in Jesus Christ. He is the *Mighty God* (Isaiah 9:6).

Let us observe, in the second place, *how the beginning of the Gospel was a fulfillment of Scripture*. John the Baptist began his ministry *as it is written in Isaiah the prophet*.

There was nothing unforeseen and suddenly contrived in the coming of Jesus Christ into the world. In the very beginning of Genesis, we find it predicted that *between your seed and her seed, He shall bruise you on the head* (Genesis 3:15). All through the Old Testament we find the same event foretold with constantly increasing clearness. It was a promise often renewed to patriarchs and repeated by prophets that a Deliverer and Redeemer should one day come. His birth, His character, His life, His death, His resurrection, and His forerunner were all prophesied long before He came. Redemption was worked out and accomplished in every step just *as it was written.*

We should always read the Old Testament with a desire to find something in it about Jesus Christ. We study that portion of the Bible with little profit if we can see in it nothing but Moses, and David, and Samuel, and the prophets. Let us search the books of the Old Testament more closely. It was said by Him whose words can never pass away, *"It is these that testify about Me"* (John 5:39).

Let us observe, in the third place, *how great were the effects which the ministry of John the Baptist produced for a time on the Jewish nation.* We are told that *all the country of Judea was going out to him, and all the people of Jerusalem; and they were being baptized by him in the Jordan River.*

The fact here recorded is one that is much overlooked. We are apt to lose sight of him who went before the face of our Lord and to see nothing but the Lord Himself. We forget the morning star in the full blaze of the sun. And yet it is clear that John's preaching arrested the attention of the whole Jewish nation and created an excitement all over Palestine. It aroused the nation from its slumbers and prepared it for the ministry of our Lord when He appeared. Jesus Himself says, *"He was the lamp that was burning and was shining and you were willing to rejoice for a while in his light"* (John 5:35).

We ought to notice here how little dependence is to be placed on what is called "popularity." If ever there was one who was a popular minister for a season, John the Baptist was that man. Yet of all the crowds who came to his baptism and heard his preaching, how few, it may be feared, were converted! Some, we may hope, like Andrew, were guided by John to Christ. But the vast majority in all probability died in their sins. Let us remember this whenever we see a crowded church. A great congregation no doubt is a pleasing sight. But the thought should often come across our minds, How many of these people will reach heaven at last? It is not enough to hear and admire popular preachers. It is no proof of our conversion that we always worship in a place where there is a crowd. Let us take care that we hear the voice of Christ Himself and follow Him.

Let us observe, in the last place, *what clear doctrine characterized John the Baptist's preaching.* He exalted Christ – *"After me One is coming who is mightier than I."* He spoke plainly of the Holy Spirit – *"He will baptize you with the Holy Spirit."*

These truths had never been so plainly proclaimed before by mortal man. More important truths than these are not to be found in the whole system of Christianity at this day. The principal work of every faithful minister of the gospel is to set the Lord Jesus fully before His people and to show them His fullness and His power to save. The next great work he has to do is to set before them the work of the Holy Spirit and the need of being born again and inwardly baptized by His grace. These two mighty truths appear to have been frequently on the lips of John the Baptist. It would be well for the church and the world if there were more ministers like him.

Let us ask ourselves, as we leave the passage, How much do we know by practical experience of the truths which John preached? What do we think of Christ? Have we felt our need of Him and fled to Him for peace? Is He king over our hearts and all things to our souls? What do we think of the Holy Spirit? Has He wrought a saving work in our hearts? Has He renewed and changed them? Has He made us partakers of the divine nature? Life or death depend on our answers to these questions. *If anyone does not have the Spirit of Christ, he does not belong to Him* (Romans 8:9).

Mark 1:9-20

In those days Jesus came from Nazareth in Galilee and was baptized by John in the Jordan. Immediately coming up out of the water, He saw the heavens opening, and the Spirit like a dove descending upon Him; and a voice came out of the heavens: "You are My beloved Son, in You I am well-pleased." Immediately the

Spirit impelled Him to go out into the wilderness. And He was
in the wilderness forty days being tempted by Satan; and He was
with the wild beasts, and the angels were ministering to Him.
Now after John had been taken into custody, Jesus came into
Galilee, preaching the gospel of God, and saying, "The time is ful-
filled, and the kingdom of God is at hand; repent and believe in
the gospel." As He was going along by the sea of Galilee, He saw
Simon and Andrew, the brother of Simon, casting a net in the
sea; for they were fishermen. And Jesus said to them, "Follow Me,
and I will make you become fishers of men." Immediately they
left their nets and followed Him. Going on a little farther, He saw
James the son of Zebedee, and John his brother, who also were in
the boat mending the nets. Immediately He called them; and they
left their father Zebedee in the boat with the hired servants, and
went away to follow Him.

This passage is singularly full of matter. It is a striking instance of that brevity of style which is the peculiar characteristic of Mark's Gospel. The baptism of our Lord, His temptation in the wilderness, the commencement of His preaching, and the calling of His first disciples are related here in twelve verses.

Let us notice, in the first place, *the voice from heaven which was heard at our Lord's baptism.* We read, *A voice came out of the heavens: "You are My beloved Son, in You I am well-pleased."*

That voice was the voice of God the Father. It declared the wondrous and ineffable love which has existed between the Father and the Son from all eternity. *"The Father loves the Son and has given all things into His hand"* (John 3:35). It proclaimed the Father's full and complete approbation of Christ's mission to seek and save the lost. It announced the Father's acceptance of the Son as the Mediator, Substitute, and Surety of the new covenant.

There is a rich mine of comfort in these words for all of Christ's believing members. In themselves and in their own doings they see nothing to please God. They are daily sensible of weakness, shortcomings, and imperfection in all their ways. But let them recollect that the

5

Father regards them as members of His beloved Son Jesus Christ. He sees no blemish in them (Song of Solomon 4:7). He beholds them as *in Christ*, clothed in His righteousness and invested with His merit. They are *accepted in the Beloved*, and when the holy eye of God looks at them, He is *well-pleased*.

Let us notice, in the second place, *the nature of Christ's preaching.* We read that He came saying, *"Repent and believe in the gospel."*

This is that old sermon which all the faithful witnesses of God have continually preached from the very beginning of the world. From Noah down to the present day, the substance of their address has been always the same: *Repent and believe.*

The apostle Paul told the Ephesian elders, when he left them for the last time, that the substance of his teaching among them had been *repentance toward God and faith in our Lord Jesus Christ* (Acts 20:21). He had the best of precedents for such teaching. The great head of the church had given him a pattern. Repentance and faith were the foundation stones of Christ's ministry. Repentance and faith must always be the main subjects of every faithful minister's instruction.

We need not wonder at this if we consider the necessities of human nature. All of us are by nature born in sin and are children of wrath, and all need to repent, be converted, and be born again if we would see the kingdom of God. All of us are by nature guilty and condemned before God, and all must flee to the hope set before us in the gospel and believe in it if we are to be saved. All of us, once penitent, need daily stirring up to deeper repentance. All of us, though believing, need constant exhortation to increased faith.

Let us ask ourselves what we know of this repentance and faith. Have we felt our sins and forsaken them? Have we laid hold on Christ and believed? We may reach heaven without learning, or riches, or health, or worldly greatness. But we shall never reach heaven if we die impenitent and unbelieving. A new heart and a lively faith in a Redeemer are absolutely needful to salvation. May we never rest until we know these things by experience and can call them our own! With them all true Christianity begins in the soul. In the exercise of them consists the life of religion. It is only through the possession of them that men have peace at the last. Church membership and priestly pardon alone save no one. They only die in the Lord who *repent and believe.*

Let us notice, in the third place, *the occupation of those who were first called to be Christ's disciples.* We read that our Lord called Simon and Andrew when they were *casting a net in the sea,* and James and John while they were *mending the nets.*

It is clear from these words that the first followers of our Lord were not the great ones of this world. They were men who had neither riches, nor rank, nor power. But the kingdom of Christ is not dependent on such things as these. His cause advances in the world, *"not by might nor by power, but by My Spirit," says the* LORD *of hosts* (Zechariah 4:6). The words of Paul will always be found true: *There were not many wise according to the flesh, not many mighty, not many noble; but God has chosen the foolish things of the world to shame the wise, and God has chosen the weak things of the world to shame the things which are strong* (1 Corinthians 1:26-27). The church which began with a few fishermen, and yet overspread half the world, must have been founded by God.

We must beware of giving way to the common notion that there is anything disgraceful in being poor and in working with our own hands. The Bible contains many instances of special privileges conferred on working men. Moses was keeping sheep when God appeared to him in the burning bush. Gideon was threshing wheat when the angel brought him a message from heaven. Elisha was ploughing when Elijah called him to be prophet in his stead. The apostles were fishing when Jesus called them to follow Him. It is disgraceful to be covetous, or proud, or a cheat, or a gambler, or a drunkard, or a glutton, or unclean. But it is no disgrace to be poor. The laborer who serves Christ faithfully is far more honorable in God's eyes than the nobleman who serves sin.

Let us notice, in the last place, *the office to which our Lord called His first disciples.* We read that He said, *"Follow Me, and I will make you become fishers of men."*

The meaning of this expression is clear and unmistakable. The disciples were to become fishers for souls. They were to labor to draw men out of darkness into light and from the power of Satan to God. They were to strive to bring men into the net of Christ's church so that they might be saved alive and not perish everlastingly.

We ought to closely observe this expression. It is full of instruction. It is the oldest name by which the ministerial office is described in the New Testament. It lies deeper down than the name of bishop, elder, or deacon. It is the first idea which should be before a minister's mind. He is not to be a mere reader of forms or an administrator of ordinances. He is to be a *fisher* of souls. The minister who does not strive to live up to this name has mistaken his calling.

Does the fisherman strive to catch fish? Does he use all means, and grieve if unsuccessful? The minister ought to do the same. Does the fisherman have patience? Does he toil on day after day, and wait, and work on in hope? Let the minister do the same. Happy is that man in whom the fisherman's skill, and diligence, and patience are all combined!

Let us resolve to pray much for ministers. Their office is no light one if they do their duty. They need the help of many intercessions from all praying people. They have not only their own souls to care for but also the souls of others. No wonder Paul cries, *Who is adequate for these things?* (2 Corinthians 2:16). If we never prayed for ministers before, let us begin to do it this day.

Mark 1:21-34

They went into Capernaum; and immediately on the Sabbath He entered the synagogue and began to teach. They were amazed at His teaching; for He was teaching them as one having authority, and not as the scribes. Just then there was a man in their synagogue with an unclean spirit; and he cried out, saying, "What business do we have with each other, Jesus of Nazareth? Have You come to destroy us? I know who You are—the Holy One of God!" And Jesus rebuked him, saying, "Be quiet, and come out of him!" Throwing him into convulsions, the unclean spirit cried out with a loud voice and came out of him. They were all amazed, so that they debated among themselves, saying, "What

*is this? A new teaching with authority! He commands even the
unclean spirits, and they obey Him." Immediately the news
about Him spread everywhere into all the surrounding district of
Galilee. And immediately after they came out of the synagogue,
they came into the house of Simon and Andrew, with James and
John. Now Simon's mother-in-law was lying sick with a fever;
and immediately they spoke to Jesus about her. And He came to
her and raised her up, taking her by the hand, and the fever left
her, and she waited on them. When evening came, after the sun
had set, they began bringing to Him all who were ill and those
who were demon-possessed. And the whole city had gathered at
the door. And He healed many who were ill with various diseases, and cast out many demons; and He was not permitting the
demons to speak, because they knew who He was.*

These verses begin the long list of miracles which Mark's Gospel contains. They tell us how our Lord cast out devils in Capernaum and
healed Simon's mother-in-law of a fever.

We learn, in the first place from these verses, *the uselessness of a
mere intellectual knowledge of religion.* Twice we are specially told that
the unclean spirits know our Lord. In one place it says *they knew who
He was.* In another, the devil cries out, *"I know who You are—the Holy
One of God!"* They knew Christ when the scribes were ignorant of Him
and the Pharisees would not acknowledge Him. And yet their knowledge was not unto salvation.

The mere belief of the facts and doctrines of Christianity will never
save our souls. Such belief is no better than the belief of devils. They all
believe and know that Jesus is the Christ. They believe that He will one
day judge the world and cast them down to endless torment in hell. It
is a solemn and sorrowful thought that on these points some professing Christians have even less faith than the devil. There are some who
doubt the reality of hell and the eternity of punishment. Such doubts as
these find no place except in the hearts of self-willed men and women.
There is no infidelity among devils. *The demons also believe, and shud-
der* (James 2:19).

9

Let us take heed that our faith be a faith of the heart as well as of the head. Let us see that our knowledge has a sanctifying influence on our affections and our lives. Let us not only know Christ but also love Him from a sense of actual benefit received from Him. Let us not only believe that He is the Son of God and the Savior of the world but also rejoice in Him and cleave to Him with purpose of heart. Let us not only be acquainted with Him by the hearing of the ear but also by daily personal application to Him for mercy and grace. "The life of Christianity," says Luther, "consists in possessive pronouns." It is one thing to say, "Christ is a Savior." It is quite another to say, "He is my Savior and my Lord." The devil can say the first. The true Christian alone can say the second.

We learn, in the second place, *to what remedy a Christian ought to resort first in time of trouble.* He ought to follow the example of the friends of Simon's mother-in-law.[1] We read that when she *was lying sick with a fever,* they *spoke to Jesus about her.*

There is no remedy like this. Means are to be used diligently without question in any time of need. Doctors are to be sent for in sickness. Lawyers are to be consulted when property or character needs defense. The help of friends is to be sought. But still, after all, the first thing to be done is to cry to the Lord Jesus Christ for help. None can relieve us so effectually as He can. None is so compassionate and so willing to relieve. When Jacob was in trouble he turned to his God first – *"Deliver me, I pray, from the hand of my brother, from the hand of Esau"* (Genesis 32:11). When Hezekiah was in trouble, he first spread Sennacherib's letter before the Lord – *"I pray, deliver us from his hand"* (2 Kings 19:19). When Lazarus fell sick, his sisters sent immediately to Jesus – *"Lord,"* they said, *"he whom You love is sick"* (John 11:3). Now let us do likewise. *Cast your burden upon the Lord and He will sustain you* (Psalm 55:22). *Casting all your anxiety on Him* (1 Peter 5:7). *In everything by prayer and supplication with thanksgiving let your requests be made known to God* (Philippians 4:6).

---

1   Let us not fail to observe here that Simon Peter, one of our Lord's principal apostles, had a wife. Yet he was called to be a disciple and afterwards chosen to be an apostle. More than this, we find Paul speaking of him as a married man in his epistle to the Corinthians many years after this (1 Corinthians 9:5).

Let us not only remember this rule but practice it too. We live in a world of sin and sorrow. The days of darkness in a man's life are many. It needs no prophet's eye to foresee that we shall all shed many a tear and feel many a heart-wrench before we die. Let us be armed with a formula against despair before our troubles come. Let us know what to do when sickness, or bereavement, or cross, or loss, or disappointment breaks in upon us like an armed man. Let us do as they did in Simon's house at Capernaum. Let us at once tell the Lord.

We learn, in the last place from these verses, *what a complete and perfect cure the Lord Jesus makes when He heals.* He took the sick woman by the hand and lifted her up, *and the fever left her.* But this was not all. A greater miracle remained behind. At once we are told that *she waited on them.* That weakness and prostration of strength which, as a general rule, a fever leaves behind, in her case was entirely removed. The fevered woman was not only made well in a moment but also in the same moment made strong and able to work.

We may see in this case a lively emblem of Christ's dealing with sin-sick souls. That blessed Savior not only gives mercy and forgiveness, He gives renewing grace besides. To as many as receive Him as their Great Physician, He gives power to become the sons of God. He cleanses them by His Spirit when He washes them in His precious blood. Those whom He justifies, He also sanctifies. When He bestows a pardon, He also bestows a new heart. When He grants free forgiveness for the past, He also grants strength to wait on Him for the time to come. The sin-sick soul is not merely cured and then left to itself. It is also supplied with a new heart and a right spirit and enabled so to live as to please God.

There is comfort in this thought for all who feel a desire to serve Christ but at present are afraid to begin. There are many in this state of mind. They fear that if they come forward boldly and take up the cross, they shall by and by fall away. They fear that they shall not be able to persevere and shall bring discredit on their profession. Let them fear no longer. Let them know that Jesus is an almighty Savior who never forsakes those who once commit themselves to Him. Once raised by His mighty hand from the death of sin and washed in His precious blood, they shall go on serving Him to their life's end. They shall have power to overcome the world, and crucify the flesh, and resist the devil. Only let them begin, and they shall go on. Jesus knows nothing of half-cured cases and half-finished work. Let them trust in Jesus and go forward. The pardoned soul shall always be enabled to serve Christ.

There is comfort here for all who are really serving Christ and are yet cast down by a sense of their own infirmity. There are many in this state of mind. They are oppressed by doubts and anxieties. They sometimes think they shall never reach heaven after all but will be cast away in the wilderness. Let them fear no longer. Their strength shall be according to their day. The difficulties they now fear shall vanish out of their path. The lion in the way which they now dread shall prove to be chained. The same gracious hand which first touched and healed shall uphold, strengthen, and lead them to the end. The Lord Jesus will never lose one of His sheep. Those whom He loves and pardons He loves unto the end. Though sometimes cast down, they shall never be cast away. The healed soul shall always go on waiting on the Lord. Grace shall always lead to glory!

Mark 1:35-39

In the early morning, while it was still dark, Jesus got up, left the house, and went away to a secluded place, and was praying there. Simon and his companions searched for Him; they found Him, and said to Him, "Everyone is looking for You." He said to them, "Let us go somewhere else to the towns nearby, so that I may preach there also; for that is what I came for." And He went into their synagogues throughout all Galilee, preaching and casting out the demons.

Every fact in our Lord's life on earth and every word which fell from His lips ought to be deeply interesting to a true Christian. We see a fact and a saying in the passage we have just read which deserve close attention.

We see, for one thing, *an example of our Lord Jesus Christ's habits of private prayer.* We are told that *in the early morning, while it was still dark, Jesus got up, left the house, and went away to a secluded place, and was praying there.*

We shall find the same thing often recorded of our Lord in the Gospel history. When He was baptized, we are told that *He was praying* (Luke 3:21). When He was transfigured, we are told that *while He was praying, the appearance of His face became different* (Luke 9:29). Before He chose the twelve apostles, we are told that *He spent the whole night in prayer to God* (Luke 6:12). When all men spoke well of Him and would sincerely have made Him king, we are told that *He went up on the mountain by Himself to pray* (Matthew 14:23). When tempted in the garden of Gethsemane, He said, *"Sit here until I have prayed"* (Mark 14:32). In short, our Lord prayed always and did not faint. Sinless as He was, He set us an example of diligent communion with His Father. His Godhead did not render Him independent of the use of all means as a man. His very perfection was a perfection kept up through the exercise of prayer.

We ought to see in all this the immense importance of private devotion. If He who was *holy, innocent, undefiled, separated from sinners* thus prayed continually, how much more ought we who are compassed with infirmity? If He found it needful to offer up supplications with strong crying and tears, how much more needful is it for us who in many things daily offend?

What shall we say to those who never pray at all in the face of such a passage as this? There are many such, it may be feared, in the list of baptized people – many who rise up in the morning without prayer and without prayer lie down at night – many who never speak one word to God. Are they Christians? It is hardly possible to say so. A praying master like Jesus can have no prayerless servants. The Spirit of adoption will always make a man call upon God. To be prayerless is to be Christless, godless, and on the high road to destruction.

What shall we say to those who pray yet give but little time to their prayers? We are obliged to say that they show at present very little of the mind of Christ. Asking little, they must expect to have little. Seeking little, they cannot be surprised if they possess little. It will always be found that when prayers are few, then grace, strength, peace, and hope are small.

We shall do well to watch our habits of prayer with a holy watchfulness. Here is the pulse of our Christianity. Here is the true test of our state before God. Here true religion begins in the soul when it does begin. Here it decays and goes backward when a man backslides from God. Let us walk in the steps of our blessed Master in this respect as well as in every other. Like Him, let us be diligent in our private devotion. Let us know what it is to go away to a secluded place and pray.

We see, for another thing in this passage, *a remarkable saying of our Lord as to the purpose for which He came into the world.* We find Him saying, *"Let us go somewhere else to the towns nearby, so that I may preach there also; for that is what I came for."*

The meaning of these words is plain and unmistakable. Our Lord declares that He came on earth to be a preacher and a teacher. He came to fulfill the prophetical office, to be the prophet greater than Moses who had been so long foretold (Deuteronomy 18:15). He left the glory which He had from all eternity with the Father to do the work of an evangelist. He came down to earth to show to man the way of peace, to proclaim deliverance to the captives and recovery of sight to the blind. One principal part of His work on earth was to go up and down and publish glad tidings, and to offer healing to the brokenhearted, light to those who sat in darkness, and pardon to the chief of sinners. He says, *"That is what I came for."*

We ought to observe here *what infinite honor the Lord Jesus puts on the office of the preacher.* It is an office which the eternal Son of God Himself undertook. He might have spent His earthly ministry in instituting and keeping up ceremonies like Aaron. He might have ruled and reigned as a king like David. But He chose a different calling. Until the time when He died as a sacrifice for our sins, His daily and almost hourly work was to preach. He says, *"That is what I came for."*

Let us never be moved by those who cry down the preacher's office and tell us that sacraments and other ordinances are of more importance than sermons. Let us give to every part of God's public worship its proper place and honor, but let us beware of placing any part of it above preaching. By preaching, the church of Christ was first gathered together, and by preaching, it has ever been maintained in health and prosperity. By preaching, sinners are awakened. By preaching, inquirers are led on. By preaching, saints are built up. By preaching, Christianity is being carried to the heathen world. There are many now who sneer at missionaries and mock those who go out into the highways of our own land to preach to crowds in the open air. But such persons would do well to pause and consider calmly what they are doing. The very work which they ridicule is the work which turned the world upside down and cast heathenism to the ground. Above all, it is the very work which Christ Himself undertook. The King of Kings and Lord of Lords Himself was once a preacher. For three long years He went to and fro proclaiming the gospel. Sometimes we see Him in a house, sometimes on the mountainside, sometimes in a Jewish synagogue, sometimes in a boat on the sea. But the great work He took up was always one and the same. He came always preaching and teaching. He says, *"That is what I came for."*

Let us leave the passage with a solemn resolution never to *despise prophetic utterances* (1 Thessalonians 5:20). The minister we hear may not be highly gifted. The sermons that we listen to may be weak and poor. But after all, preaching is God's grand ordinance for converting and saving souls. The faithful preacher of the gospel is handling the very weapon which the Son of God was not ashamed to employ. This is the work of which Christ has said, *"That is what I came for."*

Mark 1:40-45

And a leper came to Jesus, beseeching Him and falling on his knees before Him, and saying, "If You are willing, You can make me clean." Moved with compassion, Jesus stretched out His hand and touched him, and said to him, "I am willing; be cleansed." Immediately the leprosy left him and he was cleansed. And He sternly warned him and immediately sent him away, and He said to him, "See that you say nothing to anyone; but go, show

*yourself to the priest and offer for your cleansing what Moses
commanded, as a testimony to them." But he went out and began
to proclaim it freely and to spread the news around, to such an
extent that Jesus could no longer publicly enter a city, but stayed
out in unpopulated areas; and they were coming to Him from
everywhere.*

We read in these verses how our Lord Jesus Christ healed a leper. Of
all our Lord's miracles of healing, probably none were more marvelous
than those performed on leprous people. Two cases only have been fully
described in the Gospel history. Of these two, the case before us is one.

Let us try to realize, in the first place, *the dreadful nature of the
disease which Jesus cured.*

Leprosy is a complaint of which we know little or nothing in our
northern climate. In Bible lands it is far more common. It is a disease
which is utterly incurable. It is no mere skin disorder, as some igno-
rantly suppose. It is a radical disease of the whole man. It attacks not
merely the skin but also the blood, the flesh, and the bones until the
unhappy patient begins to lose his extremities and to rot by inches. Let
us remember besides this that among the Jews, the leper was reckoned
unclean and was cut off from the congregation of Israel and the ordinances of religion. He was obliged to dwell in a separate house. None
might touch him or minister to him. Let us remember all this, and then
we may have some idea of the remarkable wretchedness of a leprous
person. To use the words of Aaron when he interceded for Miriam,
he was *like one dead, whose flesh is half eaten away* (Numbers 12:12).

But is there nothing like leprosy among ourselves? Yes! Indeed there
is. There is a foul soul disease which is ingrained into our very nature
and cleaves to our bones and marrow with deadly force. That disease is
the plague of sin. Like leprosy, it is a deep-seated disease infecting every
part of our nature – heart, will, conscience, understanding, memory,
and affections. Like leprosy, it makes us loathsome and abominable,
unfit for the company of God, and unfit for the glory of heaven. Like
leprosy, it is incurable by any earthly physician and is slowly but surely
dragging us down to the second death. And, worst of all, far worse

than leprosy, it is a disease from which no mortal man is exempt. *All of us,* in God's sight, *have become like one who is unclean* (Isaiah 64:6).

Do we know these things? Have we found them out? Have we discovered our own sinfulness, guilt, and corruption? Happy indeed is that person who has been really taught to feel that he is a miserable sinner and that there is *no health in my bones because of my sin* (Psalm 38:3)! Blessed indeed is he who has learned that he is a spiritual leper and a bad, wicked, and sinful creature! To know our disease is one step towards a cure. It is the misery and the ruin of many souls that they never finally saw their sins and their need.

Let us learn, in the second place from these verses, *the wondrous and almighty power of the Lord Jesus Christ.*

We are told that the unhappy leper came to our Lord, *beseeching Him and falling on his knees before Him, and saying, "If You are willing, You can make me clean."* We are told that, *moved with compassion, Jesus stretched out His hand and touched him, and said to him, "I am willing; be cleansed."* At once the cure was effected. That very instant the deadly plague departed from the poor sufferer and he was healed. It was but a word and a touch, and there stands before our Lord not a leper but a sound and healthy man.

Who can conceive the greatness of the change in the feelings of this leper when he found himself healed? The morning sun rose upon him, a miserable being, more dead than alive, his whole frame a mass of sores and corruption, and his very existence a burden. The evening sun saw him full of hope and joy, free from pain, and fit for the society of his fellow men. Surely the change must have been like life from the dead.

Let us bless God that the Savior with whom we have to do is almighty. It is a cheering and comfortable thought that with Christ nothing is impossible. No heart disease is so deep-seated but He is able to cure it. No plague of soul is so virulent but our Great Physician can heal it. Let us never despair of anyone's salvation so long as he lives. The worst of spiritual lepers may yet be cleansed. No cases of spiritual leprosy could be worse than those of Manasseh, Saul of Tarsus, and Zacchaeus, yet they were all cured – Jesus Christ made them whole. The chief of sinners may yet be brought near to God by the blood and Spirit of Christ.

Men are not lost because they are too bad to be saved, but because they will not come to Christ that He may save them.

Let us learn, in the last place from these verses, that *there is a time to be silent about the work of Christ as well as a time to speak.*

This is a truth which is taught us in a remarkable way. We find our Lord strictly charging this man to tell no one of his cure, to *say nothing to anyone.* We find this man in the warmth of his zeal, disobeying this injunction and proclaiming and *spread[ing] the news around* about his cure in every quarter. And we are told that the result was that Jesus *could no longer publicly enter a city, but stayed out in unpopulated areas.*

There is a lesson in all this of deep importance, however difficult it may be to use it rightly. It is clear that there are times when our Lord would have us work for Him quietly and silently rather than attract public attention by a noisy zeal. There is a zeal which is *not in accordance with knowledge* as well as a zeal which is righteous and praiseworthy. Everything is beautiful in its season. Our Master's cause may on some occasions be more advanced by quietness and patience than in any other way. We are not to *give what is holy to dogs* nor *throw [our] pearls before swine.* By forgetfulness of this we may even do more harm than good and hinder the very cause we want to assist.

The subject is a delicate and difficult one without doubt. Unquestionably the majority of Christians are far more inclined to be silent about their glorious Master than to confess Him before men, and do not need the bridle so much as the spur. But still it is undeniable that there is a time for all things, and to know the time should be one great aim of a Christian. There are good men who have more zeal than discretion and even help the enemy of truth by unseasonable acts and words.

Let us all pray for the spirit of wisdom and of a sound mind. Let us seek daily to know the path of duty and ask daily for discretion and good sense. Let us be bold as a lion in confessing Christ and not be afraid to speak of Him before princes if need be. But let us never forget that *wisdom has the advantage of giving success* (Ecclesiastes 10:10), and let us beware of doing harm by an ill-directed zeal.

Mark Chapter 2

Mark 2:1-12

When He had come back to Capernaum several days afterward, it was heard that He was at home. And many were gathered together, so that there was no longer room, not even near the door; and He was speaking the word to them. And they came, bringing to Him a paralytic, carried by four men. Being unable to get to Him because of the crowd, they removed the roof above Him; and when they had dug an opening, they let down the pallet on which the paralytic was lying. And Jesus seeing their faith said to the paralytic, "Son, your sins are forgiven." But some of the scribes were sitting there and reasoning in their hearts, "Why does this man speak that way? He is blaspheming; who can forgive sins but God alone?" Immediately Jesus, aware in His spirit that they were reasoning that way within themselves, said to them, "Why are you reasoning about these things in your hearts? Which is easier, to say to the paralytic, 'Your sins are forgiven'; or to say, 'Get up, and pick up your pallet and walk'? But so that you may know that the Son of Man has authority on earth to forgive sins"—He said to the paralytic, "I say to you, get up, pick up your pallet and go home." And he got up and immediately picked up the pallet and went out in the sight of everyone, so that they were all amazed and were glorifying God, saying, "We have never seen anything like this."

THIS PASSAGE SHOWS OUR LORD ONCE MORE AT CAPERNAUM. Once more we find Him doing His accustomed work, preaching the Word, and healing those who were sick.

We see in these verses *what great spiritual privileges some people enjoy and yet make no use of them.*

This is a truth which is strikingly illustrated by the history of Capernaum. No city in Palestine appears to have enjoyed so much of our Lord's presence during His earthly ministry as did this city. It was the place where He dwelt after He left Nazareth (Matthew 4:13). It was the place where many of His miracles were worked and many of His sermons delivered. But nothing that Jesus said or did seems to have had any effect on the hearts of the inhabitants. They crowded to hear Him, as we read in this passage, until *there was no longer room, not even near the door.* They were amazed. They were astonished. They were filled with wonder at His mighty works. But they were not converted. They lived in the full noontide blaze of the Sun of Righteousness, and yet their hearts remained hard. And they drew from our Lord the heaviest condemnation that He ever pronounced against any place, except Jerusalem – *"And you, Capernaum, will not be exalted to heaven, will you? You will descend to Hades; for if the miracles had occurred in Sodom which occurred in you, it would have remained to this day. Nevertheless I say to you that it will be more tolerable for the land of Sodom in the day of judgment, than for you"* (Matthew 11:23-24).

It is good for us to closely observe this case of Capernaum. We are all apt to suppose that nothing is needed but the powerful preaching of the gospel to convert people's souls, and that if the gospel is only brought into a place, everybody must believe. We forget the amazing power of unbelief and the depth of man's enmity against God. We forget that the Capernaites heard the most faultless preaching and saw it confirmed by the most surprising miracles and yet remained dead in trespasses and sins. We need reminding that the same gospel which is the savor of life to some is the savor of death to others, and that the same fire which softens the wax will also harden the clay. Nothing, in fact, seems to harden man's heart so much as to hear the gospel regularly and yet deliberately prefer the service of sin and the world. Never was there a people so highly favored as the people of Capernaum, and never was there a people who appear to have become so hard. Let us beware of walking in their steps. We ought often to use the prayer of the Litany, "From hardness of heart, good Lord, deliver us."

We see, in the second place from these verses, *how great a blessing affliction may prove to be to a man's soul.*

We are told that one paralyzed was brought to our Lord at Capernaum in order to be healed. Helpless and impotent, he was carried on his bed by four kind friends and let down into the midst of the place where Jesus was preaching. At once the object of the man's desire was gained. The Great Physician of soul and body saw him and gave him speedy relief. He restored him to health and strength. He granted him the far greater blessing of forgiveness of sins. In short, the man who had been carried from his house that morning – weak, dependent, and bowed down both in body and soul – returned to his own house rejoicing.

Who can doubt that to the end of his days this man would thank God for his paralysis? Without it he might probably have lived and died in ignorance and have never seen Christ at all. Without it he might have kept his sheep on the green hills of Galilee all his life long and never have been brought to Christ and never have heard these blessed words, *"Your sins are forgiven."* That paralysis was indeed a blessing. Who can tell but it was the beginning of eternal life to his soul?

How many in every age can testify that this paralyzed man's experience has been their own! They have learned wisdom by affliction. Bereavements have proved mercies. Losses have proved real gains. Sicknesses have led them to the Great Physician of souls, sent them to the Bible, shut out the world, shown them their own foolishness, and taught them to pray. Thousands can say like David, *It is good for me that I was afflicted, that I may learn Your statutes* (Psalm 119:71).

Let us beware of murmuring under affliction. We may be sure there is a needs-be for every cross and a wise reason for every trial. Every sickness and sorrow is a gracious message from God and is meant to call us nearer to Him. Let us pray that we may learn the lesson that each affliction is appointed to convey. Let us see that we *do not refuse Him who is speaking.*

We see, in the last place in these verses, *the priestly power of forgiving sins which is possessed by our Lord Jesus Christ.*

21

We read that our Lord said to the paralytic, *"Son, your sins are forgiven."* He said these words with a meaning. He knew the hearts of the scribes by whom He was surrounded. He intended to show them that He laid claim to be the true High Priest and to have the power of pardoning sinners, though at present the claim was seldom put forward. But that He had the power He told them expressly. He says, *"The Son of man has authority on earth to forgive sins."* In saying, *"Your sins are forgiven,"* He had only exercised His rightful office.

Let us consider how great must be the authority of Him who has the power to forgive sins! This is the thing that none can do but God. No angel in heaven, no man upon earth, no church in council, no minister of any denomination can take away from the sinner's conscience the load of guilt and give him peace with God. They may point to the fountain open for all sin. They may declare with authority whose sins God is willing to forgive. But they cannot pardon by their own authority. They cannot put away transgressions. This is the peculiar prerogative of God and a prerogative which He has put in the hands of His Son Jesus Christ.

Let us think for a moment how great a blessing it is that Jesus is our Great High Priest and that we know where to go for pardon! We must have a priest and a sacrifice between ourselves and God. Conscience demands an atonement for our many sins. God's holiness makes it absolutely needful. Without an atoning priest, there can be no peace of soul. Jesus Christ is the very High Priest that we need, mighty to forgive and pardon, tenderhearted, and willing to save.

And now let us ask ourselves whether we have yet known the Lord Jesus as our High Priest. Have we applied to Him? Have we sought forgiveness? If not, we are yet in our sins. May we never rest until the Spirit witnesses with our spirit that we have sat at the feet of Jesus and heard His voice saying, *"Son, your sins are forgiven."*

Mark 2:13-22

And He went out again by the seashore; and all the people were coming to Him, and He was teaching them. As He passed by, He saw Levi the son of Alphaeus sitting in the tax booth, and He said to him, "Follow Me!" And he got up and followed Him. And it happened that He was reclining at the table in his house, and many tax collectors and sinners were dining with Jesus and His disciples; for there were many of them, and they were following Him. When the scribes of the Pharisees saw that He was eating with the sinners and tax collectors, they said to His disciples, "Why is He eating and drinking with tax collectors and sinners?" And hearing this, Jesus said to them, "It is not those who are healthy who need a physician, but those who are sick; I did not come to call the righteous, but sinners." John's disciples and the Pharisees were fasting; and they came and said to Him, "Why do John's disciples and the disciples of the Pharisees fast, but Your disciples do not fast?" And Jesus said to them, "While the bridegroom is with them, the attendants of the bridegroom cannot fast, can they? So long as they have the bridegroom with them, they cannot fast. But the days will come when the bridegroom is taken away from them, and then they will fast in that day. No one sews a patch of unshrunk cloth on an old garment; otherwise the patch pulls away from it, the new from the old, and a worse tear results. No one puts new wine into old wineskins; otherwise the wine will burst the skins, and the wine is lost and the skins as well; but one puts new wine into fresh wineskins."

The person who is called Levi at the beginning of this passage is the same person who is called Matthew in the first of the four Gospels. Let us not forget this. It is no less than an apostle and an evangelist whose early history is now before our eyes.

We learn from these verses *the power of Christ to call men out from the world and make them His disciples.* We read that He said to Levi while he was *sitting in the tax booth,* "Follow Me!" And at once *he got up and followed Him.* From a tax collector he became an apostle and a writer of the first book in the New Testament which is now known all over the world.

This is a truth of deep importance. Without a divine call no one can be saved. We are all so sunk in sin, and so wedded to the world, that we would never turn to God and seek salvation unless He first called us by His grace. God must speak to our hearts by His Spirit before we shall ever speak to Him. Those who are sons of God, says the seventeenth Article in the Church of England's *Articles of Religion*, are "called according to God's purpose by His Spirit working in due season." Now how blessed is the thought that this calling of sinners is committed to so gracious a Savior as Christ!

When the Lord Jesus calls a sinner to be His servant, He acts as a sovereign, but He acts with infinite mercy. He often chooses those who seem most unlikely to do His will and furthest off from His kingdom. He draws them to Himself with almighty power, breaks the chains of old habits and customs, and makes them new creatures. As the magnet attracts the iron, and the south wind softens the frozen ground, so does Christ's calling draw sinners out from the world and melt the hardest heart. The voice of the Lord is mighty in operation. Blessed are they who, when they hear it, harden not their hearts!

We ought never to despair entirely of anyone's salvation when we read this passage of Scripture. He who called Levi still lives and still works. The age of miracles is not yet past. The love of money is a powerful principle, but the call of Christ is more powerful. Let us not despair even about those who are *sitting in the tax booth* and enjoying an abundance of this world's good things. The voice which said to Levi, *"Follow Me!"* may yet reach their hearts. We may yet see them arise and take up their cross and follow Christ. Let us hope continually and pray for others. Who can tell what God may be going to do for anyone around us? No one is too bad for Christ to call. Let us pray for all.

We learn, for another thing from these verses, that *one of Christ's principal offices is that of the Great Physician.* The scribes and Pharisees found fault with Him for eating and drinking with tax collectors and sinners. But *hearing this, Jesus said to them, "It is not those who are healthy who need a physician, but those who are sick."*

The Lord Jesus did not come into the world, as some suppose, to be nothing more than a lawgiver, a king, a teacher, and an example. Had this been all the purpose of His coming, there would have been small comfort for man. Diet regimens and rules of health are all very well for the convalescent, but not suitable to the man laboring under a mortal disease. A teacher and an example might be sufficient for an unfallen being like Adam in the garden of Eden. But fallen sinners like ourselves need healing first, before we can value rules.

The Lord Jesus came into the world to be a physician as well as a teacher. He knew the necessities of human nature. He saw us all sick of a mortal disease, stricken with the plague of sin, and dying daily. He pitied us and came down to bring divine medicine for our relief. He came to give health and cure to the dying, to heal the brokenhearted, and to offer strength to the weak. No sin-sick soul is too far gone for Him. It is His glory to heal and restore to life the most desperate cases. For unfailing skill, for unwearied tenderness, for long experience of man's spiritual ailments, the Great Physician of souls stands alone. There is none like Him.

But what do we know ourselves of this special office of Christ? Have we ever felt our spiritual sickness and applied to Him for relief? We are never right in the sight of God until we do. We know nothing aright in religion if we think the sense of sin should keep us back from Christ. To feel our sins and know our sickness is the beginning of real Christianity. To be sensible of our corruption and abhor our own transgressions is the first symptom of spiritual health. Happy indeed are they who have found out their soul's disease! Let them know that Christ is the very physician they require, and let them apply to Him without delay.

We learn, in the last place from these verses, that *in religion it is worse than useless to attempt to mix things which essentially differ.* "No one," He tells the Pharisees, "*sews a patch of unshrunk cloth on an old garment.*" "*No one puts new wine into old wineskins.*"

These words, we must of course see, were a parable. They were spoken with a special reference to the question which the Pharisees had just raised – *"Why do John's disciples and the disciples of the Pharisees fast, but Your disciples do not fast?"* Our Lord's reply evidently means that to enforce fasting among His disciples would be inexpedient and unseasonable. His little flock was as yet young in grace and weak in faith, knowledge, and experience. They must be led on softly and not burdened at this early stage with requirements which they were not able to bear. Fasting, moreover, might be suitable to the disciples of him who was only the Bridegroom's friend, who lived in the wilderness, preached the baptism of repentance, was clothed in camel's hair, and ate locusts and wild honey. But fasting was not equally suitable to the disciples of Him who was the Bridegroom Himself, brought glad tidings to sinners, and came living like other men. In short, to require fasting of His disciples at present would be putting *new wine into old wineskins.* It would be trying to mingle and amalgamate things that essentially differed.

The principle laid down in these two little parables is one of great importance. It is a kind of proverbial saying and admits of a wide application. Forgetfulness of it has frequently done great harm in the church. The evils that have arisen from trying to sew the new patch on the old garment and put the new wine into old wineskins have been neither few nor small.

How was it with the Galatian church? It is recorded in Paul's epistle. Men wished in that church to reconcile Judaism with Christianity and to circumcise as well as baptize. They endeavored to keep alive the law of ceremonies and ordinances and to place it side by side with the gospel of Christ. In fact, they would gladly have put the *new wine into old wineskins.* And in so doing, they greatly erred.

How was it with the early Christian church after the apostles were dead? We have it recorded in the pages of church history. Some tried to make the gospel more acceptable by mingling it with human philosophy. Some labored to recommend it to the heathen by borrowing forms, processions, and vestments from the temples of heathen gods. In short, they sewed the patch of unshrunk cloth on the old garment. And in so doing they scattered the seeds of enormous evil! They paved the way for the whole Romish apostasy!

How is it with many professing Christians in the present day? We have only to look around us and see. There are thousands who are trying to reconcile the service of Christ and the service of the world, to have the name of *Christian* and yet live the life of the ungodly, and to keep in with the servants of pleasure and sin and yet be the followers of the crucified Jesus at the same time. In a word, they are trying to enjoy the *new wine* and yet cling to the *old wineskins*. They will find one day that they have attempted that which cannot be done!

Let us leave the passage in a spirit of serious self-inquiry. It is one which ought to raise great searchings of heart in the present day. Have we never read what the Scripture says? *"No one can serve two masters." "You cannot serve God and wealth."* Let us place side by side with these texts the concluding words of our Lord in this passage: *"One puts new wine into fresh wineskins."*[2]

Mark 2:23-28

And it happened that He was passing through the grainfields on the Sabbath, and His disciples began to make their way along while picking the heads of grain. The Pharisees were saying to Him, "Look, why are they doing what is not lawful on the Sabbath?" And He said to them, "Have you never read what David did when he was in need and he and his companions became hungry; how he entered the house of God in the time of Abiathar the high priest, and ate the consecrated bread, which is not lawful for anyone to eat except the priests, and he also gave it to those who were with him?" Jesus said to them, "The Sabbath was made for man, and not man for the Sabbath. So the Son of Man is Lord even of the Sabbath."

These verses set before us a remarkable scene in our Lord Jesus Christ's

---

2   It must always be remembered that the *wineskins* here spoken of were not bottles of glass or of earthenware, but were containers made of leather. Unless this is kept in view, the parable is unintelligible to an English mind. A similar remark applies to David's words, *Though I have become like a wineskin in the smoke* (Psalm 119:83).

earthly ministry. We see our blessed Master and His disciples *passing through the grainfields on the Sabbath*. We are told that His disciples *began to make their way along while picking the heads of grain*. At once we hear the Pharisees accusing them to our Lord, as if they had committed some great moral offense. *"Why are they doing what is not lawful on the Sabbath?"* They received an answer full of deep wisdom, which all should study well who desire to understand the subject of Sabbath observance.

We see from these verses *what extravagant importance is attached to trifles by those who are mere formalists in religion.*

The Pharisees were mere formalists, if there ever were any in the world. They seem to have thought exclusively of the outward part – the husk, the shell, and the form of religion. They even added to these externals traditions of their own. Their godliness was made up of washings, fastings, peculiarities in dress, and will-worship, while repentance, faith, and holiness were comparatively overlooked.

The Pharisees would probably have found no fault if the disciples had been guilty of some offense against the moral law. They would have winked at covetousness, or perjury, or extortions, or excess, because those were sins to which they themselves were inclined. But no sooner did they see an infringement on their man-made traditions about the right way of keeping the Sabbath than they raised an outcry and found fault.

Let us watch and pray lest we fall into the error of the Pharisees. There are never lacking professors who walk in their steps. There are thousands at the present day who plainly think more of the mere outward form of religion than of its doctrines. They make more ado about keeping saints' days, and turning to the east in the creed, and bowing at the name of Jesus than about repentance, or faith, or separation from the world. Against this spirit let us ever be on our guard. It can neither comfort, satisfy, nor save.

It ought to be a settled principle in our minds that a man's soul is in a bad state when he begins to regard man-made rites and ceremonies as things of superior importance and exalts them above the preaching of the gospel. It is a symptom of spiritual disease. There is mischief within. It is too often the resource of an uneasy conscience. The first steps of apostasy from Protestantism to Romanism have often been in this direction. No wonder that Paul said to the Galatians, *You observe days and months and seasons and years. I fear for you, that perhaps I have labored over you in vain* (Galatians 4:10-11).

We see, in the second place from these verses, *the value of a knowledge of Holy Scripture.*

Our Lord replies to this accusation of the Pharisees by a reference to Holy Scripture. He reminds His enemies of the conduct of David *when he was in need and he and his companions became hungry. "Have you never read what David did?"* They could not deny that the writer of the book of Psalms, and the man after God's own heart, was not likely to set a bad example. They knew in fact that he had not turned aside from God's commandment all the days of his life, *except in the case of Uriah the Hittite* (1 Kings 15:5). Yet what had David done? He had gone into the house of God, when pressed by hunger, and had eaten *the consecrated bread, which is not lawful for anyone to eat except the priests.* He had thus shown that some requirements of God's laws might be relaxed in case of necessity. To this scriptural example our Lord refers His adversaries. They found nothing to reply to it. The sword of the Spirit was a weapon which they could not resist. They were silenced and put to shame.

Now the conduct of our Lord on this occasion ought to be a pattern for all His people. Our grand reason for our faith and practice should always be "Thus it is written in the Bible." *What does the Scripture say?* We should endeavor to have the Word of God on our side in all debatable questions. We should seek to be able to give a scriptural answer for our behavior in all matters of dispute. We should refer our enemies to the Bible as our rule of conduct. We shall always find a plain text the most powerful argument we can use. In a world like this, we must expect our opinions to be attacked if we serve Christ, and we may be sure that nothing silences adversaries so soon as a quotation from Scripture.

Let us remember, however, that if we are to use the Bible as our Lord did, we must know it well and be acquainted with its contents. We must read it diligently, humbly, perseveringly, and prayerfully, or we shall never find its texts coming to our aid in the time of need. To use the sword of the Spirit effectually, we must be familiar with it and have it often in our hands. There is no royal road to the knowledge of the Bible. It does not come to man by intuition. The Book must be studied, pondered, prayed over, searched into, and not left always lying on a shelf or carelessly looked at now and then. It is the students of the Bible, and they alone, who will find it a weapon ready in hand in the day of battle.

We see, in the last place from these verses, the *true principle by which all questions about the observance of the Sabbath ought to be decided.* "*The Sabbath*," says our Lord, "*was made for man, and not man for the Sabbath.*"

There is a mine of deep wisdom in those words. They deserve close attention, and all the more because they are not recorded in any Gospel but that of Mark. Let us see what they contain.

The Sabbath was made for man. God made it for Adam in Paradise and renewed it to Israel on Mount Sinai. It was made for all mankind – not for the Jew only, but also for the whole family of Adam. It was made for man's benefit and happiness. It was for the good of his body, the good of his mind, and the good of his soul. It was given to him as a benefit and a blessing and not as a burden. This was the original institution.

But man was not made for the Sabbath. The observance of the day of God was never meant to be so enforced as to be an injury to his health or to interfere with his necessary requirements. The original command to keep the Sabbath day holy was not intended to be so interpreted as to do harm to his body or prevent acts of mercy to his fellow creatures. This was the point that the Pharisees had forgotten or buried under their traditions.

There is nothing in all this to warrant the rash assertion of some that our Lord has done away with the fourth commandment. On the contrary, He manifestly speaks of the Sabbath day as a privilege and a gift, and only regulates the extent to which its observance should be enforced. He shows that works of necessity and mercy may be done on the Sabbath day, but He says not a word to justify the notion that Christians need not *remember the sabbath day, to keep it holy.*

Let us be jealous over our own conduct in the matter of observing the Sabbath. There is little danger of the day being kept too strictly in the present age. There is far more danger of its being profaned and forgotten entirely. Let us contend earnestly for its preservation among us in all its integrity. We may rest assured that national prosperity and personal growth in grace are intimately bound up in the maintenance of a holy Sabbath.[3]

---

3   The concluding words of the passage now expounded are remarkable. The true meaning appears to be that our Lord claims the right to dispense with all the traditional rules and man-made laws about the Sabbath with which the Pharisees had overloaded the day of rest. As the Son of Man who came not to destroy but to save, He asserts His power to set free the blessed Sabbath from the false and superstitious notions with which the rabbis had clogged and poisoned it and to restore it to its proper meaning and use. He declares that the Sabbath is His day – His by creation and institution, since He first gave it in Paradise and at Sinai – and proclaims His determination to defend and purify His day from Jewish imposition, and to give it to His disciples as a day of blessing, comfort, and benefit, according to its original intention. According to Meyer's Commentary (1631), "It is certain that Christ, being a perfect pattern of doctrine in all things, did not transgress or maintain any transgression against any law of God. Wherefore it is to be held that all His speech here tended to nothing else but to convince the Pharisees of blindness and ignorance touching the right keeping of the Sabbath according to the commandment, it being never required to rest so strictly as they thought."

Mark Chapter 3

Mark 3:1-12

He entered again into a synagogue; and a man was there whose hand was withered. They were watching Him to see if He would heal him on the Sabbath, so that they might accuse Him. He said to the man with the withered hand, "Get up and come forward!" And He said to them, "Is it lawful to do good or to do harm on the Sabbath, to save a life or to kill?" But they kept silent. After looking around at them with anger, grieved at their hardness of heart, He said to the man, "Stretch out your hand." And he stretched it out, and his hand was restored. The Pharisees went out and immediately began conspiring with the Herodians against Him, as to how they might destroy Him. Jesus withdrew to the sea with His disciples; and a great multitude from Galilee followed; and also from Judea, and from Jerusalem, and from Idumea, and beyond the Jordan, and the vicinity of Tyre and Sidon, a great number of people heard of all that He was doing and came to Him. And He told His disciples that a boat should stand ready for Him because of the crowd, so that they would not crowd Him; for He had healed many, with the result that all those who had afflictions pressed around Him in order to touch Him. Whenever the unclean spirits saw Him, they would fall down before Him and shout, "You are the Son of God!" And He earnestly warned them not to tell who He was.

THESE VERSES SHOW US OUR LORD again working a miracle. He heals a man in the synagogue who had *the withered hand.* Always about His Father's business, always doing good – doing it in the sight of enemies as well as friends – such was the daily tenor of our Lord's earthly ministry. And He left *an example for [us] to follow in His steps* (1 Peter 2:21). Blessed indeed are those Christians who strive, however feebly, to imitate their Master!

Let us observe in these verses *how our Lord Jesus Christ was watched by His enemies.* We read that *they were watching Him to see if He would heal him on the Sabbath, so that they might accuse Him.*

What a sad proof we have here of the wickedness of human nature! It was the Sabbath day when these things happened. It was in the synagogue where men were assembled to hear the Word and worship God. Yet even on the day of God and at the time of worshiping God, these wretched formalists were plotting mischief against our Lord. The very men who pretended to such strictness and sanctity in little things were full of malicious and angry thoughts in the midst of the congregation (Proverbs 5:14).

Christ's people must not expect to fare better than their Master. They are always watched by an ill-natured and spiteful world. Their conduct is scanned with a keen and jealous eye. Their ways are noted and diligently observed. They are marked men. They can do nothing without the world noticing it. Their dress, their expenditure, their employment of time, their conduct in all the relations of life are all rigidly observed. Their adversaries wait for their halting, and if at any time they fall into an error, the ungodly rejoice.

It is good for all Christians to keep this before their minds. Wherever we go and whatever we do, let us remember that, like our Master, we are watched. The thought should make us exercise a holy jealousy over all our conduct that we may do nothing to cause the enemy to blaspheme. It should make us diligent to avoid even the appearance of evil. Above all, it should make us pray much to be kept blameless in our tempers, tongues, and daily public demeanor. That Savior who was watched Himself knows how to sympathize with His people and to supply grace to help in time of need.

Let us observe, in the second place, *the great principle that our Lord lays down about Sabbath observance.* He teaches that it is lawful *to do good* on the Sabbath.

This principle is taught by a remarkable question. He asks those around Him whether it was *lawful to do good or to do harm on the Sabbath, to save a life or to kill.* Was it better to heal this poor sufferer before Him with the withered hand or to leave him alone? Was it more sinful to restore a person to health on the Sabbath than to plot murder and nourish hatred against an innocent person, as they were doing at that moment against Him? Was He to be blamed for saving a life on the Sabbath? Were they blameless who were desirous to kill? No wonder that before such a question as this, our Lord's enemies held their peace.

It is plain from these words of our Lord that no Christian need ever hesitate to do a really good work on Sunday. A real work of mercy, such as ministering to the sick or relieving pain, may always be done without scruple. The holiness with which the fourth commandment invests the Sabbath day is not in the least degree invaded by anything of this kind.

But we must take care that the principle here laid down by our Lord is not abused and turned to bad account. We must not allow ourselves to suppose that the permission to do good implied that everyone might find his own pleasure on the Sabbath. The permission to do good was never meant to open the door to amusements, worldly festivities, traveling, journeying, and sensual gratification. It was never intended to license the Sunday railway train, or the Sunday steamboat, or the Sunday exhibition. These things do good to none and do certain harm to many. They rob many a servant of his seventh day's rest. They turn the Sunday of thousands into a day of hard toil. Let us beware of perverting our Lord's words from their proper meaning. Let us remember what kind of "doing good on the Sabbath" His blessed example sanctioned. Let us ask ourselves whether there is the slightest likeness between our Lord's works on the Sabbath and those ways of spending the Sabbath for which many contend, who yet dare to appeal to our Lord's example. Let us fall back on the plain meaning of our Lord's words and take our stand on them. He gives us liberty to do good on Sunday; but for feasting, sightseeing, party-giving, and excursions, He gives no liberty at all.

Let us observe, in the last place, *the feelings which the conduct of our*

Lord's enemies called forth in His heart. We are told that He *look[ed] around at them with anger, grieved at their hardness of heart.*

This expression is very remarkable and demands special attention. It is meant to remind us that our Lord Jesus Christ was a man like ourselves in all things, sin only excepted. Whatever sinless feelings belong to the constitution of man, our Lord partook of and knew by experience. We read that He *marveled,* that He *rejoiced,* that He *wept,* that He *loved,* and here we read that He felt *anger.*

It is plain from these words that there is an anger which is lawful, right, and not sinful. There is an indignation which is justifiable and on some occasions may be properly manifested. *Be angry, and yet do not sin* (Ephesians 4:26).

Yet it must be confessed that the subject is full of difficulty. Of all the feelings that man's heart experiences, there is none perhaps which so soon runs into sin as the feeling of anger. There is none which once excited seems less under control. There is none which leads on to so much evil. The length to which ill temper, irritability, and passion will carry even godly men, all must know. The history of the contention between Paul and Barnabas at Antioch and the story of Moses being provoked until he spoke unadvisedly with his lips are familiar to every Bible reader. The dreadful fact that passionate words are a breach of the sixth commandment is plainly taught in the Sermon on the Mount. And yet here we see that there is anger which is lawful.

Let us leave this subject with an earnest prayer that we may all be enabled to take heed to our spirit in the matter of anger. We may rest assured that there is no human feeling which needs so much cautious guarding as this. A sinless wrath is a very rare thing. The wrath of man is seldom for the glory of God. In every case a righteous indignation should be mingled with grief and sorrow for those who cause it, even as it was in the case of our Lord. And this, at all events, we may be sure of: it is better never to be angry than to be angry and sin.

Mark 3:13-21

And He went up on the mountain and summoned those whom
He Himself wanted, and they came to Him. And He appointed
twelve, so that they would be with Him and that He could
send them out to preach, and to have authority to cast out the
demons. And He appointed the twelve: Simon (to whom He
gave the name Peter), and James, the son of Zebedee, and John
the brother of James (to them He gave the name Boanerges,
which means, "Sons of Thunder"); and Andrew, and Philip, and
Bartholomew, and Matthew, and Thomas, and James the son
of Alphaeus, and Thaddaeus, and Simon the Zealot; and Judas
Iscariot, who betrayed Him. And He came home, and the crowd
gathered again, to such an extent that they could not even eat a
meal. When His own people heard of this, they went out to take
custody of Him; for they were saying, "He has lost His senses."

The beginning of this passage describes the appointment of the twelve apostles. It is an event in our Lord's earthly ministry which should always be read with deep interest. What a vast amount of benefit these few men have conferred on the world! The names of a few Jewish fishermen are known and loved by millions all over the globe, while the names of many kings and rich men are lost and forgotten. It is those who do good to souls who *will be remembered forever* (Psalm 112:6).

Let us notice in these verses *how many of the twelve who are here named had been called to be disciples before they were ordained apostles.*

There are six at least, out of the number, whose first call to follow Christ is specially recorded. These six are Peter and Andrew, James and John, and Philip and Matthew. In short, there can be little doubt that eleven of our Lord's apostles were converted before they were ordained.

It ought to be the same with all ministers of the gospel. They ought to be men who have been first called by the Spirit before they are set apart for the great work of teaching others. The rule should be the same with them as with the apostles – first converted, then ordained.

It is impossible to overrate the importance of this to the interests of true religion. Bishops and presbyteries can never be too strict and particular in the inquiries they make about the spiritual character of candidates for orders. An unconverted minister is utterly unfit for his office. How can he speak experientially of that grace which he has never tasted himself? How can he commend that Savior to his people whom he himself only knows by name? How can he urge on souls the need of that conversion and new birth which he himself has not experienced? Miserably mistaken are those parents who persuade their sons to become clergymen in order to obtain a good living or follow a respectable profession! What is it but persuading them to say what is not true and to take the Lord's name in vain! None do such injury to the cause of Christianity as unconverted, worldly ministers. They are a support to the infidel, a joy to the devil, and an offense to God.

Let us notice, in the second place, *the nature of the office to which the apostles were ordained.* They were to *be with Him.* They were to be sent *out to preach.* They were to *cast out the demons.*

These three points deserve attention. They contain much instruction. Our Lord's twelve apostles, beyond doubt, were a distinct order of men. They had no successors when they died. Strictly and literally speaking, there is no such thing as apostolic succession. No man can be really called a successor of the apostles unless he can work miracles and teach infallibly as they did. But still, in saying this, we must not forget that in many things the apostles were intended to be patterns and models for all ministers of the gospel. Bearing this in mind, we may draw most useful lessons from this passage as to the duties of a faithful minister.

Like the apostles, the faithful minister ought to keep up close communion with Christ. He should be much *with Him.* His fellowship should be *with [the] Son* (1 John 1:3). He should abide in Him. He should be separate from the world and daily sit, like Mary, at Jesus' feet and hear His Word. He should study Him, copy Him, drink into His Spirit, and walk in His steps. He should strive to be able to say when he enters the pulpit, *What we have seen and heard we proclaim to you* (1 John 1:3).

Like the apostles, the faithful minister ought to be a preacher. This must ever be his principal work and receive the greatest part of his thoughts. An unpreaching minister is of little use to the church of Christ. He is a lampless lighthouse, a silent trumpeter, a sleeping watchman, a painted fire.

Like the apostles, the faithful minister must labor to do good in every way. Though he cannot heal the sick, he must seek to alleviate sorrow and to increase happiness among all with whom he has to do. He must strive to be known as the comforter, the counselor, the peacemaker, the helper, and the friend of all. Men should know him not as one who rules and domineers, but as one who is *their bond-servant for Jesus' sake* (2 Corinthians 4:5).

Like the apostles, the faithful minister must oppose every work of the devil. Though perhaps not called now to cast out evil spirits from the body, he must be ever ready to resist the devil's devices and to denounce his snares for the soul. He must expose the tendency of races, theaters, balls, gambling, drunkenness, Sabbath profanation, and sensual gratifications. Every age has its own peculiar temptations. Many are the devices of Satan. But whatever be the direction in which the devil is most busy, there ought the minister to be, ready to confront and withstand him.

How great is the responsibility of ministers! How heavy their work if they do their duty! How much they need the prayers of all praying people in order to support and strengthen their hands! No wonder that Paul says so often to the churches, *Pray for us.*

Let us notice, in the last place, *how our Lord Jesus Christ's zeal was misunderstood.* We are told that they *went out to take custody of Him; for they were saying, "He has lost His senses."*

There is nothing in this fact that should surprise us. The prophet who came to anoint Jehu was called a *mad fellow* (2 Kings 9:11). Festus told Paul that he was *mad.* Few things show the corruption of human nature more clearly than man's inability to understand zeal in religion. Zeal about money, or science, or war, or commerce, or business is intelligible to the world. But zeal about religion is too often reckoned foolishness, fanaticism, and the sign of a weak mind. If a man injures his health by study or excessive attention to business, no fault is found; it is said, "He is a diligent man." But if he wears himself out with preaching or spends his whole time in doing good to souls, the cry is raised,

"He is an enthusiast and overly righteous." The world has not changed. The things of the Spirit are always foolishness to the natural man (1 Corinthians 2:14).

Let it not shake our faith if we have to drink of the same cup as our blessed Lord. Hard as it may be to flesh and blood to be misunderstood by our relatives, we must remember it is no new thing. Let us call to mind our Lord's words: *"He who loves father or mother more than Me is not worthy of Me"* (Matthew 10:37). Jesus knows the bitterness of our trials; Jesus feels for us. Jesus will give us help.

Let us bear patiently the unreasonableness of unconverted men, even as our Lord did. Let us pity their blindness and lack of knowledge and not love them one whit the less. Above all, let us pray that God would change their hearts. Who can tell but the very persons who now try to turn us away from Christ may one day become new creatures, see all things differently, and follow Christ themselves.

Mark 3:22-30

The scribes who came down from Jerusalem were saying, "He is possessed by Beelzebul," and "He casts out the demons by the ruler of the demons." And He called them to Himself and began speaking to them in parables, "How can Satan cast out Satan? If a kingdom is divided against itself, that kingdom cannot stand. If a house is divided against itself, that house will not be able to stand. If Satan has risen up against himself and is divided, he cannot stand, but he is finished! But no one can enter the strong man's house and plunder his property unless he first binds the strong man, and then he will plunder his house. Truly I say to you, all sins shall be forgiven the sons of men, and whatever blasphemies they utter; but whoever blasphemes against the Holy Spirit never has forgiveness, but is guilty of an eternal sin"— because they were saying, "He has an unclean spirit."

We all know how painful it is to have our conduct misunderstood and misrepresented when we are doing right. It is a trial which our Lord Jesus Christ had to endure continually, all through His earthly ministry. We have an instance in the passage before us. The *scribes who came down from Jerusalem* saw the miracles which He worked. They could not deny their reality. What then did they do? They accused our blessed Savior of being in league and union with the devil. They said, *"He is possessed by Beelzebul,"* and *"He casts out the demons by the ruler of the demons."*

In our Lord's answer to this wicked accusation, there are expressions which deserve special attention. Let us see what lessons they contain for our use.

We ought to notice, in the first place, *how great is the evil of dissension and divisions.*

This is a lesson which is strongly brought out in the beginning of our Lord's reply to the scribes. He shows the absurdity of supposing that Satan would *cast out Satan* and so help to destroy his own power. He appeals to the notorious fact, which even His enemies must allow, that there can be no strength where there is division. *"If a kingdom is divided against itself, that kingdom cannot stand."*

This truth is one which does not receive sufficient consideration. On no point has the abuse of the right of private judgment produced so much evil. The divisions of Christians are one great cause of the weakness of the visible church. They often absorb energy, time, and power which might have been well bestowed on better things. They furnish the infidel with a prime argument against the truth of Christianity. They help the devil. Satan indeed is the chief promoter of religious divisions. If he cannot extinguish Christianity, he labors to make Christians quarrel with one another and to set every man's hand against his neighbor. None knows better than the devil that "to divide is to conquer."

Let us resolve, so far as in us lies, to avoid all differences, dissensions, and disputes in religion. Let us loathe and abhor them as the plague of the churches. We cannot be too jealous about all saving truths. But it is easy to mistake morbid scrupulosity for conscientiousness, and zeal about mere trifles for zeal about the truth. Nothing justifies separation from a church but the separation of that church from the gospel. Let us be ready to concede much and make many sacrifices for the sake of unity and peace.

We ought to notice, in the second place, *what a glorious declaration our Lord makes in these verses about the forgiveness of sins.* He says, "All sins shall be forgiven the sons of men, and whatever blasphemies they utter."

These words fall lightly on the ears of many persons. They see no particular beauty in them. But to the man who is alive to his own sinfulness and deeply sensible of his need of mercy, these words are sweet and precious. *All sins shall be forgiven.* The sins of youth and age; the sins of head, and hand, and tongue, and imagination; the sins against all God's commandments; the sins of persecutors, like Saul; the sins of idolaters, like Manasseh; the sins of open enemies of Christ, like the Jews who crucified Him; and the sins of backsliders from Christ, like Peter – all, all may be forgiven. The blood of Christ can cleanse all away. The righteousness of Christ can cover all and hide all from God's eyes.

The doctrine here laid down is the crown and glory of the gospel. The very first thing it proposes to man is free pardon, full forgiveness, and complete remission without money and without price. *Through Him forgiveness of sins is proclaimed to you, and through Him everyone who believes is freed from all things* (Acts 13:38-39).

Let us lay hold on this doctrine without delay, if we never received it before. It is for us as well as for others. We too, this very day, if we come to Christ, may be completely forgiven. *"Though your sins are as scarlet, they will be as white as snow"* (Isaiah 1:18).

Let us cleave firmly to this doctrine, if we have received it already. We may sometimes feel faint, and unworthy, and cast down. But if we have really come to Jesus by faith, our sins are fully forgiven. They are cast behind God's back – blotted out of the book of His remembrance – sunk into the depths of the sea. Let us believe and not be afraid.

We ought to notice, in the last place, that *it is possible for a man's soul to be lost forever in hell.* The words of our Lord are distinct and precise. He speaks of one who *never has forgiveness, but is guilty of an eternal sin.*

This is a dreadful truth, beyond doubt. But it is a truth, and we must not shut our eyes against it. We find it asserted over and over again in

Scripture. Figures of all kinds are multiplied, and language of every sort is employed in order to make it plain and unmistakable. In short, if there is no such thing as *an eternal sin*, we may throw the Bible aside and say that words have no meaning at all.

We have great need to keep this dreadful truth steadily in view in these latter days. Teachers have risen up who are openly attacking the doctrine of the eternity of punishment or laboring hard to explain it away. Men's ears are being tickled with plausible sayings about the love of God and the impossibility of a loving God permitting an everlasting hell. The eternity of punishment is spoken of as a mere speculative question about which men may believe anything they please. In the midst of all this flood of false doctrine, let us hold firmly the old truth. Let us not be ashamed to believe that there is an eternal God, an eternal heaven, and an eternal hell. Let us recollect that sin is an infinite evil. It needed an atonement of infinite value to deliver the believer from its consequences – and it entails an infinite loss on the unbeliever who rejects the remedy provided for it. Above all, let us fall back on plain scriptural statements like that before us this day. One plain text is worth a thousand deep arguments.

Finally, if it be true that there is *an eternal sin*, let us give diligence that we ourselves do not fall into it. Let us escape for our lives and not linger (Genesis 19:16-17). Let us flee for refuge to the hope set before us in the gospel and never rest until we know and feel that we are safe. And never, never let us be ashamed of seeking safety. Of sin, worldliness, and the love of pleasure we may well be ashamed. But we never need be ashamed of seeking to be delivered from an eternal hell.[4]

---

4   From this passage it seems that there is such a thing as an unpardonable sin. It must be frankly confessed that its precise nature is nowhere defined in Holy Scripture. The most probable view is that it is a combination of clear intellectual knowledge of the gospel with deliberate rejection of it and willful choice of sin. It is the union of light in the head and hatred in the heart. The limits which knowledge combined with unbelief must pass in order to become the unpardonable sin are graciously withheld from us. It is mercifully ordered of God that man doesn't need to decide positively for any brother that he has committed a sin which cannot be forgiven. But although it is difficult to define what the unpardonable sin is, it is far less difficult to point out what it is not. We may lay it down as nearly certain that those who are troubled with fears that they have committed the unpardonable sin are the very people who have not committed it. The very fact that they are afraid and anxious about it is the strongest possible evidence in their favor.

Mark 3:31-35

Then His mother and His brothers arrived, and standing out-
side they sent word to Him and called Him. A crowd was sitting
around Him, and they said to Him, "Behold, Your mother and
Your brothers are outside looking for You." Answering them, He
said, "Who are My mother and My brothers?" Looking about at
those who were sitting around Him, He said, "Behold My mother
and My brothers! For whoever does the will of God, he is My
brother and sister and mother."

In the verses which immediately precede this passage, we see our
blessed Lord accused by the scribes of being in league with the devil.
They said, *"He is possessed by Beelzebul," and "He casts out the demons*
by the ruler of the demons."

In the verses we have now read, we find that this absurd charge of
the scribes was not all that Jesus had to endure at this time. We are told
that *then His mother and His brothers arrived, and standing outside they*
sent word to Him and called Him. They could not yet understand the
beauty and usefulness of the life that our Lord was living. Though they
doubtless loved Him well, they would sincerely have persuaded Him to
cease from His work and spare Himself. Little did they know what they
were doing! Little had they observed or understood our Lord's words
when He was only twelve years old: *"Did you not know that I had to be*
in my Father's house?" (Luke 2:49).

It is interesting to consider the quiet, firm perseverance of our Lord
in the face of all discouragements. None of these things moved Him. The
slanderous suggestions of enemies and the well-meant remonstrances
of ignorant friends were alike powerless to turn Him from His course.
He had set His face as a flint towards the cross and the crown. He knew
the work He had come into the world to do. He had a baptism to be
baptized and was distressed until it was accomplished (Luke 12:50).

So let it be with all true servants of Christ. Let nothing turn them
for a moment out of the narrow way or make them stop and look back.
Let them not heed the ill-natured remarks of enemies. Let them not

give way to the well-intentioned but mistaken entreaties of unconverted relatives and friends. Let them reply in the words of Nehemiah, *"I am doing a great work and I cannot come down"* (Nehemiah 6:3). Let them say, "I have taken up the cross, and I will not cast it away."

We learn from these verses one mighty lesson. We learn *who they are that are reckoned the relatives of Jesus Christ.* They are those who are His disciples and do the will of God. Of such the great head of the church says, *"He is My brother and sister and mother."*

How much there is in this single expression! What a rich mine of consolation it opens to all true believers! Who can conceive the depth of our Lord's love towards Mary the mother who bore Him and on whose bosom He had been nursed? Who can imagine the breadth of His love towards His brethren according to the flesh with whom the tender years of His childhood had been spent? Doubtless no heart ever had within it such deep wellsprings of affection as the heart of Christ. Yet even He says of everyone who *does the will of God*, that each *is [His] brother and sister and mother.*

Let all true Christians drink comfort out of these words. Let them know that there is one at least who knows them, loves them, cares for them, and reckons them as His own family. What if they be poor in this world? They have no cause to be ashamed when they remember that they are the brethren and sisters of the Son of God. What if they be persecuted and ill-treated in their own homes because of their religion? They may remember the words of David and apply them to their own case: *For my father and my mother have forsaken me, but the* LORD *will take me up* (Psalm 27:10).

Finally, let all who persecute and ridicule others because of their religion take warning by these words and repent. Whom are they persecuting and ridiculing? The relations of Jesus the Son of God! The family of the King of Kings and Lord of Lords! Surely they would do wisely to hold their peace and consider well what they are doing. These whom they persecute have a mighty Friend – *Their redeemer is strong; He will plead their case* (Proverbs 23:11).

Mark Chapter 4

Mark 4:1-20

He began to teach again by the sea. And such a very large crowd gathered to Him that He got into a boat in the sea and sat down; and the whole crowd was by the sea on the land. And He was teaching them many things in parables, and was saying to them in His teaching, "Listen to this! Behold, the sower went out to sow; as he was sowing, some seed fell beside the road, and the birds came and ate it up. Other seed fell on the rocky ground where it did not have much soil; and immediately it sprang up because it had no depth of soil. And after the sun had risen, it was scorched; and because it had no root, it withered away. Other seed fell among the thorns, and the thorns came up and choked it, and it yielded no crop. Other seeds fell into the good soil, and as they grew up and increased, they yielded a crop and produced thirty, sixty, and a hundredfold." And He was saying, "He who has ears to hear, let him hear." As soon as He was alone, His followers, along with the twelve, began asking Him about the parables. And He was saying to them, "To you has been given the mystery of the kingdom of God, but those who are outside get everything in parables, so that while seeing, they may see and not perceive, and while hearing, they may hear and not understand, otherwise they might return and be forgiven." And He said to them, "Do you not understand this parable? How will you understand all the parables? The sower sows the word. These are the ones who are beside the road where the word is sown; and when they hear, immediately Satan comes and takes away the word which has been sown in them. In a similar way these are the ones

*on whom seed was sown on the rocky places, who, when they
hear the word, immediately receive it with joy; and they have
no firm root in themselves, but are only temporary; then, when
affliction or persecution arises because of the word, immediately
they fall away. And others are the ones on whom seed was sown
among the thorns; these are the ones who have heard the word,
but the worries of the world, and the deceitfulness of riches, and
the desires for other things enter in and choke the word, and it
becomes unfruitful. And those are the ones on whom seed was
sown on the good soil; and they hear the word and accept it and
bear fruit, thirty, sixty, and a hundredfold."*

THESE VERSES CONTAIN THE PARABLE of the sower. Of all the
parables spoken by our Lord, none is probably so well-known as this.
There is none which is so easily understood by all from the gracious
familiarity of the figures which it contains.[5] There is none which is of
such universal and perpetual application. So long as there is a church of
Christ and a congregation of Christians, so long there will be employment for this parable.

The language of the parable requires no explanation. To use the
words of an ancient writer, "It needs application, not exposition." Let
us now see what it teaches.

We are taught, in the first place, *that there are some hearers of the
gospel whose hearts are like the wayside in a field.*

These are they who hear sermons but pay no attention to them. They
go to a place of worship for form or fashion or to appear respectable
before men. But they take no interest whatsoever in the preaching. It
seems to them a mere matter of words and names and unintelligible
talk. It is neither money, nor food, nor drink, nor clothes, nor company;
and as they sit under the sound of it, they are taken up with thinking of

---

5 "Our Savior borrowed his comparisons from easy and familiar things, such as the sower,
the seed, the ground, the growth, the withering, the answering or failing of the sower's
expectations, all of them things well-known, and by all these would teach us some spiritual
instruction. . . . Christ cannot look upon the sun, the wind, the fire, water, a hen, a little
grain of mustard seed . . . but he applies all to some special use of edification in grace.
Earthly things must remind us of heavenly. We must translate the book of nature into the
book of grace." – Thomas Taylor, 1634.

other things. It matters nothing whether it is law or gospel. It produces no more effect on them than water on a stone. And at the end they go away knowing no more than when they came in.

There are myriads of professing Christians in this state of soul. There is hardly a church or chapel where scores of them are not to be found. Sunday after Sunday they allow the devil to catch away the good seed that is sown on the surface of their hearts. Week after week they live on without faith, or fear, or knowledge, or grace – feeling nothing, caring nothing, taking no more interest in religion than if Christ had never died on the cross at all. And in this state they often die and are buried and are lost forever in hell. This is a mournful picture but only too true.

We are taught, in the second place, that *there are some hearers of the gospel whose hearts are like the stony ground in a field.*

These are they on whom preaching produces temporary impressions but no deep, lasting, and abiding effect. They take pleasure in hearing sermons in which the truth is faithfully set forth. They can speak with apparent joy and enthusiasm about the sweetness of the gospel and the happiness which they experience in listening to it. They can be moved to tears by the appeals of preachers and talk with apparent earnest-ness of their own inward conflicts, hopes, struggles, desires, and fears. But unfortunately there is no stability about their religion. *"They have no firm root in themselves, but are only temporary."* There is no real work of the Holy Spirit within their hearts. Their impressions are like Jonah's plant which came up in a night and perished in a night. They fade as rapidly as they grow. No sooner does *affliction or persecution [arise] because of the word,* than they fall away. Their goodness proves as *a morning cloud and like the dew which goes away early* (Hosea 6:4). Their religion has no more life in it than the cut flower. It has no root and soon withers away.

There are many in every congregation who hear the gospel who are just in this state of soul. They are not careless and inattentive hearers, like many around them, and are therefore tempted to think well of their own condition. They feel a pleasure in the preaching to which they listen and therefore flatter themselves that they must have grace in their hearts. And yet they are thoroughly deceived. Old things have not yet passed away. There is no real work of conversion in their inward man. With all their feelings, affections, joys, hopes, and desires, they are actually on the high road to destruction.

We are taught, in the third place, that *there are some hearers of the gospel whose hearts are like the thorny ground in a field.*

These are they who attend to the preaching of Christ's truth and to a certain extent obey it. Their understanding assents to it. Their judgment approves of it. Their conscience is affected by it. Their affections are in favor of it. They acknowledge that it is all right, and good, and worthy of all reception. They even abstain from many things which the gospel condemns and adopt many habits which the gospel requires. But here, unfortunately, they stop short. Something appears to chain them fast, and they never get beyond a certain point in their religion. And the grand secret of their condition is the world. *But the worries of the world, and the deceitfulness of riches, and the desires for other things* prevent the Word from having its full effect on their souls. With everything apparently that is promising and favorable in their spiritual state, they stand still. They never come up to the full standard of New Testament Christianity. They bring no fruit to perfection.

There are few faithful ministers of Christ who could not point to cases like these. Of all cases they are the most grieving. To go so far and yet go no further – to see so much and yet not see all – to approve so much and yet not give Christ the heart, this is indeed most deplorable! And there is but one verdict that can be given about such people. Without a decided change, they will never enter the kingdom of heaven. Christ wants all of our heart. *Whoever wishes to be a friend of the world makes himself an enemy of God* (James 4:4).

We are taught, in the last place, that *there are some hearers of the gospel whose hearts are like the good ground in a field.*

These are they who really receive Christ's truth into the bottom of their hearts, believe it implicitly, and obey it thoroughly. In these the fruits of that truth will be seen – uniform, plain, and unmistakable results in heart and life. Sin will be truly hated, mourned over, resisted, and renounced. Christ will be truly loved, trusted in, followed, and obeyed. Holiness will show itself in all their life in humility, spiritual-mindedness, patience, meekness, and charity. There will be something that can be seen. The true work of the Holy Spirit cannot be hidden.

There will always be some people in this state of soul where the gospel is faithfully preached. Their numbers may very likely be few compared to the worldly around them. Their experience and degree of spiritual attainment may differ widely, with some bringing forth thirty, some sixty, and some a hundredfold. But the fruit of the seed falling into good ground will always be of the same kind. There will always be visible repentance, visible faith in Christ, and visible holiness of life. Without these things, there is no saving religion.

And now let us ask ourselves, What are we? Under which class of hearers ought we to be ranked? With what kind of hearts do we hear the Word? Never, never may we forget that there are three ways of hearing without profit and only one way of hearing aright! Never, never may we forget that there is only one infallible characteristic of being a right-hearted hearer! That mark is to bear fruit. To be without fruit is to be in the way to hell.

Mark 4:21-25

And He was saying to them, "A lamp is not brought to be put under a basket, is it, or under a bed? Is it not brought to be put on the lampstand? For nothing is hidden, except to be revealed; nor has anything been secret, but that it would come to light. If anyone has ears to hear, let him hear." And He was saying to them, "Take care what you listen to. By your standard of measure it will be measured to you; and more will be given you besides. For whoever has, to him more shall be given; and whoever does not have, even what he has shall be taken away from him."

These verses seem intended to enforce the parable of the sower on the attention of those who heard it. They are remarkable for the succession of short, proverbial sayings which they contain. Such sayings are eminently calculated to arrest an ignorant hearer. They often strike and stick in the memory when the main subject of the sermon is forgotten.

We learn from these verses that *we ought not only to receive knowledge but also to impart it to others.*

A candle is not lit in order to be hidden and concealed but to be set on a candlestick and used. Religious light is not given to a man for himself alone but for the benefit of others. We are to try to spread and diffuse our knowledge. We are to display to others the precious treasure that we have found and persuade them to seek it for themselves. We are to tell them of the good news that we have heard and endeavor to make them believe and value it themselves.

We shall all have to give account of our use of knowledge one day. The books of God in the day of judgment will show what we have done. If we have buried our talent in the earth – if we have been content with a lazy, idle, do-nothing Christianity and cared nothing about what happened to others so long as we went to heaven ourselves – there will be a fearful exposure at last. *For nothing is hidden, except to be revealed.*

It becomes all Christians to lay these things to heart. It is high time that the old tradition – that the clergy alone ought to teach and spread religious knowledge – should be exploded and cast aside forever. To do good and diffuse light is a duty for which all members of Christ's church are responsible, whether ministers or laymen. Neighbors ought to tell neighbors if they have found an unfailing remedy in a time of plague. Christians ought to tell others that they have found medicine for their souls if they see them ignorant and dying for lack of it. What says the apostle Peter? *As each one has received a special gift, employ it in serving one another* (1 Peter 4:10). They will be happy days for the church when that text is obeyed.

We learn, in the second place from these verses, *the importance of hearing, and of considering well what we hear.*

This is a point to which our Lord evidently attaches great weight. We have seen it already brought out in the parable of the sower. We see it here enforced in two remarkable expressions: *If anyone has ears to hear, let him hear. Take care what you listen to.*

Hearing the truth is one principal avenue through which grace is conveyed to the soul of man. *Faith comes from hearing* (Romans 10:17). One of the first steps towards conversion is to receive from the Spirit a hearing ear. Seldom are men brought to repentance and faith in Christ without *hearing*. The general rule is that of which Paul reminds the Ephesians: *You also, after listening to the message of truth, the gospel of your salvation—having also believed* (Ephesians 1:13).

Let us bear this in mind when we hear preaching decried as a means of grace. There are never lacking men who seek to cast it down from the high place which the Bible gives it. There are many who proclaim loudly that it is of far more importance to the soul to hear liturgical forms read and to receive the Lord's Supper than to hear God's Word expounded. Of all such notions let us beware. Let it be a settled principle with us that hearing the Word is one of the foremost means of grace that God has given to man. Let us give to every other means and ordinance its proper value and proportion. But never let us forget the words of Paul: *Do not despise prophetic utterances* (1 Thessalonians 5:20), and his dying charge to Timothy: *Preach the word* (2 Timothy 4:2).

We learn, in the last place from these verses, *the importance of a diligent use of religious privileges*. What says our Lord? *"More will be given you besides. For whoever has, to him shall more be given; and whoever does not have, even what he has shall be taken away from him."*

This is a principle which we find continually brought forward in Scripture. All that believers have is undoubtedly of grace. Their repentance, faith, and holiness are all the gift of God. But the degree to which a believer attains in grace is ever set before us as closely connected with his own diligence in the use of means and his own faithfulness in living fully up to the light and knowledge which he possesses. Indolence and laziness are always discouraged in God's Word. Labor and pains in hearing, reading, and prayer are always represented as bringing their own reward. *The soul of the diligent is made fat* (Proverbs 13:4). *An idle man will suffer hunger* (Proverbs 19:15).

Attention to this great principle is the main secret of spiritual prosperity. The man who makes rapid progress in spiritual attainments – who grows visibly in grace, and knowledge, and strength, and usefulness – will always be found to be a diligent man. He leaves no stone unturned

53

to promote his soul's well-doing. He is diligent over his Bible, diligent in his private devotions, diligent as a hearer of sermons, and diligent in his attendance at the Lord's Table. And he reaps according as he sows. Just as the muscles of the body are strengthened by regular exercise, so are the graces of the soul increased by diligence in using them.

Do we wish to grow in grace? Do we desire to have stronger faith, brighter hope, and clearer knowledge? Beyond doubt we do if we are true Christians. Then let us live fully up to our light and improve every opportunity. Let us never forget our Lord's words in this passage. *"By your standard of measure"* to your souls, *"it will be measured to you."* The more we do for our souls, the more shall we find God does for them.

Mark 4:26-29

And He was saying, "The kingdom of God is like a man who casts seed upon the soil; and he goes to bed at night and gets up by day, and the seed sprouts and grows—how, he himself does not know. The soil produces crops by itself; first the blade, then the head, then the mature grain in the head. But when the crop permits, he immediately puts in the sickle, because the harvest has come."

The parable contained in these verses is short and only recorded in Mark's Gospel. But it is one that ought to be deeply interesting to all who have reason to hope that they are true Christians. It sets before us the history of the work of grace in an individual soul. It summons us to an examination of our own experience in divine things.

There are some expressions in the parable which we must not press too far. Such are the *goes to bed* and the *gets up* of the farmer and the *night* and *day*. In this, as in many of our Lord's parables, we must carefully keep in view the main scope and objective of the whole story and not lay too much stress on lesser points. In the case before us, the main thing taught is the close resemblance between some familiar operations in the culture of grain and the work of grace in the heart. To this let us rigidly confine our attention.

We are taught firstly, that as in the growth of grain, so in the work of grace, *there must be a sower.*

The earth, as we all know, never brings forth grain of itself. It is a mother of weeds but not of wheat. The hand of man must plough it and scatter the seed, or else there would never be a harvest.

The heart of man, in like manner, will never of itself turn to God, repent, believe, and obey. It is utterly barren of grace. It is entirely dead towards God and unable to give itself spiritual life. The Son of Man must break it up by His Spirit and give it a new nature. He must scatter over it by the hand of His laboring ministers the good seed of the Word.

Let us not fail to observe this truth. Grace in the heart of man is an exotic thing. It is a new principle from outside, sent down from heaven and implanted in his soul. Left to himself, no man living would ever seek God. And yet in communicating grace, God ordinarily works by means. To despise the instrumentality of teachers and preachers is to expect corn where no seed has been sown.

We are taught secondly, that as in the growth of grain, so in the work of grace, *there is much that is beyond man's comprehension and control.*

The wisest farmer on earth can never explain all that takes place in a grain of wheat when he has sown it. He knows the broad fact that unless he puts it into the soil and covers it up, there will not be a kernel of wheat in time of harvest. But he cannot command the prosperity of each grain. He cannot explain why some grains come up and others die. He cannot specify the hour or the minute when life shall begin to show itself. He cannot define what that life is. These are matters he must leave alone. He sows his seed and leaves the growth to God. It is *God who causes the growth* (1 Corinthians 3:7).

The workings of grace in the heart in like manner are utterly mysterious and unsearchable. We cannot explain why the Word produces effects on one person in a congregation and not upon another. We cannot explain why in some cases – with every possible advantage and in spite of every entreaty – people reject the Word and continue dead in trespasses and sins. We cannot explain why in other cases – with every possible difficulty and with no special encouragement – people are born again and become decided Christians. We cannot define the manner in which the Spirit of God conveys life to a soul and the exact process by which a believer receives a new nature. All these are hidden things to us. We see certain results, but we can go no further. *"The wind blows where it wishes and you hear the sound of it, but do not know where it comes from and where it is going; so is everyone who is born of the Spirit"* (John 3:8).

Let us observe this truth also, for it is deeply instructive. It is humbling, no doubt, to ministers and teachers of others. The highest abilities, the most powerful preaching, the most diligent working cannot command success. God alone can give spiritual life. But it is a truth at the same time which supplies an admirable antidote to over-anxiety and despondency. Our principal work is to sow the seed. That done, we may wait with faith and patience for the result. We may go *to bed at night and [get] up by day* and leave our work with the Lord. He alone can, and if He thinks fit, He will give success.

We are taught thirdly, that as in the growth of grain, so in the work of grace, *life manifests itself gradually.*

There is a true proverb which says, "Nature does nothing at a bound." The ripe ear of wheat does not appear at once as soon as the seed bursts forth into life. The plant goes through many stages before it arrives at perfection – *first the blade, then the head, then the mature grain in the head.* But in all these stages one great thing is true about it: even at its weakest, it is a living plant.

The work of grace in like manner goes on in the heart by degrees. The children of God are not born perfect in faith, or hope, or knowledge, or experience. Their beginning is generally a *day of small things.* They see in part their own sinfulness, and Christ's fullness, and the beauty of holiness. But for all that, the weakest child in God's family is a true child of God. With all his weakness and infirmity he is alive. The seed of grace has really come up in his heart, though at present it be only in the blade. He is *alive from the dead.* And the wise man says, *A live dog is better than a dead lion* (Ecclesiastes 9:4).

Let us observe this truth also, for it is full of consolation. Let us not despise grace because it is weak, or think people are not converted because they are not yet as strong in the faith as Paul. Let us remember that grace, like everything else, must have a beginning. The mightiest oak was once an acorn. The strongest man was once a babe. Better a thousand times to have grace in the blade than no grace at all.

We are taught lastly, that as in the growth of grain, so in the work of grace, *there is no harvest until the seed is ripe.*

No farmer thinks of cutting his wheat when it is green. He waits until the sun, and rain, and heat, and cold have done their appointed work, and the golden ears hang down. Then, and not until then, he puts in the sickle and gathers the wheat into his barn.

God deals with His work of grace exactly in the same way. He never removes His people from this world until they are ripe and ready. He never takes them away until their work is done. They never die at the wrong time, however mysterious their deaths appear sometimes to man. Josiah and James, the brother of John, were both cut off in the midst of usefulness. Our own King Edward VI was not allowed to reach a mature state. But we shall see in the resurrection morning that there was a needs-be. All was done well about their deaths as well as about their births. The Great Husbandman never cuts His grain until it is ripe.

Let us leave the parable with this truth on our minds and take comfort about the death of every believer. Let us rest satisfied that there is no chance, no accident, and no mistake about the decease of any of God's children. They are all "God's field," and God knows best when they are ready for the harvest.

Mark 4:30-34

And He said, "How shall we picture the kingdom of God, or by what parable shall we present it? It is like a mustard seed, which, when sown upon the soil, though it is smaller than all the seeds that are upon the soil, yet when it is sown, it grows up and becomes larger than all the garden plants and forms large branches; so that the birds of the air can nest under its shade." With many such parables He was speaking the word to them, so far as they were able to hear it; and He did not speak to them without a parable; but He was explaining everything privately to His own disciples.

The parable of the mustard seed is one of those parables which partake of the character both of history and prophecy. It seems intended to illustrate the history of Christ's visible church on earth from the time of the first advent down to the judgment day. The seed cast into the earth in the preceding parable showed us the work of grace in a heart. The mustard seed shows us the progress of professing Christianity in the world.

We learn, in the first place, that like the mustard seed, *Christ's visible church was to be small and weak in its beginnings.*

A mustard seed was a proverbial expression among the Jews for something very small and insignificant. Our Lord calls it *smaller than all the seeds that are upon the soil.* Twice in the Gospels we find our Lord using the figure as a word of comparison when speaking of a weak faith (Matthew 17:20; Luke 17:6). The idea was doubtless familiar to a Jewish mind, however strange it may sound to us. Here, as in other places, the Son of God shows us the wisdom of using language familiar to the minds of those whom we may address.

It would be difficult to find an emblem which more faithfully represents the history of the visible church of Christ than this mustard seed.

Weakness and apparent insignificance were undoubtedly the characteristics of its beginning. How did its Head and King come into the world? He came as a feeble infant, born in a manger at Bethlehem without riches, or armies, or attendants, or power. Who were the men that the head of the church gathered around Himself and appointed as His apostles? They were poor and unlearned people – fishermen, publicans, and men of like occupations, to all appearances the most unlikely people to shake the world. What was the last public act of the earthly ministry of the great head of the church? He was crucified like a malefactor between two thieves, after having been forsaken by nearly all His disciples, betrayed by one, and denied by another. What was the doctrine which the first builders of the church went forth from the upper chamber in Jerusalem to preach to mankind? It was a doctrine which to the Jews was a stumbling block and to the Greeks foolishness. It was a proclamation that the great Head of their new religion had been put to death on a cross, and that notwithstanding this, they offered life through His death to the world! In all this the mind of man can perceive nothing but weakness and feebleness. Truly the emblem of a mustard seed was verified and fulfilled to the very letter. To the eyes of man the beginning of the visible church was contemptible, insignificant, powerless, and small.

We learn, in the second place, that like the mustard seed, *the visible church, once planted, was to grow and greatly increase.*

"A mustard seed," says our Lord, *"when it is sown, it grows up and becomes larger than all the garden plants."* These words may sound startling to an English ear. We are not accustomed to such a growth in our cold northern climate. But to those who know eastern countries, there is nothing surprising in it. The testimony of well-informed and experienced travelers is distinct – that such an increase is both possible and probable.

No figure could be chosen more strikingly applicable to the growth and increase of Christ's visible church in the world. It began to grow from the day of Pentecost and grew with a rapidity which nothing could account for but the finger of God. It grew wonderfully when three thousand souls were converted at once and five thousand more in a few days afterwards. It grew wonderfully when at Antioch, and Ephesus, and Philippi, and Corinth, and Rome, congregations were gathered together and Christianity firmly established. It grew wonderfully when at last the despised religion of Christ overspread the greater part of Europe, and Asia Minor, and North Africa, and, in spite of fierce persecution and opposition, supplanted heathen idolatry and became the professed creed of the whole Roman Empire. Such growth must have been marvelous in the eyes of many. But it was only what our Lord foretold in the parable before us. *The kingdom of God . . . is like a mustard seed.*

The visible church of Christ is not yet done growing. Notwithstanding the grievous apostasy of some of its branches and the deplorable weakness of others, it is still extending and expanding over the world. New branches have continually been springing up in America, in India, in Australia, in Africa, in China, and in the islands of the South Seas during the last fifty years. Evils undoubtedly there are many. False profession and corruption abound. But still, on the whole, heathenism is waning, wearing out, and melting away. In spite of all the predictions of Voltaire and Paine, in spite of foes without and treachery within, the visible church progresses – the mustard plant still grows!

And the prophecy, we may rest assured, is not yet exhausted. A day shall yet come when the great head of the church shall take to Himself His power, and will reign and put down every enemy under His feet. The earth shall yet be filled with the knowledge of God as the waters cover the sea (Habakkuk 2:14). Satan shall yet be bound. The heathen shall yet be our Lord's inheritance and the utmost parts of the earth His possession. And then this parable shall receive its full accomplishment. The little seed shall become a great tree and fill the whole earth.

Let us leave the parable with a resolution never to despise any movement or instrumentality in the church of Christ because at first it is weak and small. Let us remember the manger of Bethlehem and learn wisdom. The name of Him who lay there, a helpless infant, is now known all over the globe. The little seed which was planted in the day when Jesus was born has become a great tree, and we ourselves are rejoicing under its shadow. Let it be a settled principle in our religion never to *despise the day of small things* (Zechariah 4:10). One child may be the beginning of a flourishing school, one conversion the beginning of a mighty church, one word the beginning of some blessed Christian enterprise, and one seed the beginning of a rich harvest of saved souls.

Mark 4:35-41

On that day, when evening came, He said to them, "Let us go over to the other side." Leaving the crowd, they took Him along with them in the boat, just as He was; and other boats were with Him. And there arose a fierce gale of wind, and the waves were breaking over the boat so much that the boat was already filling up. Jesus Himself was in the stern, asleep on the cushion;

and they woke Him and said to Him, "Teacher, do You not care
that we are perishing?" And He got up and rebuked the wind
and said to the sea, "Hush, be still." And the wind died down
and it became perfectly calm. And He said to them, "Why are
you afraid? Do you still have no faith?" They became very much
afraid and said to one another, "Who then is this, that even the
wind and the sea obey Him?"

These verses describe a storm on the Sea of Galilee when our Lord and His disciples were crossing it, and a miracle performed by our Lord in calming the storm in a moment. Few miracles recorded in the Gospel were so likely to strike the minds of the apostles as this. At least four of the apostles were fishermen. Peter, Andrew, James, and John had probably known the Sea of Galilee and its storms from their youth. Few events in our Lord's journeyings to and fro upon earth contain more rich instruction than the one related in this passage.

Let us learn, in the first place, that *Christ's service does not exempt His servants from storms.* Here were the twelve disciples in the path of duty. They were obediently following Jesus wherever He went. They were daily attending upon His ministry and hearkening to His word. They were daily testifying to the world that whatever scribes and Pharisees might think, they believed on Jesus, loved Jesus, and were not ashamed to give up all for His sake. Yet here we see these men in trouble, tossed up and down by a tempest, and in danger of being drowned.

Let us closely observe this lesson. If we are true Christians, we must not expect everything to be smooth in our journey to heaven. We must count it no strange thing if we have to endure sicknesses, losses, bereavements, and disappointments just like other men. Free pardon and full forgiveness, grace along the way, and glory at the end – all this our Savior has promised to give. But He has never promised that we shall have no affliction. He loves us too well to promise that. By affliction He teaches us many precious lessons which without it we would never learn. By affliction He shows us our emptiness and weakness, draws us to the throne of grace, purifies our affections, weans us from the world, and makes us long for heaven. In the resurrection morning, we shall all say, *It is good for me that I was afflicted* (Psalm 119:71).We shall thank God for every storm.

Let us learn, in the second place, that *our Lord Jesus Christ was really and truly man.* We are told in these verses that when the storm began and the waves beat over the ship, He was in the back part of the boat asleep. He had a body exactly like our own – a body that could hunger, and thirst, and feel pain, and be weary, and need rest. No wonder that His body needed repose at this time. He had been diligent in His Father's business all the day. He had been preaching to a great multitude in the open air. No wonder that *when evening came,* and His work finished, He fell asleep.

Let us observe this lesson also attentively. The Savior in whom we are bid to trust is as really a man as He is God. He knows the trials of a man, for He has experienced them. He knows the bodily infirmities of a man, for He has felt them. He can well understand what we mean when we cry to Him for help in this world of need. He is just the Savior that men and women with weary frames and aching heads in a weary world require for their comfort every morning and night. *For we do not have a high priest who cannot sympathize with our weaknesses* (Hebrews 4:15).

Let us learn, in the third place, that *our Lord Jesus Christ, as God, has almighty power.* We see Him in these verses doing that which is proverbially impossible. He speaks to the winds and they obey Him. He speaks to the waves and they submit to His command. He turns the raging storm into a calm with a few words – *"Hush, be still."* Those words were the words of Him who first created all things. The elements knew the voice of their Master and, like obedient servants, were quiet at once.

Let us observe this lesson also and lay it up in our minds. With the Lord Jesus Christ, nothing is impossible. No stormy passions are so strong that He can't tame them. No temper is so rough and violent that He can't change it. No conscience is so disturbed that He can't speak peace to it and make it calm. No man ever need despair if he will only bow down his pride and come as a humbled sinner to Christ. Christ can do miracles upon his heart. No man ever need despair of reaching his journey's end if he has once committed his soul to Christ's keeping. Christ will carry him through every danger. Christ will make him conqueror over every foe. What if our relatives oppose us? What if our neighbors laugh us to scorn? What if our place be hard? What if our temptations be great? It is all nothing if Christ is on our side and we are in the ship with Him. Greater is He that is for us than all those who are against us.

Finally, we learn from this passage that *our Lord Jesus Christ is exceedingly patient and piteous in dealing with His own people.* We see the disciples on this occasion showing great lack of faith and giving way to most improper fears. They forgot their Master's miracles and care for them in days gone by. They thought of nothing but their present peril. They woke our Lord hastily and cried, *"Teacher, do You not care that we are perishing?"* We see our Lord dealing most gently and tenderly with them. He gives them no sharp reproof. He makes no threat of casting them off because of their unbelief. He simply asks the touching question, *"Why are you afraid? Do you still have no faith?"*

Let us closely observe this lesson. The Lord Jesus is very empathetic and full of tender mercy. *Just as a father has compassion on his children, so the LORD has compassion on those who fear Him* (Psalm 103:13). He does not deal with believers according to their sins, nor reward them according to their iniquities. He sees their weakness. He is aware of their shortcomings. He knows all the defects of their faith, and hope, and love, and courage. And yet He will not cast them off. He bears with them continually. He loves them even to the end. He raises them when they fall. He restores them when they err. His patience, like His love, is a patience that passes knowledge. When He sees a heart right, it is His glory to pass over many a shortcoming.

Let us leave these verses with the comfortable recollection that Jesus has not changed. His heart is still the same as it was when He crossed the Sea of Galilee and stilled the storm. High in heaven at the right hand of God, Jesus is still sympathizing – still almighty – still piteous and patient towards His people. Let us be more charitable and patient towards our brethren in the faith. They may err in many things, but if Jesus has received them and can bear with them, surely we may bear with them too. Let us be more hopeful about ourselves. We may be very weak, and frail, and unstable; but if we can truly say that we do

EXPOSITORY THOUGHTS ON THE GOSPEL OF MARK

come to Christ and believe on Him, we may take comfort. The question for conscience to answer is not, Are we like the angels? Are we perfect as we shall be in heaven? The question is, Are we real and true in our approaches to Christ? Do we truly repent and believe?[6]

---

6   The Sea of Galilee, or Tiberias, is an inland lake through which the river Jordan flows, about fifteen miles long and six broad. It lies in a deep valley, much depressed below the level of the sea – its surface being 652 feet below that of the Mediterranean – and is surrounded on most sides by steep hills. Owing to these last circumstances, sudden squalls or storms are reported by all travelers to be very common on the lake. The Sea of Galilee and the country surrounding it were favored with more of our blessed Lord's presence during His earthly ministry than any other part of Palestine.

Mark Chapter 5

Mark 5:1-17

They came to the other side of the sea, into the country of the Gerasenes. When He got out of the boat, immediately a man from the tombs with an unclean spirit met Him, and he had his dwelling among the tombs. And no one was able to bind him anymore, even with a chain; because he had often been bound with shackles and chains, and the chains had been torn apart by him and the shackles broken in pieces, and no one was strong enough to subdue him. Constantly, night and day, he was screaming among the tombs and in the mountains, and gashing himself with stones. Seeing Jesus from a distance, he ran up and bowed down before Him; and shouting with a loud voice, he said, "What business do we have with each other, Jesus, Son of the Most High God? I implore You by God, do not torment me!" For He had been saying to him, "Come out of the man, you unclean spirit!" And He was asking him, "What is your name?" And he said to Him, "My name is Legion; for we are many." And he began to implore Him earnestly not to send them out of the country. Now there was a large herd of swine feeding nearby on the mountain. The demons implored Him, saying, "Send us into the swine so that we may enter them." Jesus gave them permission. And coming out, the unclean spirits entered the swine; and the herd rushed down the steep bank into the sea, about two thousand of them; and they were drowned in the sea. Their herdsmen ray away and reported it in the city and in the country. And the people came to see what it was that had happened. They came to Jesus and observed the man who had been demon-possessed sitting down, clothed and in his right mind, the very man who had the "legion"; and they became frightened. Those who had seen it described to them how it had happened to the demon-possessed man, and all about the swine. And they began to implore Him to leave their region.

THESE VERSES DESCRIBE ONE OF THOSE mysterious miracles which the Gospels frequently record – the casting out of a devil. Of all the cases of this kind in the New Testament, none is so fully described as this one. Of all the three evangelists who relate the history, none gives it so fully and minutely as Mark.

We see, in the first place in these verses, that *the possession of a man's body by the devil was a real and true thing in the time of our Lord's earthly ministry.*

It is a painful fact that there are never lacking professing Christians who try to explain away our Lord's miracles. They endeavor to account for them by natural causes and to show that they were not worked by any extraordinary power. Of all miracles, there are none which they assault so strenuously as the casting out of devils. They do not scruple to deny satanic possession entirely. They tell us that it was nothing more than lunacy, or frenzy, or epilepsy, and that the idea of the devil inhabiting a man's body is absurd.

The best and simplest answer to such skeptical objections is a reference to the plain narratives of the Gospels and especially to the one before us at this moment. The facts here detailed are utterly inexplicable if we do not believe in satanic possession. It is widely known that lunacy, and frenzy, and epilepsy are not infectious complaints and at any rate cannot be communicated to a herd of swine! And yet men ask us to believe that as soon as this man was healed, two thousand swine ran violently down a steep place into the sea from a sudden impulse without any apparent cause to account for their so doing! Such reasoning is the height of credulity. When men can satisfy themselves with such explanations, they are in a pitiable state of mind.

Let us beware of a skeptical and incredulous spirit in all matters relating to the devil. No doubt there is much in the subject of satanic possession which we do not understand and cannot explain. But let us not therefore refuse to believe it. The eastern king who would not believe in the possibility of ice because he lived in a hot country and had never seen it was not more foolish than the man who refuses to believe in satanic possession because he never saw a case himself and cannot understand it. We may be sure that upon the subject of the devil and his power, we are far more likely to believe too little than too much. Unbelief about the existence and personality of Satan has often proved the first step to unbelief about God.

We see, in the second place in these verses, *what an awfully cruel, powerful, and malicious being Satan is.* On all these three points, the passage before us is full of instruction.

The *cruelty* of Satan appears in the miserable condition of the unhappy man of whose body he had possession. We read that he dwelt *among the tombs,* that *no one was able to bind him anymore, even with a chain,* that *no one was strong enough to subdue him,* and that *constantly, night and day, he was screaming among the tombs and in the mountains, and gashing himself with stones.* Such is the state to which the devil would bring us all if he only had the power. He would rejoice to inflict upon us the utmost misery both of body and mind. Cases like this are faint types of the miseries of hell.

The *power* of Satan appears in the dreadful words which the unclean spirit used when our Lord asked, *"What is your name?"* He answered, saying, *"My name is Legion; for we are many."* We probably have not the faintest idea of the number, subtlety, and activity of Satan's agents. We forget that he is king over an enormous host of subordinate spirits who do his will. We would probably find, if our eyes were opened to see spirits, that they are about our path, and about our bed, and observing all our ways to an extent of which we have no conception. In private and in public, in church and in the world, there are busy enemies ever near us of whose presence we are not aware.

The *malice* of Satan appears in the strange petition, *"Send us into the swine."* Cast forth from the man whose body they had so long inhabited and possessed, they still thirsted to do mischief. Unable to injure anymore an immortal soul, they desired leave to injure the dumb beasts which were feeding nearby. Such is the true character of Satan. It is the bent of his nature to do harm, to kill, and to destroy. No wonder that he is called Apollyon, the destroyer.

Let us beware of giving way to the senseless habit of jesting about the devil. It is a habit which furnishes dreadful evidence of the blindness and corruption of human nature and one which is far too common. When it is seemly in the condemned criminal to jest about his executioner, then and not until then, it will be seemly for mortal man to talk lightly about Satan. Well would it be for us all if we strove more to realize the power and presence of our great spiritual enemy and prayed more to be delivered from him. It was a true saying of an eminent Christian, now gone to rest: "No prayer is complete which does not contain a petition to be kept from the devil."

We see, in the last place from these verses, *how complete is our Lord's power and authority over the devil.* We see it in the cry of the unclean spirit, *"I implore You by God, do not torment me!"* We see it in the command, *"Come out of the man, you unclean spirit!"* and the immediate obedience that followed. We see it in the blessed change that at once took place in him who was possessed: he was found *sitting down, clothed and in his right mind.* We see it in the petition of all the devils: *"Send us into the swine,"* confessing their consciousness that they could do nothing without permission. All these things show that one mightier than Satan was there. Strong as the great enemy of man was, he was in the presence of one stronger than him. Numerous as his hosts were, he was confronted with one who could command more than twelve legions of angels, *since the word of the king is authoritative* (Ecclesiastes 8:4).

The truth here taught is full of strong consolation for all true Christians. We live in a world full of difficulties and snares. We are ourselves weak and compassed with infirmity. The dreadful thought that we have a mighty, spiritual enemy ever near us – subtle, powerful, and malicious as Satan is – might well disquiet us and cast us down. But thanks be unto God, we have in Jesus an almighty Friend who *is able also to save forever.* He has already triumphed over Satan on the cross. He will ever triumph over him in the hearts of all believers and intercede for them that their faith fail not. And He will finally triumph over Satan completely when He shall come forth at the second advent and bind him in the bottomless pit.

And now, are we ourselves delivered from Satan's power? This, after all, is the grand question that concerns our souls. He still reigns and rules in the hearts of all who are children of disobedience (Ephesians 2:3). He is still a king over the ungodly. Have we, by grace, broken his bonds and escaped his hand? Have we really renounced him and all his works? Do we daily resist him and make him flee? Do we put on the whole armor of God and stand against his wiles? May we never rest until we can give satisfactory answers to these questions.

Mark 5:18-20

As He was getting into the boat, the man who had been demon-possessed was imploring Him that he might accompany Him. And He did not let him, but He said to him, "Go home to your people and report to them what great things the Lord has done for you, and how He had mercy on you." And he went away and began to proclaim in Decapolis what great things Jesus had done for him; and everyone was amazed.

The after-conduct of those whom our Lord Jesus Christ healed and cured when upon earth is a thing which is not often related in the Gospels. The story often describes the miraculous cure and then leaves the after-history of the person cured in obscurity and passes on to other things.

But there are some deeply interesting cases in which the after-conduct of persons cured is described; and the man from whom the devil was cast out in the country of the Gadarenes is one. The verses before us tell the story. Few as they are, they are full of precious instruction.

We learn from these verses that *the Lord Jesus knows better than His people what is the right position for them to be in.* We are told that when our Lord was on the point of leaving the country of the Gadarenes, *the man who had been demon-possessed was imploring Him that he might*

69

accompany Him. We can well understand that request. He felt grateful for the blessed change that had taken place in him. He felt full of love towards his Deliverer. He thought he could not do better than follow our Lord and go with Him as His companion and disciple. He was ready to give up home and country and go after Christ. And yet, strange as it appears at first sight, the request was refused. *And He did not let him.* Our Lord had other work for him to do. Our Lord saw better than he did in what way he could glorify God most. *"Go home to your people,"* He says, *"and report to them what great things the Lord has done for you, and how He had mercy on you."*

There are lessons of profound wisdom in these words. The place that Christians wish to be is not always the place which is best for their souls. The position that they would choose, if they could have their own way, is not always that which Jesus would have them occupy.

There are none who need this lesson so much as believers newly converted to God. Such people are often very poor judges of what is really for their good. Full of the new views which they have been graciously taught, excited with the novelty of their present position, seeing everything around them in a new light, knowing little yet of the depths of Satan and the weakness of their own hearts, knowing only that a little time ago they were blind, and now through mercy, they see – of all people they are in the greatest danger of making mistakes. With the best intentions, they are apt to fall into mistakes about their plans in life, their choices, their moves, their professions. They forget that what we like best is not always best for our souls, and that the seed of grace needs winter as well as summer, cold as well as heat to ripen it for glory.

Let us pray that God would guide us in all our ways after conversion and not allow us to err in our choices or to make hasty decisions. That place and position is most healthful for us in which we are kept most humble, most taught our own sinfulness, drawn most to the Bible and prayer, and led most to live by faith and not by sight. It may not be quite what we like. But if Christ by His providence has placed us in it, let us not be in a hurry to leave it. Let us therein abide with God. The great thing is to have no will of our own and to be where Jesus would have us be.[7]

We learn, for another thing from these verses, that *a believer's own home has the first claims on his attention*. We are taught this in the striking words which our Lord addresses to the man who had been possessed with the devil. *"Go home,"* He says, *"to your people and report to them what great things the Lord has done for you."* The friends of this man had probably not seen him for some years, except under the influence of Satan. Most likely he had been as one dead to them, or worse than dead, and a constant cause of trouble, anxiety, and sorrow. Here then was the path of duty. Here was the way by which he could most glorify God. Let him go home and tell his friends what Jesus had done for him. Let him be a living witness before their eyes of the compassion of Christ. Let him deny himself the pleasure of being in Christ's bodily presence in order to do the higher work of being useful to others.

How much there is in these simple words of our Lord! What thoughts they ought to stir up in the hearts of all true Christians! *"Go home to your people and report to them."* Home is the place above all others where the child of God ought to make his first endeavors to do good. Home is the place where he is most continually seen and where the reality of his grace ought most truly to appear. Home is the place where his best affections ought to be concentrated. Home is the place where he should strive daily to witness for Christ. Home is the place where he was daily doing harm by his example, so long as he served the world. Home is the place where he is specially bound to be a living epistle of Christ as soon as he has been mercifully taught to serve God. May we all remember these things daily! May it never be said of us that we are saints abroad but wicked by our own fireside – talkers about religion abroad but worldly and ungodly at home!

---

7   I doubt whether men who have been suddenly converted to God in the army, the navy, the law, or the merchant's office do not sometimes forsake their professions with undue hastiness in order to become clergymen. It seems to be forgotten that conversion alone is not proof that we are called and qualified to become teachers of others. God may be glorified as really and truly in the secular calling as in the pulpit. Converted men can be eminently useful as landlords, magistrates, soldiers, sailors, barristers, or merchants. We want witnesses for Christ in all these professions. As a general rule, I believe that the rule of Paul ought to be carefully observed: *Each one is to remain with God in that condition in which he was called* (1 Corinthians 7:24).

71

But after all, have we anything to tell others? Can we testify to any work of grace in our hearts? Have we experienced any deliverance from the power of the world, the flesh, and the devil? Have we ever tasted the graciousness of Christ? These are indeed serious questions. If we have never yet been born again and made new creatures, we can of course have nothing to *report*.

If we have anything to tell others about Christ, let us resolve to tell it. Let us not be silent if we have found peace and rest in the gospel. Let us speak to our relations, and friends, and families, and neighbors according as we have opportunity, and tell them what the Lord has done for our souls. All are not called to be ministers. All are not intended to preach. But all can walk in the steps of the Man of whom we have been reading and in the steps of Andrew, and Philip, and the Samaritan woman (John 1:41, 45; 4:29). Happy is he who is not ashamed to say to others, *Come and hear, . . . and I will tell of what He has done for my soul* (Psalm 66:16).

Mark 5:21-34

When Jesus had crossed over again in the boat to the other side, a large crowd gathered around Him; and so He stayed by the seashore. One of the synagogue officials named Jairus came up, and on seeing Him, fell at His feet and implored Him earnestly, saying, "My little daughter is at the point of death; please come and lay Your hands on her, so that she will get well and live." And He went off with him; and a large crowd was following Him and pressing in on Him. A woman who had had a hemorrhage for twelve years, and had endured much at the hands of many physicians, and had spent all that she had and was not helped at all, but rather had grown worse—after hearing about Jesus, she came up in the crowd behind Him and touched His cloak. For she thought, "If I just touch His garments, I will get well." Immediately the flow of her blood was dried up; and she felt in her body that she was healed of her affliction. Immediately

Jesus, perceiving in Himself that the power proceeding from Him had gone forth, turned around in the crowd and said, "Who touched My garments?" And His disciples said to Him, "You see the crowd pressing in on You, and You say, 'Who touched Me?'" And He looked around to see the woman who had done this. But the woman fearing and trembling, aware of what had happened to her, came and fell down before Him and told Him the whole truth. And He said to her, "Daughter, your faith has made you well; go in peace and be healed of your affliction."

The main subject of these verses is the miraculous healing of a sick woman. Great is our Lord's experience in cases of disease! Great is His sympathy with His sick and ailing members! The gods of the heathen are generally represented as terrible and mighty in battle, delighting in bloodshed, the strong man's patrons, and the warrior's friends. The Savior of the Christian is always set before us as gentle and easy to be entreated, the healer of the brokenhearted, the refuge of the weak and helpless, the comforter of the distressed, and the sick man's best friend. And is not this just the Savior that human nature needs? The world is full of pain and trouble. The weak on earth are far more numerous than the strong.

Let us observe in these verses *what misery sin has brought into the world.* We read of one who had had a most painful disease *for twelve years.* She *had endured much at the hands of many physicians, and had spent all that she had and was not helped at all, but rather had grown worse.* Means of every kind had been tried in vain. Medical skill had proved unable to cure. Twelve long, weary years had been spent in battling with disease, and relief seemed no nearer than at first. *Hope deferred* might well *make the heart sick* (Proverbs 13:12).

How incredible it is that we do not hate sin more than we do! Sin is the cause of all the pain and disease in the world. God did not create man to be an ailing and suffering creature. It was sin and nothing but sin which brought in all the ills that flesh is heir to. It was sin to which we owe every racking pain, and every loathsome infirmity, and every humbling weakness to which our poor bodies are liable. Let us keep this ever in mind. Let us hate sin with a godly hatred.

Let us observe, in the second place, *how different are the feelings with which people draw near to Christ*. We are told in these verses that *a large crowd was following Him and pressing in on Him*. But we are only told of one person who *came up in the crowd behind Him* and touched Him with faith and was healed. Many followed Jesus from curiosity and derived no benefit from Him. One, and only one, followed under a deep sense of her need and of our Savior's power to relieve her, and that one received a mighty blessing.

We see the same thing going on continually in the church of Christ at the present day. Multitudes go to our places of worship and fill our pews. Hundreds come up to the Lord's Table and receive the bread and wine. But of all these worshipers and communicants, how few really obtain anything from Christ! Fashion, custom, ritual, habit, the love of excitement, or an itching ear are the true motives of the vast majority. There are but few here and there who touch Christ by faith and go home *in peace*. These may seem to be hard sayings. But they are unfortunately too true!

Let us observe, in the third place, *how immediate and instantaneous was the cure which this woman received*. No sooner did she touch our Lord's clothes than she was healed. The thing that she had sought in vain for twelve years was done in a moment. The cure that many physicians could not effect was wrought in an instant of time. *She felt in her body that she was healed of her affliction.*

We need not doubt that we are meant to see here an emblem of the relief that the gospel confers on souls. The experience of many a weary conscience has been exactly like that of this woman with her disease. Many a man has spent sorrowful years in search of peace with God and failed to find it. He has gone to earthly remedies and obtained no relief. He has wearied himself in going from place to place, and church to church, and has felt after all *not helped at all, but rather [has] grown worse*. But at last he has found rest. And where has he found it? He has found it where this woman found hers – in Jesus Christ. He has ceased from his own works. He has stopped looking to his own endeavors and doings for relief. He has come to Christ Himself, as a humble sinner, and committed himself to His mercy. At once the burden has fallen from off his shoulders. Heaviness is turned to joy and anxiety to peace. One touch of real faith can do more for the soul than a hundred self-imposed austerities. One look at Jesus is more efficacious than years of sackcloth and ashes. May we never forget this to our dying day! Personal application to Christ is the real secret of peace with God.

Let us observe, in the fourth place, *how much it becomes Christians to confess before men the benefit they receive from Christ.* We see that this woman was not allowed to go home when cured without her cure being noticed. Our Lord inquired who had touched Him and *looked around to see the woman who had done this.* No doubt He knew perfectly the name and history of the woman. He needed not that any should tell Him. But He desired to teach her, and all those around Him, that healed souls should make public acknowledgment of mercies received.

There is a lesson here which all true Christians would do well to remember. We are not to be ashamed to confess Christ before men and to let others know what He has done for our souls. If we have found peace through His blood and have been renewed by His Spirit, we must not shrink from avowing it on every proper occasion. It is not necessary to blow a trumpet in the streets and force our experience on everybody's notice. All that is required is a willingness to acknowledge Christ as our Master without flinching from the ridicule or persecution which by so doing we may bring on ourselves. More than this is not required, but less than this ought not to content us. If we are ashamed of Jesus before men, He will one day be ashamed of us before His Father and the angels.

Let us observe, in the last place, *how precious a grace is faith.* "Daughter," says our Lord to the woman who was healed, "*your faith has made you well; go in peace.*"

Of all the Christian graces, none is so frequently mentioned in the New Testament as faith, and none is so highly commended. No grace brings such glory to Christ. Hope brings an eager expectation of good things to come. Love brings a warm and willing heart. Faith brings an empty hand, receives everything, and can give nothing in return. No grace is so important to the Christian's own soul. By faith we begin. By faith we live. By faith we stand. We walk by faith and not by sight. By faith we overcome. By faith we have peace. By faith we enter into rest. No grace should be the subject of so much self-inquiry. We should often ask ourselves, Do I really believe? Is my faith true, genuine, and the gift of God?

May we never rest until we can give a satisfactory answer to these questions! Christ has not changed since the day when this woman was healed. He is still gracious and still mighty to save. There is but one thing needful if we want salvation. That one thing is the hand of faith. Let a man only "touch" Jesus, and he shall be made whole.

Mark 5:35-43

While He was still speaking, they came from the house of the synagogue official, saying, "Your daughter has died; why trouble the Teacher anymore?" But Jesus, overhearing what was being spoken, said to the synagogue official, "Do not be afraid any longer, only believe." And He allowed no one to accompany Him, except Peter and James and John the brother of James. They came to the house of the synagogue official; and He saw a commotion, and people loudly weeping and wailing. And entering in, He said to them, "Why make a commotion and weep? The child has not died, but is asleep." They began laughing at Him. But putting them all out, He took along the child's father and mother and His own companions, and entered the room where the child was. Taking the child by the hand, He said to her, "Talitha kum!" (which translated means, "Little girl, I say to you, get up!"). Immediately the girl got up and began to walk, for she was twelve years old. And immediately they were completely astounded. And He gave them strict orders that no one should know about this, and He said that something should be given her to eat.

A great miracle is recorded in these verses. A dead girl is restored to life. Mighty as the king of terrors is, there is one mightier than he. The keys of death are in our Lord Jesus Christ's hands. He will one day *swallow up death for all time* (Isaiah 25:8).

Let us learn from these verses that *rank places no man beyond the reach of sorrow.* Jairus was an *official;* yet sickness and trouble came to his house. Jairus probably had wealth and all the medical help that wealth can command; yet money could not keep death away from his child. The daughters of officials are liable to sickness as well as the daughters of poor men. The daughters of officials die.

It is good for us all to remember this. We are too apt to forget it. We often think and talk as if the possession of riches was the great antidote to sorrow and as if money could secure us against sickness and death. But it is the very extreme of blindness to think so. We have only to look around us and see a hundred proofs to the contrary. Death comes to palaces as well as to cottages – to landlords as well as to tenants – to the rich as well as to the poor. It caters to no man's leisure or convenience. It will not be kept out by locks and bars. *It is appointed for men to die once and after this comes judgment* (Hebrews 9:27). All are going to one place: the grave.

We may be sure there is far more equality in the portions appointed to men than at first sight appears. Sickness is a great leveler. It makes no distinction. Heaven is the only place where *no resident will say, "I am sick"* (Isaiah 33:24). Happy are they who set their affections on things above! They, and they only, have a treasure which is incorruptible. Yet a little while and they will be where they shall hear no more evil tidings. All tears shall be wiped from their faces. They shall mourn no more. Never again shall they hear those sorrowful words, "Your daughter – your son – your wife – your husband – is dead." The former things will have passed away.

Let us learn, for another thing, *how almighty is the power of our Lord Jesus Christ.* That message which pierced the official's heart, telling him that his child was dead, did not stop our Lord for a moment. At once He cheered the father's fainting spirit with these gracious words: *"Do not be afraid any longer, only believe."* He comes to the house where many are weeping and wailing and enters the room where the girl is lying. He takes her by the hand and says, *"Little girl, I say to you, get up!"* At once the heart begins to beat again and the breath returns to the lifeless body. *The girl got up and began to walk.* No wonder that we read the words, *And immediately they were completely astounded.*

Let us think for a moment how wonderful was the change which took place in that house. From weeping to rejoicing, from mourning to congratulation, and from death to life – how great and marvelous must have been the transition! They only can tell of that, who have seen death face to face, and had the light of their households quenched, and felt the iron entering into their own souls. They, and they only, can conceive what the family of Jairus must have felt when they saw their beloved one given back once more into their bosom by the power of Christ. There must have been a happy family gathering that night!

Let us see in this glorious miracle *a proof of what Jesus can do for dead souls.* He can raise our children from the death of trespasses and sins and make them walk before Him in newness of life. He can take our sons and daughters by the hand and say to them, *"Get up!"* and bid them live not to themselves but to Him who died for them and rose again. Have we a dead soul in our family? Let us call on the Lord to come and revive him (Ephesians 2:1). Let us send to Him message after message and entreat Him to help. He that came to the support of Jairus is still plenteous in mercy and mighty in power.

Finally, let us see in this miracle *a blessed pledge of what our Lord will do in the day of His second appearing.* He will call His believing people from their graves. He will give them a better, more glorious, and more beautiful body than they had in the days of their pilgrimage. He will gather together His elect from north, and south, and east, and west to part no more and die no more. Believing parents shall once more see believing children. Believing husbands shall once more see believing wives. Let us beware of sorrowing like those who have no hope over friends who fall asleep in Christ. The youngest and loveliest believer can never die before the right time. Let us look forward. There is a glorious resurrection morning yet to come. *God will bring with Him those who have fallen asleep in Jesus* (1 Thessalonians 4:14). Those words shall one day receive a complete fulfillment: *Shall I ransom them from the power of Sheol? Shall I redeem them from death? O Death, where are your thorns? O Sheol, where is your sting?* (Hosea 13:14). He that raised the daughter of Jairus still lives! When He gathers His flock around Him at the last day, not one lamb shall be found missing.

Mark Chapter 6

Mark 6:1-6

Jesus went out from there and came into His hometown; and His disciples followed Him. When the Sabbath came, He began to teach in the synagogue; and the many listeners were astonished, saying, "Where did this man get these things, and what is this wisdom given to Him, and such miracles as these performed by His hands? Is not this the carpenter the son of Mary, and brother of James and Joses and Judas and Simon? Are not His sisters here with us?" And they took offense at Him. Jesus said to them, "A prophet is not without honor except in his hometown and among his own relatives and in his own household." And He could do no miracle there except that He laid His hands on a few sick people and healed them. And He wondered at their unbelief. And He was going around the villages teaching.

THIS PASSAGE SHOWS US OUR LORD JESUS CHRIST in *His hometown* at Nazareth. It is a sad illustration of the wickedness of man's heart and deserves special attention.

We see, in the first place, *how apt men are to undervalue things with which they are familiar.* The men of Nazareth *took offense* at our Lord. They could not think it possible that one who had lived so many years among themselves and whose brethren and sisters they knew could deserve to be followed as a public teacher.

Never had any place on earth such privileges as Nazareth. For thirty years the Son of God resided in this town and went to and fro in its streets. For thirty years He walked with God before the eyes of its inhabitants, living a blameless, perfect life. But it was all lost upon them. They were not ready to believe the gospel when the Lord came among them and taught in their synagogue. They would not believe that one whose face they knew so well and who had lived so long eating, and drinking, and dressing like one of themselves had any right to claim their attention. *They took offense at Him.*

There is nothing in all this that should surprise us. The same thing is going on around us every day in our own land. The Holy Scriptures, the preaching of the gospel, the public ordinances of religion, the abundance of churches that our country enjoys are continually undervalued by English people. They are so accustomed to them that they do not know their privileges. It is a solemn truth that in religion more than in anything else, familiarity breeds contempt.

There is comfort in this part of our Lord's experience for some of the Lord's people. There is comfort for faithful ministers of the gospel who are cast down by the unbelief of their parishioners or regular hearers. There is comfort for true Christians who stand alone in their families and see all around them a cleaving to the world. Let both remember that they are drinking the same cup as their beloved Master. Let them remember that He too was despised most by those who knew Him best. Let them learn that the utmost consistency of conduct will not make others adopt their views and opinions any more than it did the people of Nazareth. Let them know that the sorrowful words of their Lord will generally be fulfilled in the experience of His servants: *"A prophet is not without honor except in his hometown and among his own relatives and in his own household."*

We see, in the second place, *how humble was the rank of life which our Lord condescended to occupy before He began His public ministry.* The people of Nazareth said of Him, in contempt, *"Is not this the carpenter?"*

This is a remarkable expression and is only found in the Gospel of Mark. It shows us plainly that for the first thirty years of His life, our Lord was not ashamed to work with His own hands. There is something marvelous and overwhelming in the thought! He who made heaven, and earth, and sea, and all that is therein – He, without whom nothing was made that was made – the Son of God Himself took upon Himself the form of a servant and *by the sweat of [His] face* He ate bread as a working man. This is indeed that *love of Christ which passes knowledge.* Though He was rich, yet for our sakes He became poor. Both in life and in death He humbled Himself that through Him sinners might live and reign forevermore.

Let us remember, when we read this passage, that there is no sin in poverty. We never need be ashamed of poverty unless our own sins have brought it upon us. We never ought to despise others because they are poor. It is disgraceful to be a gambler, or a drunkard, or a covetous man, or a liar; but it is no disgrace to work with our own hands and earn our bread by our own labor. The thought of the carpenter's shop at Nazareth should cast down the high thoughts of all who make an idol of riches. It cannot be dishonorable to occupy the same position as the Son of God and Savior of the world.

We see, in the last place, *how exceedingly sinful is the sin of unbelief.* Two remarkable expressions are used in teaching this lesson. One is that our Lord *could do no miracle* at Nazareth by reason of the hardness of the people's hearts. The other is that *He wondered at their unbelief.* The one shows us that unbelief has a power to rob men of the highest blessings. The other shows that it is so suicidal and unreasonable a sin that even the Son of God regards it with surprise.

We can never be too much on our guard against unbelief. It is the oldest sin in the world. It began in the garden of Eden when Eve listened to the devil's promises instead of believing God's words, *"You will die."* It is the most ruinous of all sins in its consequences. It brought death into the world. It kept Israel for forty years out of Canaan. It is the sin that especially fills hell. *"He who has disbelieved shall be condemned."* It is the most foolish and inconsistent of all sins. It makes a man refuse the plainest evidence, shut his eyes against the clearest testimony, and yet believe lies. Worst of all, it is the most common sin in the world. Thousands are guilty of it on every side. In profession they are Christians. They know nothing of Paine and Voltaire. But in practice they are really unbelievers. They do not implicitly believe the Bible and receive Christ as their Savior.

Let us watch our own hearts carefully in the matter of unbelief.

The heart, and not the head, is the seat of its mysterious power. It is neither the lack of evidence nor the difficulties of Christian doctrine that makes men unbelievers. It is the lack of will to believe. They love sin. They are wedded to the world. In this state of mind they never lack showy reasons to confirm their will. The humble, childlike heart is the heart that believes.

Let us go on watching our hearts even after we have believed. The root of unbelief is never entirely destroyed. We have only to leave off watching and praying, and a noxious crop of unbelief will soon spring up. No prayer is so important as that of the disciples to their Lord: *"Increase our faith!"*

Mark 6:7-13

And He summoned the twelve and began to send them out in pairs, and gave them authority over the unclean spirits; and He instructed them that they should take nothing for their journey, except a mere staff—no bread, no bag, no money in their belt—but to wear sandals; and He added, "Do not put on two tunics." And He said to them, "Wherever you enter a house, stay there until you leave town. Any place that does not receive you or listen to you, as you go out from there, shake the dust off the soles of your feet for a testimony against them." They went out and preached that men should repent. And they were casting out many demons and were anointing with oil many sick people and healing them.

These verses describe the first sending forth of the apostles to preach. The great head of the church made proof of His ministers before He left them alone in the world. He taught them to try their own powers of teaching and to find out their own weaknesses while He was yet with them. Thus, on the one hand, He was enabled to correct their mistakes. Thus, on the other hand, they were trained for the work they were one day to do and were not novices when finally left to themselves. Well would it be for the church if all ministers of the gospel were prepared for their duty in like manner and did not so often take up their office untried, unproved, and inexperienced.

Let us observe in these verses *how our Lord Jesus Christ sent forth His apostles "in pairs."* Mark is the only evangelist who mentions this fact. It is one that deserves special notice.

There can be no doubt that this fact is meant to teach us the advantages of Christian company to all who work for Christ. The wise man had good reason for saying, *Two are better than one* (Ecclesiastes 4:9). Two men together will do more work than two men singly. They will help one another in judgment and commit fewer mistakes. They will aid one another in difficulties and less often fail of success. They will stir one another up when tempted to idleness and less often relapse into indolence and indifference. They will comfort one another in times of trial and be less often cast down. *Woe to the one who falls when there is not another to lift him up* (Ecclesiastes 4:10).

It is probable that this principle is not sufficiently remembered in the church of Christ in these latter days. The harvest is undoubtedly great all over the world, both at home and abroad. The laborers are unquestionably few, and the supply of faithful men far less than the demand. The arguments for sending out men one by one under existing circumstances are undeniably strong and weighty. But still the conduct of our Lord in this place is a striking fact. The fact that there is hardly a single case in the book of Acts where we find Paul or any other apostle working entirely alone is another remarkable circumstance. It is difficult to avoid the conclusion that if the rule of going forth *in pairs* had been more strictly observed, the missionary field would have yielded larger results than it has.

One thing at all events is clear, and that is the duty of all workers for Christ to work together and help one another whenever they can. *Iron sharpens iron, so one man sharpens another.* Ministers and missionaries, and district visitors, and Sunday school teachers should take opportunities for meeting and taking sweet counsel together. The words of Paul contain a truth which is too much forgotten: *And let us consider how to stimulate one another to love and good deeds, not forsaking our own assembling together, as is the habit of some, but encouraging one another; and all the more as you see the day drawing near* (Hebrews 10:24-25).

Let us observe, in the second place, *what solemn words our Lord uses about those who will not receive nor hear His ministers.* He says, *"It will be more tolerable for the land of Sodom and Gomorrah in the day of judgment than for that city."*

This is a truth which we find very frequently laid down in the Gospels. It is painful to think how entirely it is overlooked by many. Thousands appear to suppose that so long as they go to church and do not murder, or steal, or cheat, or openly break any of God's commandments, they are in no great danger. They forget that it needs something more than mere abstinence from outward irregularities to save a man's soul. They do not see that one of the greatest sins a man can commit in the sight of God is to hear the gospel of Christ and not believe it – to be invited to repent and believe and yet to remain careless and unbelieving. In short, to reject the gospel will sink a man to the lowest place in hell.

Let us never turn away from a passage like this without asking ourselves, What are we doing with the gospel? We live in a Christian land. We have the Bible in our houses. We hear of the salvation of the gospel frequently every year. But have we received it into our hearts? Have we really obeyed it in our lives? Have we, in short, laid hold on the hope set before us, taken up the cross, and followed Christ? If not, we are far worse than the heathen who bow down to stocks and stones. We are far more guilty than the people of Sodom and Gomorrah. They never heard the gospel and therefore never rejected it. But as for us, we hear the gospel and yet will not believe. May we search our own hearts and take heed that we do not ruin our own souls!

Let us observe, in the last place, *what was the doctrine which our Lord's apostles preached.* We read that *they went out and preached that men should repent.*

The necessity of repentance may seem at first sight a very simple and elementary truth. And yet volumes might be written to show the fullness of the doctrine and the suitableness of it to every age and time and to every rank and class of mankind. It is inseparably connected with right views of God, of human nature, of sin, of Christ, of holiness, and of heaven. All have sinned and come short of the glory of God. All need to be brought to a sense of their sins, to a sorrow for them, to a willing-ness to give them up, and to a hunger and thirst after pardon. All, in a word, need to be born again and to flee to Christ. This is repentance unto life. Nothing less than this is required for the salvation of any man. Nothing less than this ought to be pressed on men by everyone who professes to teach Bible religion. We must bid men repent if we would walk in the steps of the apostles, and when they have repented, we must bid them repent more and more to their last day.

Have we ourselves repented? This, after all, is the question that con-cerns us most. It is well to know what the apostles taught. It is well to be familiar with the whole system of Christian doctrine. But it is far better to know repentance by experience and to feel it inwardly in our own hearts. May we never rest until we know and feel that we have repented! There are no impenitent people in the kingdom of heaven. All who enter in there have felt, mourned over, forsaken, and sought pardon for sin. This must be our experience if we hope to be saved.

Mark 6:14-29

And King Herod heard of it, for His name had become well known; and people were saying, "John the Baptist has risen from the dead, and that is why these miraculous powers are at work in Him." But others were saying, "He is Elijah." And others were saying, "He is a prophet, like one of the prophets of old." But when Herod heard of it, he kept saying, "John, whom I beheaded, has risen!" For Herod himself had sent and had John arrested and bound in prison on account of Herodias, the wife of his brother Philip, because he had married her. For John had been saying to Herod, "It is not lawful for you to have your brother's wife." Herodias had a grudge against him and wanted to put him to death and could not do so; for Herod was afraid of John, knowing that he was a righteous and holy man, and he kept him safe. And when he heard him, he was very perplexed; but he

*used to enjoy listening to him. A strategic day came when Herod
on his birthday gave a banquet for his lords and military com-
manders and the leading men of Galilee; and when the daughter of Herodias herself came in and danced, she pleased Herod
and his dinner guests; and the king said to the girl, "Ask me for
whatever you want and I will give it to you." And he swore to
her, "Whatever you ask of me, I will give it to you; up to half of
my kingdom." And she went out and said to her mother, "What
shall I ask for?" And she said, "The head of John the Baptist."
Immediately she came in a hurry to the king and asked, saying,
"I want you to give me at once the head of John the Baptist on a
platter." And although the king was very sorry, yet because of his
oaths and because of his dinner guests, he was unwilling to refuse
her. Immediately the king sent an executioner and commanded
him to bring back his head. And he went and had him beheaded
in the prison, and brought his head on a platter, and gave it to
the girl; and the girl gave it to her mother. When his disciples
heard about this, they came and took away his body and laid it
in a tomb.*

These verses describe the death of one of the most eminent saints of
God. They relate the murder of John the Baptist. Of all the evangelists,
none tells this sad story so fully as Mark. Let us see what practical lessons the passage contains for our own souls.

We see, in the first place, *the amazing power of truth over the conscience.* Herod is *afraid of* John the Baptist while he lives and is troubled
about him after he dies. A friendless, solitary preacher with no other
weapon than God's truth disturbs and terrifies a king.

Everybody has a conscience. Here lies the secret of a faithful minister's
power. This is the reason why Felix *became frightened* and Agrippa was
almost persuaded when Paul the prisoner spoke before them. God has
not left Himself without witness in the hearts of unconverted people.
Fallen and corrupt as man is, there are thoughts within him accusing
or excusing, according as he lives – thoughts that will not be shut out
– thoughts that can make even kings like Herod restless and afraid.

None ought to remember this so much as ministers and teachers. If they preach and teach Christ's truth, they may rest assured that their work is not in vain. Children may seem inattentive in schools. Hearers may seem careless in congregations. But in both cases there is often far more going on in the conscience than our eyes see. Seeds often spring up and bear fruit when the sower, like John the Baptist, is dead or gone.

We see, in the second place, *how far people may go in religion and yet miss salvation by yielding to one master sin.*

King Herod went further than many. He *was afraid of John.* He knew *that he was a righteous and holy man.* He observed him. He heard him and did many things in consequence. He even *used to enjoy listening to him.* But there was one thing Herod would not do. He would not cease from adultery. He would not give up Herodias. And so he ruined his soul forevermore.

Let us take warning from Herod's case. Let us keep back nothing – cleave to no favorite vice – spare nothing that stands between us and salvation. Let us often look within and make sure that there is no darling lust or pet transgression which, Herodias-like, is murdering our souls. Let us rather cut off the right hand and pluck out the right eye than go into hellfire. Let us not be content with admiring favorite preachers and gladly hearing evangelical sermons. Let us not rest until we can say with David, *I esteem right all Your precepts concerning everything, I hate every false way* (Psalm 119:128).

We see, in the third place, *how boldly a faithful minister of God ought to rebuke sin.* John the Baptist spoke plainly to Herod about the wickedness of his life. He did not excuse himself under the plea that it was imprudent, or impolitic, or untimely, or useless to speak out. He did not say smooth things and palliate the king's ungodliness by using soft words to describe his offense. He told his royal hearer the plain truth, regardless of all consequences – *"It is not lawful for you to have your brother's wife."*

Here is a pattern that all ministers ought to follow. Publicly and privately, from the pulpit and in private visits, they ought to rebuke all open sin and deliver a faithful warning to all who are living in it.

It may give offense. It may entail immense unpopularity. With all this they have nothing to do. Duties are theirs. Results are God's.

No doubt it requires great grace and courage to do this. No doubt a reprover, like John the Baptist, must go to work wisely and lovingly in carrying out his Master's commission and rebuking the wicked. But it is a matter in which his character for faithfulness and charity are manifestly at stake. If he believes a man is injuring his soul, he ought surely to tell him so. If he loves him truly and tenderly, he ought not to let him ruin himself unwarned. Great as the present offense may be, in the long run the faithful reprover will generally be respected. *He who rebukes a man will afterward find more favor than he who flatters with the tongue* (Proverbs 28:23).

We see, in the fourth place, *how bitterly people hate a reprover when they are determined to keep their sins.* Herodias, the king's unhappy partner in iniquity, seems to have sunk even deeper in sin than Herod. Hardened and seared in conscience by her wickedness, she hated John the Baptist for his faithful testimony and never rested until she had procured his death.

We need not wonder at this. When men and women have chosen their line and resolved to have their own wicked way, they dislike anyone who tries to turn them. They want to be let alone. They are irritated by opposition. They are angry when they are told the truth. The prophet Elijah was called the *troubler of Israel.* The prophet Micaiah was hated by Ahab because *he never prophesie[d] good concerning [him] but always evil.* The prophets and faithful preachers of every age have been treated in like manner. They have been hated by some as well as not believed.

Let it never surprise us when we hear of faithful ministers of the gospel being spoken against, hated, and reviled. Let us rather remember that they are ordained to bear witness against sin, the world, and the devil, and that if they are faithful, they cannot help giving offense. It is no disgrace to a minister's character to be disliked by the wicked and ungodly. It is no real honor to a minister to be thought well of by everybody. Those words of our Lord are not enough considered: "*Woe to you when all men speak well of you.*"

We see, in the fifth place, *how much sin may sometimes follow from feasting and reveling.* Herod keeps his birthday with a splendid banquet. Company, drinking, and dancing fill up the day. In a moment of excitement, he grants a wicked girl's request to have the head of John the Baptist cut off. The next day, in all probability, he repented bitterly of his conduct. But the deed was done. It was too late.

This is a faithful picture of what often results from feasting and merrymaking. People do things at such seasons from heated feelings which they afterwards deeply regret. Happy are they who keep clear of temptations and avoid giving occasion to the devil. Men never know what they may do when they once venture off safe ground. Late hours, crowded rooms, splendid entertainments, mixed company, music, and dancing may seem harmless to many people. But the Christian should never forget that to take part in these things is to open a wider door to temptation.

We see finally, in these verses, *how little reward some of God's best servants receive in this world.* An unjust imprisonment and a violent death were the last fruit that John the Baptist reaped in return for his labor. Like Stephen and James and others of whom the world was not worthy, he was called to seal his testimony with his blood.

Histories like these are meant to remind us that the true Christian's best things are yet to come. His rest, his crown, his wages, and his reward are all on the other side of the grave. Here, in this world, he must walk by faith and not by sight; and if he looks for the praise of man, he will be disappointed. Here, in this life, he must sow, and labor, and fight, and endure persecution; and if he expects a great earthly reward, he expects what he will not find. But this life is not all. There is to be a day of retribution. There is a glorious harvest yet to come. Heaven will make amends for all. Eye has not seen and ear has not heard the glorious things that God has laid up for all who love Him. The value of real religion is not to be measured by the things seen but the things unseen. *The sufferings of this present time are not worthy to be compared with the glory that is to be revealed to us* (Romans 8:18). *For momentary, light affliction is producing for us an eternal weight of glory far beyond all comparison* (2 Corinthians 4:17).

Mark 6:30-34

The apostles gathered together with Jesus; and they reported to Him all that they had done and taught. And He said to them, "Come away by yourselves to a secluded place and rest a while." (For there were many people coming and going, and they did not even have time to eat.) They went away in the boat to a secluded place by themselves. The people saw them going, and many recognized them and ran there together on foot from all the cities, and got there ahead of them. When Jesus went ashore, He saw a large crowd, and He felt compassion for them because they were like sheep without a shepherd; and He began to teach them many things.

Let us observe in this passage *the conduct of the apostles when they returned from their first mission as preachers.* We read that they *gathered together with Jesus; and they reported to Him all that they had done and taught.*

These words are deeply instructive. They are a bright example to all ministers of the gospel and to all laborers in the great work of doing good to souls. All such should daily do as the apostles did on this occasion. They should tell all their proceedings to the great head of the church. They should spread all their work before Christ and ask of Him counsel, guidance, strength, and help.

Prayer is the main secret of success in spiritual business. It moves Him who can move heaven and earth. It brings down the promised aid of the Holy Spirit without whom the finest sermons, the clearest teaching, and the most diligent labors are all alike in vain. It is not always those who have the most eminent gifts who are most successful laborers for God. It is generally those who keep up closest communion with Christ and are most constant in prayer. It is those who cry with the prophet Ezekiel, *"Come from the four winds, O breath, and breathe on these slain, that they come to life"* (Ezekiel 37:9). It is those who follow most exactly the apostolic model and *devote [themselves] to prayer and to the ministry of the word* (Acts 6:4). Happy is that church which has a praying as well as a preaching ministry! The question we should ask about a new minister is not merely, Can he preach well? but also, Does he pray much for his people and his work?

Let us observe, in the second place, *the words of our Lord to the apostles when they returned from their first public ministry.* Jesus said to them, *"Come away by yourselves to a secluded place and rest a while."*

These words are full of tender consideration. Our Lord knows well that His servants are flesh as well as spirit and have bodies as well as souls. He knows that at best they have a treasure in earthen vessels and are themselves encompassed with many infirmities. He shows them that He does not expect from them more than their bodily strength can do. He asks for what we can do and not for what we cannot do. *"Come away by yourselves to a secluded place and rest a while."*

These words are full of deep wisdom. Our Lord knows well that His servants must attend to their own souls as well as the souls of others. He knows that a constant attention to public work is apt to make us forget our own private soul business, and that while we are keeping the vineyards of others, we are in danger of neglecting our own (Song of Solomon 1:6). He reminds us that it is good for ministers to withdraw occasionally from public work and look within. *"Come away by yourselves to a secluded place and rest a while."*

There are few unfortunately in the church of Christ who need these admonitions. There are but few in danger of overworking themselves and injuring their own bodies and souls by excessive attention to others. The vast majority of professing Christians are indolent and slothful and do nothing for the world around them. There are few comparatively who need the bridle nearly so much as the spur. Yet these few ought to lay to heart the lessons of this passage. They should economize their health as a talent and not squander it away like gamblers. They should be content with spending their daily income of strength and should not draw recklessly on their principal. They should remember that to do a little and do it well is often the way to do most in the long run. Above all, they should never forget to watch their own hearts jealously and to make time for regular self-examination and calm meditation. The prosperity of a man's ministry and public work is intimately bound up with the prosperity of his own soul. Occasional retirement is one of the most useful ordinances.

Finally, let us observe the *feelings of our Lord Jesus Christ towards the people who came together to Him.* We read that He *felt compassion for them because they were like sheep without a shepherd.* They were destitute of teachers. They had no guides but the blind scribes and Pharisees. They had no spiritual food but man-made traditions. Thousands of immortal souls stood before our Lord, ignorant, helpless, and on the high road to ruin. It touched the gracious heart of our Lord Jesus Christ. He *felt compassion for them . . . and He began to teach them many things.*

Let us never forget that our Lord is the same yesterday, today, and forever. He never changes. High in heaven at God's right hand, He still looks with compassion on the children of men. He still pities the ignorant and those who are out of the way. He is still willing to *teach them many things.* Special as His love is towards His own sheep who hear His voice, He still has a mighty general love towards all mankind – a love of real pity, a love of compassion. We must not overlook this. It is a poor theology which teaches that Christ cares for none except believers. There is warrant in Scripture for telling the chief of sinners that Jesus pities them and cares for their souls, that Jesus is willing to save them and invites them to believe and be saved.

Let us ask ourselves, as we leave the passage, whether we know anything of the mind of Christ. Are we, like Him, tenderly concerned about the souls of the unconverted? Do we, like Him, feel deep compassion for all who are yet as sheep without a shepherd? Do we care about the impenitent and ungodly near our own doors? Do we care about the heathen, the Jew, the Muslim, and the Roman Catholic in foreign lands? Do we use every means and give our money willingly to spread the gospel in the world? These are serious questions and demand a serious reply. The man who cares nothing for the souls of other people is not like Jesus Christ. It may well be doubted whether he is converted himself and knows the value of his own soul.

Mark 6:35-46

When it was already quite late, His disciples came to Him and said, "This place is desolate and it is already quite late; send them away so that they may go into the surrounding countryside and villages and buy themselves something to eat." But He answered them, "You give them something to eat!" And they said to Him, "Shall we go and spend two hundred denarii on bread and give them something to eat?" And He said to them, "How many loaves do you have? Go look!" And when they found out, they said, "Five, and two fish." And He commanded them all to sit down by groups on the green grass. They sat down in groups of hundreds and of fifties. And He took the five loaves and the two fish, and looking up toward heaven, He blessed the food and broke the loaves and He kept giving them to the disciples to set before them; and He divided up the two fish among them all. They all ate and were satisfied, and they picked up twelve full baskets of the broken pieces, and also of the fish. There were five thousand men who ate the loaves. Immediately Jesus made His disciples get into the boat and go ahead of Him to the other side to Bethsaida, while He Himself was sending the crowd away. After bidding them farewell, He left for the mountain to pray.

Of all our Lord Jesus Christ's miracles, none is so frequently described in the Gospels as that which we have now read. Each of the four evangelists was inspired to record it. It is evident that it demands more than ordinary attention from every reader of God's Word.

Let us observe, for one thing in this passage, *what an example this miracle affords of our Lord Jesus Christ's almighty power.* We are told that He fed five thousand men with five loaves and two fish. We are distinctly told that this multitude had nothing to eat. We are no less distinctly told that the whole provision for their sustenance consisted of only five loaves and two fish. And yet we read that our Lord took these loaves and fish, blessed, broke, and gave them to His disciples to set before the people. And the conclusion of the narrative tells us that *they all ate and were satisfied, and they picked up twelve full baskets of the broken pieces.*

Here was creative power beyond all question. Something real, solid, and substantial must manifestly have been called into being which did not exist before. There is no room left for the theory that the people were under the influence of an optical delusion or a heated imagination. Five thousand hungry people would never have been satisfied if they had not received into their mouths material bread. Twelve baskets full of broken pieces would never have been picked up if the five loaves had not been miraculously multiplied. In short, it is plain that the hand of Him who made the world out of nothing was present on this occasion. None but He who at the first created all things and sent down manna in the desert could thus have *prepare[d] a table in the wilderness.*

It becomes all true Christians to store up facts like these in their minds and to remember them in time of need. We live in the midst of an evil world and see few with us and many against us. We carry within us a weak heart too ready at any moment to turn aside from the right way. We have near us at every moment a busy devil watching continually for our halting and seeking to lead us into temptation. Where shall we turn for comfort? What shall keep faith alive and preserve us from sinking into despair? There is only one answer. We must look to Jesus. We must think on His almighty power and His wonders of old time. We must call to mind how He can create food for His people out of nothing and supply the needs of those who follow Him, even in the wilderness. And as we think these thoughts, we must remember that this Jesus still lives, never changes, and is on our side.

Let us observe, for another thing in this passage, *our Lord Jesus Christ's conduct when the miracle of feeding the multitude had been performed.* We read that *after bidding them farewell, He left for the mountain to pray.*

There is something deeply instructive in this circumstance. Our Lord never sought the praise of man. After one of His greatest miracles, we find Him immediately seeking solitude and spending His time in prayer. He practiced what He had taught elsewhere when He said, *"Go into your inner room, close your door and pray to your Father who is in secret."* None ever did such mighty works as He did. None ever spoke such words. None ever was so constant in prayer.

Let our Lord's conduct in this respect be our example. We cannot work miracles as He did; in this He stands alone. But we can walk in His steps in the matter of private devotion. If we have the Spirit of adoption, we can pray. Let us resolve to pray more than we have done hitherto. Let us strive to make time, and place, and opportunity for being alone with God. Above all, let us not only pray before we attempt to work for God, but pray also after our work is done.

It would be well for us all if we examined ourselves more frequently as to our habits about private prayer. What time do we give to it in the twenty-four hours of the day? What progress can we observe, one year with another, in the fervency, fullness, and earnestness of our prayers? What do we know by experience of *laboring earnestly* in prayer (Colossians 4:12)? These are humbling questions, but they are useful for our souls. There are few things, it may be feared, in which Christians come so far short of Christ's example as they do in the matter of prayer. Our Master's strong crying and tears – His continuing all night in prayer to God – His frequent withdrawal to private places to hold close communion with the Father are things more talked of and admired than imitated. We live in an age of hurry, bustle, and so-called activity. Men are tempted continually to cut short their private devotions and abridge their prayers. When this is the case, we need not wonder that the church of Christ does little in proportion to its machinery. The church must learn to copy its Head more closely. Its members must be more in their closets. *You do not have because you do not ask* (James 4:2).

Mark 6:47-56

When it was evening, the boat was in the middle of the sea, and He was alone on the land. Seeing them straining at the oars, for the wind was against them, at about the fourth watch of the night He came to them, walking on the sea; and He intended to pass by them. But when they saw Him walking on the sea, they supposed that it was a ghost, and cried out; for they all saw Him and were terrified. But immediately He spoke with them and said to them, "Take courage; it is I, do not be afraid." Then He got into the boat with them, and the wind stopped; and they were utterly astonished, for they had not gained any insight from the incident of the loaves, but their heart was hardened. When they had crossed over they came to land at Gennesaret, and moored to the shore. When they got out of the boat, immediately the people recognized Him, and ran about that whole country and began to carry here and there on their pallets those who were sick, to the place they heard He was. Wherever He entered villages, or cities, or countryside, they were laying the sick in the market places, and imploring Him that they might just touch the fringe of His cloak; and as many as touched it were being cured.

The event first recorded in these verses is a beautiful emblem of the position of all believers between the first and second advents of Jesus Christ. Like the disciples, we are now tossed to and fro by storms and do not at the moment enjoy the visible presence of our Lord. But like the disciples, we shall see our Lord face to face again, though it may be a time of great extremity when He returns. Like the disciples, we shall see all things changed for the better when our Master comes to us. We shall no longer be buffeted by storms. There will be a great calm.

There is nothing fanciful in such an application of the passage. We need not doubt that there is a deep meaning in every step of His life who was God *revealed in the flesh*. For the present, however, let us confine ourselves to the plain, practical lessons which these verses contain.

Let us notice, in the first place, *how our Lord sees the troubles of His believing people and in due time will help them*. We read that when *the boat was in the middle of the sea, and He was alone on the land*, He saw His disciples *straining at the oars*; He *came to them, walking on the sea*; He cheered them with the gracious words, *"It is I, do not be afraid"*; and He changed the storm into a calm.

There are thoughts of comfort here for all true believers. Wherever they may be or whatever their circumstances, the Lord Jesus sees them.

Alone or in company, in sickness or in health, by sea or by land, in perils in the city, and in perils in the wilderness – the same eye which saw the disciples tossed on the lake is ever looking at us. We are never beyond the reach of His care. Our way is never hidden from Him. He knows the path that we take and is still able to help. He may not come to our aid at the time we like best, but He will never allow us utterly to fail. He who walked upon the water never changes. He will always come at the right time to uphold His people. Though He tarry, let us wait patiently. Jesus sees us and will not forsake us.

Let us notice, in the second place, *the fears of the disciples when they first saw our Lord walking upon the sea.* We are told that *they supposed that it was a ghost, and cried out; for they all saw Him and were terrified.*

What a faithful picture of human nature we have in these words! How many thousands in the present day, if they had seen what the disciples saw, would have behaved in the same manner! How few, if they were on board a ship in a storm at midnight and suddenly saw one walking on the water and drawing near to the ship – how few would preserve their composure and be altogether free from fears! Let men laugh, if they please, at the superstitious fears of these unlearned disciples. Let them boast, if they like, of the march of intellect and the spread of knowledge in these latter times. There are few, we may confidently assert, who, placed in the same position as the apostles, would have shown more courage than they did. The boldest skeptics have sometimes proved the greatest cowards when appearances have been seen at night which they could not explain.

The truth is that there is an instinctive feeling in all men which makes them shrink from anything which seems to belong to another world. There is a consciousness which many try in vain to conceal by affected composure that there are beings unseen as well as seen, and that the life which we now live in the flesh is not the only life in which man has a portion. The common stories about ghosts and apparitions are undoubtedly foolish and superstitious. They are almost always traceable to the fears and imaginations of weak-minded people. Yet the universal attention which such stories obtain all over the world is a fact that deserves notice. It is an indirect evidence of latent belief in unseen things, just as a counterfeit coin is an evidence that there is true money. It forms a peculiar testimony which the infidel would find it hard to explain away. It proves that there is something within men which testifies of a world beyond the grave, and that when men feel it, they are afraid.

The plain duty of the true Christian is to live provided with an antidote against all fears of the great unseen world. That antidote is faith in an unseen Savior and constant communion with Him. Armed with that antidote and seeing Him who is invisible, nothing need make us afraid. We travel on towards a world of spirits. We are surrounded even now by many dangers. But with Jesus for our Shepherd, we have no cause for alarm. With Him for our Shield, we are safe.

Let us notice, in the conclusion of the chapter, *what a bright example we have of our duty to one another*. We are told that when our Lord came into the land of Gennesaret, the people *ran about that whole country* and brought to Him on pallets *those who were sick*. We read that *wherever He entered villages, or cities, or countryside, they were laying the sick in the market places, and imploring Him that they might just touch the fringe of His cloak*.

Let us see here a pattern for ourselves. Let us go and do likewise. Let us strive to bring all around us who are in need of spiritual medicine to Jesus, the Great Physician, that they may be healed. Souls are dying every day. Time is short. Opportunities are rapidly passing away. The night comes when no man can work.

Let us spare no pains in laboring to bring men and women to the knowledge of Jesus Christ that they may be saved. It is a comfortable thought that as many as touch Him will be made whole.

Mark Chapter 7

Mark 7:1-13

The Pharisees and some of the scribes gathered around Him when they had come from Jerusalem, and had seen that some of His disciples were eating their bread with impure hands, that is, unwashed. (For the Pharisees and all the Jews do not eat unless they carefully wash their hands, thus observing the traditions of the elders; and when they come from the market place, they do not eat unless they cleanse themselves; and there are many other things which they have received in order to observe, such as the washing of cups and pitchers and copper pots.) The Pharisees and the scribes asked Him, "Why do Your disciples not walk according to the tradition of the elders, but eat their bread with impure hands?" And He said to them, "Rightly did Isaiah prophesy of you hypocrites, as it is written:

> *'This people honors Me with their lips,*
> *But their heart is far away from Me.*
> *'But in vain do they worship Me,*
> *Teaching as doctrines the precepts of men.'*

Neglecting the commandment of God, you hold to the tradition of men." He was also saying to them, "You are experts at setting aside the commandment of God in order to keep your tradition. For Moses said, 'Honor your father and your mother'; and, 'He who speaks evil of father or mother, is to be put to death'; but you say, 'If a man says to his father or his mother, whatever I have that would help you is Corban (that is to say, given to God),' you

no longer permit him to do anything for his father or his mother;
thus invalidating the word of God by your tradition which you
have handed down; and you do many things such as that."

THIS PASSAGE CONTAINS A HUMBLING PICTURE of what human nature is capable of doing in religion. It is one of those Scriptures which ought to be frequently and diligently studied by all who desire the success of the church of Christ.

The first thing which demands our attention in these verses is *the low and degraded condition of Jewish religion when our Lord was upon earth.* What can be more deplorable than the statement now before us? We find the principal teachers of the Jewish nation finding fault because *some of His disciples were eating their bread with impure hands, that is, unwashed.* We are told that they attached great importance to *the washing of cups and pitchers and copper pots.* In short, the man who paid most rigid attention to mere external observances of human invention was reckoned the holiest man!

The nation, be it remembered, in which this state of things existed was the most highly favored in the world. To it was given the law on Mount Sinai, the service of God, the priesthood, the covenants, and the promises. Moses, and Samuel, and David, and the prophets lived and died among its people. No nation upon earth ever had so many spiritual privileges. No nation ever misused its privileges so fearfully and so thoroughly forsook its own mercies. Never did fine gold become so dim! From the religion of the books of Deuteronomy and Psalms to the religion of washing hands and pots and cups – how great was the fall! No wonder that in the time of our Lord's earthly ministry He found the people like sheep without a shepherd. External observances alone feed no consciences and sanctify no hearts!

Let the history of the Jewish Church be a warning to us never to trifle with false doctrine. If we once tolerate it, we never know how far it may go or into what degraded state of religion we may at last fall. If we once leave the King's highway of truth, we may end with washing pots and cups like Pharisees and scribes. There is nothing too base, trifling, or irrational for a man if he once turns his back on God's Word. There are branches of the church of Christ at this day in which the Scriptures are never read and the gospel never preached – branches in which the only religion now remaining consists of using a few unmeaning forms and keeping certain man-made fasts and feasts – branches which began well like the Jewish Church but, like the Jewish Church, have now fallen into utter barrenness and decay. We can never be too jealous about false doctrine. A little leaven leavens the whole lump. Let us earnestly contend for the whole faith once delivered to the saints.

The second thing that demands our attention is *the uselessness of mere lip service in the worship of God.* Our Lord enforces this lesson by a quotation from the Old Testament – *"You hypocrites, rightly did Isaiah prophesy of you: 'This people honors Me with their lips, but their heart is far away from Me'"* (Matthew 15:7-8).

The heart is the part of man which God chiefly notices in religion. The bowed head and the bended knee, the grave face and the rigid posture, the ritual response and the formal amen – all these together do not make up a spiritual worshipper. The eyes of God look further and deeper. He requires the worship of the heart. *Give me your heart, my son,* He says to every one of us.

Let us remember this in the public congregation. It must not content us to take our bodies to church if we leave our hearts at home. The eye of man may detect no flaw in our service. Our minister may look at us with approval. Our neighbors may think us patterns of what a Christian ought to be. Our voice may be heard foremost in the praise and prayer. But it is all worse than nothing in God's sight if our hearts are far away. It is only wood, hay, and stubble before Him who discerns thoughts and reads the secrets of the inward man.

Let us remember this in our private devotions. It must not satisfy us to say good words if our heart and our lips do not go together. What does it profit us to be fluent and lengthy if our imaginations are roving far away while we are upon our knees? It profits us nothing at all. God sees what we are really doing and rejects our offering. Heart prayers are the prayers He loves to hear. Heart prayers are the only prayers that He will answer. Our petitions may be weak, and stammering, and poor in our eyes. They may be presented with no fine words or well-chosen language and might seem almost unintelligible, if they were written down. But if they come from a right heart, God understands them. Such prayers are His delight.

The last thing that demands our attention in these verses is *the tendency of man's inventions in religion to supplant God's Word.* Three times we find this charge brought forward by our Lord against the Pharisees. *"Neglecting the commandment of God, you hold to the tradition of men." "Setting aside the commandment of God in order to keep your tradition." "Invalidating the word of God by your tradition."* The first step of the Pharisees was to add their traditions to the Scriptures as useful supplements. The second was to place them on a level with the Word of God and give them equal authority. The last was to honor them above the Scriptures and to degrade Scripture from its lawful position. This was the state of things which our Lord found when He was upon earth. Practically, the traditions of man were everything, and the Word of God was nothing at all. Obedience to the traditions constituted true religion. Obedience to the Scriptures was lost sight of altogether.

It is a mournful fact that Christians have far too often walked in the steps of Pharisees in this matter. The very same process has taken place over and over again. The very same consequences have resulted. Religious observances of man's inventions have been pressed on the acceptance of Christians – observances to all appearances useful and at all events well-meant, but observances nowhere commanded in the Word of God. These very observances have by and by been required with more vigor than God's own commandments and defended with more zeal than the authority of God's own Word. We need not look far for examples. The history of our own church will supply them.

Let us beware of attempting to add anything to the Word of God as necessary to salvation. It provokes God to give us over to judicial blindness. It is as good as saying that His Bible is not perfect and that we know better than He does what is necessary for man's salvation. It is just as easy to destroy the authority of God's Word by addition as by subtraction, by burying it under man's inventions as by denying its truth. The whole Bible, and nothing but the Bible, must be our rule of faith, nothing added and nothing taken away.

Finally, let us draw a broad line of distinction between those things in religion which have been devised by man and those which are plainly commanded in God's Word. What God commands is necessary to salvation. What man commands is not. What man devises may be useful and expedient for the times, but salvation does not hinge on obedience to it. What God requires is essential to life eternal. He that willfully disobeys it ruins his own soul.

Mark 7:14-23

After He called the crowd to Him again, He began saying to them, "Listen to Me, all of you, and understand: there is nothing outside the man which can defile him if it goes into him; but the things which proceed out of the man are what defile the man. [If anyone has ears to hear, let him."] When he had left the crowd and entered the house, His disciples questioned Him about the parable. And He said to them, "Are you so lacking in understanding also? Do you not understand that whatever goes into the man from outside cannot defile him, because it does not go into his heart, but into his stomach, and is eliminated?" (Thus He declared all foods clean.) And He was saying, "That which proceeds out of the man, that is what defiles the man. For from within, out of the heart of men, proceed the evil thoughts, fornications, thefts, murders, adulteries, deeds of coveting and wickedness, as well as deceit, sensuality, envy, slander, pride and foolishness. All these evil things proceed from within and defile the man."

We see in the beginning of this passage *how slow of understanding men are in spiritual things.* Our Lord says to the people, *"Listen to Me, all of you, and understand." "Are you so lacking in understanding also?"* He says to His disciples, *"Do you not understand?"*

The corruption of human nature is a universal disease. It affects not only a man's heart, will, and conscience, but also his mind, memory, and understanding. The very same person who is quick and clever in worldly things will often utterly fail to comprehend the simplest truths of Christianity. He will often be unable to grasp the plainest reasonings of the gospel. He will see no meaning in the clearest statements of evangelical doctrine. They will sound to him either foolish or mysterious. He will listen to them like one listening to a foreign language, catching a word here and there but not seeing the drift of the whole. *The world through its wisdom did not come to know God* (1 Corinthians 1:21). It hears but does not understand.

We must pray daily for the teaching of the Holy Spirit if we would make progress in the knowledge of divine things. Without the Holy Spirit, the mightiest intellect and the strongest reasoning powers will carry us but a little way. In reading the Bible and hearing sermons, everything depends on the spirit in which we read and hear. A humble, teachable, childlike frame of mind is the grand secret of success. Happy is he who often says with David, *Teach me Your statutes* (Psalm 119:64). Such a one will understand as well as hear.

We see, in the second place from this passage, that *the heart is the chief source of defilement and impurity in God's sight*. Moral purity does not depend on washing or not washing – touching things or not touching them – eating things or not eating them, as the scribes and Pharisees taught. *"There is nothing outside the man which can defile him if it goes into him; but the things which proceed out of the man are what defile the man."*

There is a deep truth in these words which is frequently overlooked. Our original sinfulness and natural inclination to evil are seldom sufficiently considered. The wickedness of men is often attributed to bad examples, bad company, peculiar temptations, or the snares of the devil. It seems forgotten that every man carries within him a fountain of wickedness. We need no bad company to teach us and no devil to tempt us in order to run into sin. We have within us the beginning of every sin under heaven.

We ought to remember this in the training and education of children.

In all our management we must never forget that the seeds of all mischief and wickedness are in their hearts. It is not enough to keep boys and girls at home and shut out every outward temptation. They carry within them a heart ready for any sin, and until that heart is changed, they are not safe, no matter what we do. When children do wrong, it is a common practice to lay all the blame on bad companions. But it is mere ignorance, blindness, and foolishness to do so. Bad companions are a great evil, no doubt, and an evil to be avoided as much as possible. But no bad companion teaches a boy or girl half as much sin as their own hearts will suggest to them unless they are renewed by the Spirit. The beginning of all wickedness is within. If parents were half as diligent in praying for their children's conversion as they are in keeping them from bad company, their children would turn out far better than they do.

We see, in the last place from this passage, *what a black catalogue of evils the human heart contains. "For from within, out of the heart of men, proceed the evil thoughts, fornications, thefts, murders, adulteries, deeds of coveting and wickedness, as well as deceit, sensuality, envy, slander, pride and foolishness. All these evil things proceed from within and defile the man."*

Let us distinctly understand when we read these words that our Lord is speaking of the human heart generally. He is not speaking only of the notorious profligate or the prisoner in the jail. He is speaking of all mankind. All of us, whether high or low, rich or poor, masters or servants, old or young, learned or unlearned – all of us have by nature such a heart as Jesus here describes. The seeds of all the evils here mentioned lie hidden within us all. They may lie dormant all our lives. They may be kept down by the fear of consequences, the restraint of public opinion, the dread of discovery, the desire to be thought respectable, and, above all, by the almighty grace of God. But every man has within him the root of every sin.

How humble we ought to be when we read these verses! *All of us have become as one who is unclean* in God's sight (Isaiah 64:6). He sees in each one of us countless evils which the world never sees at all, for He reads our hearts. Surely, of all sins to which we are liable, self-righteousness is the most unreasonable and unfitting.

How thankful we ought to be for the gospel when we read these verses! That gospel contains a complete provision for all the needs of our poor defiled natures. The blood of Christ can cleanse us from all sin. The Holy Spirit can change even our sinful hearts and keep them clean when changed. The man who does not glory in the gospel can surely know little of the plague that is within him.

How watchful we ought to be when we remember these verses! What a careful guard we ought to keep over our imaginations, our tongues, and our daily behavior! At the head of the blacklist of our heart's contents stand *evil thoughts*. Let us never forget that. Thoughts are the parents of words and deeds. Let us pray daily for grace to keep our thoughts in order, and let us cry earnestly and fervently, *"Lead us not into temptation."*

Mark 7:24-30

Jesus got up and went away from there to the region of Tyre. And when He had entered a house, He wanted no one to know of it; yet He could not escape notice. But after hearing of Him, a woman whose little daughter had an unclean spirit immediately came and fell at His feet. Now the woman was a Gentile, of the Syrophoenician race. And she kept asking Him to cast the demon out of her daughter. And He was saying to her, "Let the children be satisfied first, for it is not good to take the children's bread and throw it to the dogs." But she answered and said to Him, 'Yes, Lord, but even the dogs under the table feed on the children's crumbs." And He said to her, "Because of this answer go; the demon has gone out of your daughter." And going back to her home, she found the child lying on the bed, the demon having left.

We know nothing of the woman who is here mentioned beyond the facts that we here read. Her name, her former history, the way in which she was led to seek our Lord, though a Gentile and dwelling in the region of Tyre – all these things are hidden from us. But the few facts that are related about this woman are full of precious instruction. Let us observe them and learn wisdom.

In the first place, *this passage is meant to encourage us to pray for others.* The woman who came to our Lord in the history now before us must doubtless have been in deep affliction. She saw a beloved child possessed by an unclean spirit. She saw her in a condition in which no teaching could reach the mind and no medicine could heal the body – a condition only one degree better than death itself. She hears of Jesus and beseeches Him to *cast the demon out of her daughter.* She prays for one who could not pray for herself and never rests until her prayer is granted. By prayer she obtains the cure which no human means could obtain. Through the prayer of the mother, the daughter is healed. On her own behalf that daughter did not speak a word, but her mother spoke for her to the Lord and did not speak in vain. Hopeless and desperate as her case appeared, she had a praying mother, and where there is a praying mother there is always hope.

The truth here taught is one of deep importance. The case here recorded is one that does not stand alone. Few duties are so strongly recommended by scriptural example as the duty of intercessory prayer. There is a long catalogue of instances in Scripture which show the benefits that may be conferred on others by praying for them. The official's son at Capernaum – the centurion's servant – the daughter of Jairus are all striking examples. Incredible as it may seem, God is pleased to do great things for souls when friends and relations are moved to pray for them. *The effective prayer of a righteous man can accomplish much* (James 5:16).

Fathers and mothers are especially bound to remember the case of this woman. They cannot give their children new hearts. They can give them a Christian education and show them the way of life, but they cannot give them a will to choose Christ's service and a heart to love God. Yet there is one thing they can always do – they can pray for them. They can pray for the conversion of profligate sons who will have their own way and run greedily into sin. They can pray for the conversion of worldly daughters who set their affections on things below and love pleasure more than God. Such prayers are heard on high. Such prayers will often bring down blessings. Never, never let us forget that the children for whom many prayers have been offered seldom finally perish. Let us pray more for our sons and daughters. Even when they will not let us speak to them about religion, they cannot prevent us from speaking for them to God.

In the second place, *this passage is meant to teach us to persevere in praying for others.* The woman whose history we are now reading appeared at first to obtain nothing by her application to our Lord. On the contrary, our Lord's reply was discouraging. Yet she did not give up in despair. She prayed on and did not faint. She pressed her suit with sincere arguments. She would take no refusal. She pleaded for a few *crumbs* of mercy rather than none at all. And through this holy importunity, she succeeded. She heard at last these joyful words: *"Because of this answer go; the demon has gone out of your daughter."*

Perseverance in prayer is a point of great moment. Our hearts are apt to become cool and indifferent and to think that it is no use to draw near to God. Our hands soon hang down, and our knees wax faint. Satan is ever laboring to draw us off from our prayers and filling our minds with reasons why we should give them up. These things are true with respect to all prayers, but they are especially true with respect to intercessory prayer. It is always far more meager than it ought to be. It is often attempted for a little season and then left off. We see no immediate answer to our prayers. We see the people for whose souls we pray going on still in sin. We draw the conclusion that it is useless to pray for them and we allow our intercession to come to an end.

In order to arm our minds with arguments for perseverance in intercessory prayer, let us often study the case of this woman. Let us remember how she prayed on and did not faint in the face of great discouragement. Let us notice how at last she went home rejoicing, and let us resolve, by God's grace, to follow her example.

Do we know what it is to pray for ourselves? This, after all, is the first question for self-inquiry. The man who never speaks to God about his own soul can know nothing of praying for others. He is as yet godless,

Christless, and hopeless, and has to learn the very rudiments of religion. Let him awake and call upon God.

But do we pray for ourselves? Then let us take heed that we pray for others also. Let us beware of selfish prayers – prayers which are wholly taken up with our own affairs and in which there is no place for other souls besides our own. Let us name all whom we love before God continually. Let us pray for all – the worst, the hardest, and the most unbelieving. Let us continue praying for them year after year, in spite of their continued unbelief. God's time of mercy may be a distant one. Our eyes may not see an answer to our intercession. The answer may not come for ten, fifteen, or twenty years. It may not come until we have exchanged prayer for praise and are far away from this world. But while we live, let us pray for others. It is the greatest kindness we can do to anyone, to speak for him to our Lord Jesus Christ. The day of judgment will show that one of the greatest links in drawing some souls to God has been the intercessory prayer of friends.

Mark 7:31-37

Again He went out from the region of Tyre, and came through Sidon to the Sea of Galilee, within the region of Decapolis. They brought to Him one who was deaf and spoke with difficulty, and they implored Him to lay His hand on him. Jesus took him aside from the crowd, by himself, and put His fingers into his ears, and after spitting, He touched his tongue with the saliva; and looking up to heaven with a deep sigh, He said to him, "Ephphatha!" that is, "Be opened!" And his ears were opened, and the impediment of his tongue was removed, and he began speaking plainly. And He gave them orders not to tell anyone; but the more He ordered them, the more widely they continued to proclaim it. They were utterly astonished, saying, "He has done all things well; He makes even the deaf to hear and the mute to speak."

The first thing that demands our notice in these verses is *the mighty miracle that is here recorded.* We read that they brought unto our Lord *one who was deaf and spoke with difficulty,* and besought Him that He would *lay His hand on him.* At once the petition is granted, and the cure is wrought. Speech and hearing are instantaneously given to the man by a word and a touch. *And his ears were opened, and the impediment of his tongue was removed, and he began speaking plainly.*

We see but half the instruction of this passage, if we only regard it as an example of our Lord's divine power. It is such an example, beyond doubt, but it is something more than that. We must look further, deeper, and lower than the surface, and we shall find in the passage precious spiritual truths.

Here we are meant to see our Lord's power to heal the spiritually deaf. He can give the chief of sinners a hearing ear. He can make him delight in listening to the very gospel which he once ridiculed and despised. Here also we are meant to see our Lord's power to heal the spiritually dumb. He can teach the hardest of transgressors to call upon God. He can put a new song in the mouth of him whose talk was once only of this world. He can make the vilest of men speak of spiritual things and testify to the gospel of the grace of God.

When Jesus pours forth His Spirit, nothing is impossible. We must never despair of others. We must never regard our own hearts as too bad to be changed. He that healed the deaf and dumb still lives. The cases which society pronounces hopeless are not incurable if they are brought to Christ.

The second thing which demands our notice in these verses is *the peculiar manner in which our Lord thought good to work the miracle here recorded.* We are told that when the deaf and dumb person was brought to Jesus, He *took him aside from the crowd, by himself, and put His fingers into his ears, and after spitting, He touched his tongue with the saliva; and looking up to heaven with a deep sigh, He said to him, "Ephphatha!" that is, "Be opened!"*

There is undoubtedly much that is mysterious in these actions. We know not why they were used. It would have been as easy to our Lord to speak the word and command health to return at once as to do what He did here. His reasons for the course He adopted are not recorded.

We only know that the result was the same as on other occasions – the man was cured.

But there is one simple lesson to be learned from our Lord's conduct on this occasion. That lesson is that Christ was not tied to the use of any one means in doing His works among men. Sometimes He thought fit to work in one way, sometimes in another. His enemies were never able to say that unless He employed a certain invariable agency He could not work at all.

We see the same thing going on still in the church of Christ. We see continual proof that the Lord is not tied to the use of any one means exclusively in conveying grace to the soul. Sometimes He is pleased to work by the Word preached publicly, sometimes by the Word read privately. Sometimes He awakens people by sickness and affliction, sometimes by the rebukes or counsel of friends. Sometimes He employs preaching to turn people out of the way of sin. Sometimes He arrests their attention by some providence without any preaching at all. He will not have any preaching made an idol and exalted to the disparagement of other means. He will not have any means despised as useless and neglected as of no value. All are good and valuable. All are in their turn employed for the same great end: the conversion of souls. All are in the hands of Him who *does not give an account of all His doings*, and knows best which to use in each separate case that He heals.

The last thing which demands our notice in these verses is *the remarkable testimony which was borne by those who saw the miracle here recorded*. They said of our Lord, *"He has done all things well."*

It is more than probable that those who said these words were hardly cognizant of their full meaning when applied to Christ. Like Caiaphas, they *did not say this on [their] own initiative* (John 11:51). But the truth to which they gave utterance is full of deep and unspeakable comfort and ought to be daily remembered by all true Christians. Let us remember it as we look back over the days past of our lives from the hour of our conversion. Our Lord *has done all things well*. In the first, bringing us out of darkness into marvelous light; in humbling us and teaching us our weakness, guilt, and folly; in stripping us of our idols and choosing all our portions in placing us where we are and giving us what we have – how well everything has been done! How great the mercy that we have not had our own way!

Let us remember it as we look forward to the days yet to come. We know not what they may be – bright or dark, many or few. But we know that we are in the hands of Him who *has done all things well.* He will not err in any of His dealings with us. He will take away and give – He will afflict and bereave – He will move and He will settle with perfect wisdom at the right time in the right way. The great Shepherd of the sheep makes no mistakes. He leads every lamb of His flock by the right way to the city of habitation.

We shall never see the full beauty of these words until the resurrection morning. We shall then look back over our lives and know the meaning of everything that happened from first to last. We shall remember all the way by which we were led and confess that all was *done well.* The why and the wherefore, the causes and the reasons of everything which now perplexes, will be clear and plain as the sun at noonday. We shall wonder at our own past blindness and marvel that we could ever have doubted our Lord's love. *Now we see in a mirror dimly, but then face to face; now I know in part, but then I will know fully just as I also have been fully known* (1 Corinthians 13:12).

Mark Chapter 8

Mark 8:1-13

In those days, when there was again a large crowd and they had nothing to eat, Jesus called His disciples and said to them, "I feel compassion for the people because they have remained with Me now three days and have nothing to eat. If I send them away hungry to their homes, they will faint on the way; and some of them have come from a great distance." And His disciples answered Him, "Where will anyone be able to find enough bread here in this desolate place to satisfy these people?" And He was asking them, "How many loaves do you have?" And they said, "Seven." And He directed the people to sit down on the ground; and taking the seven loaves, He gave thanks and broke them, and started giving them to His disciples to serve to them, and they served them to the people. They also had a few small fish; and after He had blessed them, He ordered these to be served as well. And they ate and were satisfied; and they picked up seven large baskets full of what was left over of the broken pieces. About four thousand were there; and He sent them away. And immediately He entered the boat with His disciples and came to the district of Dalmanutha. The Pharisees came out and began to argue with Him, seeking from Him a sign from heaven, to test Him. Sighing deeply in His spirit, He said, "Why does this generation seek for a sign? Truly I say to you, no sign will be given to this generation." Leaving them, He again embarked and went away to the other side.

ONCE MORE WE SEE OUR LORD FEEDING a great multitude with a few loaves and fish. He knew the heart of man. He saw the rise of quibblers and skeptics who would question the reality of the wonderful works He performed. By repeating the mighty miracle here recorded, He stops the mouths of all who are not willfully blind to evidence. Publicly and before four thousand witnesses, He shows His almighty power a second time.

Let us observe in this passage *how great is the kindness and compassion of our Lord Jesus Christ.* He saw around Him a *large crowd* who had nothing to eat. He knew that the great majority were following Him from no other motive than idle curiosity and had no claim whatsoever to be regarded as His disciples. Yet when He saw them hungry and destitute, He pitied them – *"I feel compassion for the people because they have remained with Me now three days and have nothing to eat."*

The feeling heart of our Lord Jesus Christ appears in these words. He has compassion even on those who are not His people – the faithless, the graceless, the followers of this world. He feels tenderly for them, though they know it not. He died for them, though they care little for what He did on the cross. He would receive them graciously and pardon them freely if they would only repent and believe on Him. Let us ever beware of measuring the love of Christ by any human measure. He has a special love, beyond doubt, for His own believing people. But He has also a general love of compassion even for the unthankful and the evil. His love *surpasses knowledge* (Ephesians 3:19).

Let us strive to make Jesus our pattern in this as well as in everything else. Let us be kind, and compassionate, and piteous, and courteous to all men. Let us be ready to do good to all men and not only to friends and the household of faith. Let us carry into practice our Lord's injunction: *"Love your enemies and pray for those who persecute you"* (Matthew 5:44). This is to show the mind of Christ. This is the right way to heap coals of fire on an enemy's head and to melt foes into friends (Romans 12:20).

Let us observe, in the second place from this passage, that *with Christ nothing is impossible.* The disciples said, *"Where will anyone be able to find enough bread here in this desolate place to satisfy these people?"*

They might well say so. Without the hand of Him who first made the world out of nothing, the thing could not be. But in the almighty hands of Jesus, seven loaves and a few fish were made sufficient to satisfy four thousand men. Nothing is too hard for the Lord.

We must never allow ourselves to doubt Christ's power to supply the spiritual needs of all His people. He has *more than enough bread* for every soul that trusts in Him. Weak, infirm, corrupt, and empty as believers feel themselves, let them never despair while Jesus lives. In Him there is a boundless store of mercy and grace laid up for the use of all His believing members and ready to be bestowed on all who ask in prayer. *It was the Father's good pleasure for all the fullness to dwell in Him* (Colossians 1:19).

Let us never doubt Christ's providential care for the temporal needs of all His people. He knows their circumstances. He is acquainted with all their necessities. He will never allow them to lack anything that is really for their good. His heart has not changed since He ascended up on high and sat down at the right hand of God. He still lives who had compassion on the hungry crowd in the wilderness and supplied their need. How much more, may we suppose, will He supply the need of those who trust Him? He will supply them without fail. Their faith may occasionally be tried. They may sometimes be kept waiting and be brought very low. But the believer shall never be left entirely destitute. *His bread will be given him, his water will be sure* (Isaiah 33:16).

Let us observe, in the last place, *how much sorrow unbelief brings to our Lord Jesus Christ*. We are told that when *the Pharisees came out and began to argue with Him, seeking from Him a sign from heaven, to test Him*, He *sigh[ed] deeply in His spirit*. There was a deep meaning in that sigh! It came from a heart which mourned over the ruin that these wicked men were bringing on their own souls. Enemies as they were, Jesus could not behold them hardening themselves in unbelief without sorrow.

The feeling which our Lord Jesus Christ here expressed will always be the feeling of all true Christians. Grief over the sins of others is one leading evidence of true grace. The man who is really converted will always regard the unconverted with pity and concern. This was the mind of David – *I behold the treacherous and loathe them* (Psalm 119:158). This was the mind of the godly in the days of Ezekiel regarding Jerusalem – they *sigh and groan over all the abominations which are being committed in its midst* (Ezekiel 9:4). This was the mind of Lot of those around him – he *felt his righteous soul tormented day after day by their lawless deeds* (2 Peter 2:8). This was the mind of Paul for his brethren – *I have great sorrow and unceasing grief in my heart* (Romans 9:2). In all these cases we see something of the mind of Christ. As the great Head feels, so feel the members. They all grieve when they see sin.

Let us leave the passage with solemn self-inquiry. Do we know anything of likeness to Christ and fellow feeling with Him? Do we feel hurt, and pained, and sorrowful when we see men continuing in sin and unbelief? Do we feel grieved and concerned about the state of the unconverted? These are heart-searching questions and demand serious consideration. There are few surer marks of an unconverted heart than carelessness and indifference about the souls of others.

Finally, let us never forget that unbelief and sin are just as great a cause of grief to our Lord now as they were eighteen hundred years ago. Let us strive and pray that we may not add to that grief by any act or deed of ours. The sin of grieving Christ is one which many commit continually without thought or reflection. He who sighed over the unbelief of the Pharisees is still unchanged. Can we doubt that when He sees some persisting in unbelief at the present day He is grieved? From such sin may we be delivered!

Mark 8:14-21

And they had forgotten to take bread, and did not have more than one loaf in the boat with them. And He was giving orders to them, saying, "Watch out! Beware of the leaven of the Pharisees and the leaven of Herod." They began to discuss with one another the fact that they had no bread. And Jesus, aware of this, said to them, "Why do you discuss the fact that you have no bread? Do you not yet see or understand? Do you have a hardened heart?

*Having eyes, do you not see? And having ears, do you not hear?
And do you not remember, when I broke the five loaves for the
five thousand, how many baskets full of broken pieces you picked
up?" They said to Him, "Twelve." "When I broke the seven for the
four thousand, how many large baskets full of broken pieces did
you pick up?" And they said to Him, "Seven." And He was saying
to them, "Do you not yet understand?"*

Let us notice *the solemn warning which our Lord gives to His disciples*
at the beginning of this passage. He says, *"Watch out! Beware of the
leaven of the Pharisees and the leaven of Herod."*

We are not left to conjecture the meaning of this warning. This is
made clear by the parallel passage in Matthew's Gospel. We there read
that Jesus did not mean the leaven of *bread*, but the leaven of *doctrine*.
The self-righteousness and formalism of the Pharisees – the worldliness and skepticism of the courtiers of Herod – were the object of our
Lord's caution. Against both He bids His disciples be on their guard.

Such warnings are of deep importance. It would be well for the
church of Christ if they had been more remembered. The assaults of
persecution from without have never done half so much harm to the
church as the rise of false doctrines within. False prophets and false
teachers within the camp have done far more mischief in Christendom
than all the bloody persecutions of the emperors of Rome. The sword of
the foe has never done such damage to the cause of truth as the tongue
and the pen.

The doctrines which our Lord specifies are precisely those which have
always been found to inflict most injury on the cause of Christianity.
Formalism on the one hand, and skepticism on the other, have been
chronic diseases in the professing church of Christ. In every age multitudes of Christians have been infected by them. In every age men need
to watch against them and be on their guard.

The expression used by our Lord in speaking of false doctrine is
singularly forcible and appropriate. He calls it *leaven*. No word more
suitable could have been employed. It exactly describes the small beginnings of false doctrine – the subtle, quiet way in which it insensibly

pervades a man's religion – the deadly power with which it changes the whole character of his Christianity. Here, in fact, lies the great danger of false doctrine. If it approached us under its true colors, it would do little harm. The great secret of its success is its subtlety and likeness to truth. Every error in religion has been said to be a truth abused.

Let us often *test ourselves to see if we are in the faith* and beware of *leaven*. Let us no more trifle with a little false doctrine than we would trifle with a little immorality or a little lie. Once we admit it into our hearts, we never know how far it may lead us astray. The beginning of departure from the pure truth is like the letting out of waters – first a drop, and at last a torrent. A little leaven leavens the whole lump (Galatians 5:9).

Let us notice *the dull understanding of the disciples* when our Lord gave the warning of this passage. They thought that the *leaven* of which He spoke must be the leaven of bread. It never struck them that He was speaking of doctrines. They drew from Him the sharp reproof – *"Do you not yet see or understand? Do you have a hardened heart? Having eyes, do you not see? And having ears, do you not hear? And do you not remember?"* As believers, converted and renewed as the disciples were, they were still dull of apprehension in spiritual things. Their eyes were still dim and their perception slow in the matters of the kingdom of God.

We shall find it useful to ourselves to remember what is here recorded of the disciples. It may help to correct the high thoughts which we are apt to entertain of our own wisdom and to keep us humble and lowly minded. We must not fancy that we know everything as soon as we are converted. Our knowledge, like all our graces, is always imperfect and never so far from perfection as at our first beginning in the service of Christ. There is more ignorance in our hearts than we are at all aware of. *If anyone supposes that he knows anything, he has not yet known as he ought to know* (1 Corinthians 8:2).

Above all, we shall find it useful to remember what is here recorded in dealing with young Christians. We must not expect perfection in a new convert. We must not set him down as graceless and godless and a false professor of Christ because at first he sees but half the truth and commits many mistakes. His heart may be right in the sight of God, and yet, like the disciples, he may be very slow of understanding in the things of the Spirit. We must bear with him patiently and not cast him aside. We must give him time to grow in grace and knowledge, and his latter end may find him ripe in wisdom like Peter and John. It is a blessed thought that Jesus, our Master in heaven, despises none of His people. Incredible and blameworthy as their slowness to learn undoubtedly is, His patience never gives way. He goes on teaching them, *order on order, line on line.* Let us do likewise. Let it be a rule with us never to despise the weakness and dullness of young Christians. Wherever we see a spark of true grace, however dim and mixed with infirmity, let us be helpful and kind. Let us do as we would be done by.

Mark 8:22-26

And they came to Bethsaida. And they brought a blind man to Jesus and implored Him to touch him. Taking the blind man by the hand, He brought him out of the village; and after spitting on his eyes and laying His hands on him, He asked him, "Do you see anything?" And he looked up and said, "I see men, for I see them like trees, walking around." Then again He laid His hands on his eyes; and he looked intently and was restored, and began to see everything clearly. And He sent him to his home, saying, "Do not even enter the village."

We do not know the reason for the peculiar means employed by our Lord Jesus Christ in working the miracle recorded in these verses. We see a blind man miraculously healed. We know that a word from our Lord's mouth or a touch of His hand would have been sufficient to effect a cure. But we see Jesus taking this blind man by the hand, leading him out of the town, spitting on his eyes, putting His hands on him, and then, and not until then, restoring his sight. And the meaning of all these actions the passage before us leaves entirely unexplained.

But it is well to remember, in reading passages of this kind, that *the Lord is not tied to the use of any one means.* In the conversion of men's souls, there are diversities of operation, but it is the same Spirit who converts. So also in the healing of men's bodies there were varieties of agency employed by our Lord, but it was the same divine power that effected the cure. In all His works God is a sovereign. He gives no account of any of His matters.

One thing in the passage demands our special observation. That thing is *the gradual nature of the cure which our Lord performed on this blind man*. He did not deliver him from his blindness at once, but by degrees. He might have done it in a moment, but He chose to do it step by step. First the blind man said that he only saw *men, . . . like trees, walking around*. Afterwards, his eyesight was restored completely and he saw *everything clearly*. In this respect the miracle stands entirely alone.

We need hardly doubt that this gradual cure was meant to be an emblem of spiritual things. We may be sure that there was a deep meaning in every word and work of our Lord's earthly ministry, and here, as in other places, we shall find a useful lesson.

Let us see then in this gradual restoration to sight *a vivid illustration of the manner in which the Spirit frequently works in the conversion of souls*. We are all naturally blind and ignorant in the matters which concern our souls. Conversion is an illumination, a change from darkness to light, from blindness to seeing the kingdom of God. Yet few converted people see things distinctly at first. The nature and proportion of doctrines, practices, and ordinances of the gospel are dimly seen by them and imperfectly understood. They are like the man before us who at first saw men as trees walking. Their vision is dazzled and unaccustomed to the new world into which they have been introduced. It is not until the work of the Spirit has become deeper and their experience has been somewhat matured that they see all things clearly and give to each part of religion its proper place. This is the history of thousands of God's children. They begin with seeing men as trees walking; they end with seeing everything clearly. Happy is he who has learned this lesson well and is humble and distrustful of his own judgment.

Finally, let us see in the gradual cure of this blind man *a striking picture of the present position of Christ's believing people in the world, compared with that which is to come*. We see in part and know in part in the present dispensation. We are like those who travel by night. We know not the meaning of much that is passing around us. In the providential dealings of God with His children and in the conduct of many of God's saints, we see much that we cannot understand – and cannot alter. In short, we are like him that saw *men, . . . like trees, walking around.*

But let us look forward and take comfort. The time comes when we shall see all *clearly.* The night is far spent. The day is at hand. Let us be content to wait, and watch, and work, and pray. When the day of the Lord comes, our spiritual eyesight will be perfected. We shall see as we have been seen and know as we have been known.

Mark 8:27-33

Jesus went out, along with His disciples, to the villages of Caesarea Philippi; and on the way He questioned His disciples, saying to them, "Who do people say that I am?" They told Him, saying, "John the Baptist; and others say Elijah; but others, one of the prophets." And He continued by questioning them, "But who do you say that I am?" Peter answered and said to Him, "You are the Christ." And He warned them to tell no one about Him. And He began to teach them that the Son of Man must suffer many things and be rejected by the elders and the chief priests and the scribes, and be killed, and after three days rise again. And He was stating the matter plainly. And Peter took Him aside and began to rebuke Him. But turning around and seeing His disciples, He rebuked Peter and said, "Get behind Me, Satan; for you are not setting your mind on God's interests, but man's."

The circumstances here recorded are of great importance. They took place during a journey and arose out of a conversation *on the way.* Happy are those journeys in which time is not wasted on trifles, but redeemed as far as possible for the consideration of serious things.

Let us observe *the variety of opinions about Christ* which prevailed among the Jews. Some said that He was John the Baptist – some Elijah

121

– and others one of the prophets. In short, every kind of opinion appears to have been current, except that one which was true.

We may see the same thing on every side at the present day. Christ and His gospel are just as little understood in reality and are the subject of just as many different opinions as they were eighteen hundred years ago. Many know the name of Christ, acknowledge Him as one who came into the world to save sinners, and regularly worship in buildings set apart for His service. Few thoroughly realize that He is very God, the one Mediator, the one High Priest, the only source of life and peace, their own Shepherd, and their own Friend. Vague ideas about Christ are still very common. Intelligent experimental acquaintance with Christ is still very rare. May we never rest until we can say of Christ, *"My beloved is mine, and I am his"* (Song of Solomon 2:16). This is saving knowledge. This is life eternal.

Let us observe *the good confession of faith which the apostle Peter witnessed.* He replied to our Lord's question, *"Who do you say that I am?"* with *"You are the Christ."*

This was a noble answer, when the circumstances under which it was made are duly considered. It was made when Jesus was poor in condition, without honor, majesty, wealth, or power. It was made when the heads of the Jewish nation, both in church and state, refused to receive Him as the Messiah. Yet even then Simon Peter says, *"You are the Christ."* His strong faith was not stumbled by our Lord's poverty and low estate. His confidence was not shaken by the opposition of scribes and Pharisees and the contempt of rulers and priests. None of these things moved Simon Peter. He believed that He whom he followed, Jesus of Nazareth, was the promised Savior, the true prophet greater than Moses, the long-predicted Messiah. He declared it boldly and unhesitatingly as the creed of himself and his few companions – *"You are the Christ."*

There is much that we may profitably learn from Peter's conduct on this occasion. Erring and unstable as he sometimes was, the faith he exhibited in the passage now before us is well worthy of imitation. Such bold confessions as his are the truest evidence of living faith and are required in every age, if men will prove themselves to be Christ's disciples. We too must be ready to confess Christ even as Peter did. We shall never find our Master and His doctrine popular. We must be prepared to confess Him with few on our side and many against us. But let us take courage and walk in Peter's steps, and we shall not fail of receiving Peter's reward. Jesus takes notice of those who confess Him before men and will one day confess them as His servants before an assembled world.

Let us observe *the full declaration which our Lord makes of His own coming death and resurrection.* We read that *He began to teach them that the Son of Man must suffer many things and be rejected by the elders and the chief priests and the scribes, and be killed, and after three days rise again.*

The events here announced must have sounded strange to the disciples. To be told that their beloved Master, after all His mighty works, would soon be put to death, must have been heavy tidings and beyond their understanding. But the words which convey the announcement are scarcely less remarkable than the event: He *must* suffer – He *must* be killed – He *must* rise again.

Why did our Lord say *must*? Did He mean that He was unable to escape suffering – that He must die by compulsion of a stronger power than His own? Impossible. This could not have been His meaning. Did He mean that He must die to give a great example to the world of self-sacrifice and self-denial, and that this, and this alone, made His death necessary? Once more it may be replied, "Impossible." There is a far deeper meaning in the word *must* suffer and be killed. He meant that His death and passion were necessary in order to make atonement for man's sin. Without shedding His blood there could be no remission. Without the sacrifice of His body on the cross, there could be no satisfaction of God's holy law. He *must* suffer to make reconciliation for iniquity. He *must* die, because without His death as a propitiatory offering, sinners could never have life. He *must* suffer, because without His vicarious sufferings, our sins could never be taken away. In a word, He *must* be delivered for our offenses and raised again for our justification.

Here is the center truth of the Bible. Let us never forget that. All other truths compared to this are of secondary importance. Whatever views we hold of religious truth, let us see that we have a firm grasp upon the atoning efficacy of Christ's death. Let the truth so often proclaimed by our Lord to His disciples and so diligently taught by the disciples to the world be the foundational truth in our Christianity. In life and in death, in health and in sickness, let us lean all our weight on this mighty fact – that though we have sinned, Christ has died for sinners – and that though we deserve nothing, Christ has suffered on the cross for us, and by that suffering purchased heaven for all who believe in Him.

Finally, let us observe in this passage *the strange mixture of grace and infirmity which may be found in the heart of a true Christian.* We see that very Peter who had just witnessed so noble a confession, presuming to rebuke his Master because He spoke of suffering and dying. We see him drawing down on himself the sharpest rebuke which ever fell from our Lord's lips during His earthly ministry – *"Get behind Me, Satan; for you are not setting your mind on God's interests, but man's."*

We have here a humbling proof that the best of saints is a poor fallible creature. Here was *ignorance* in Simon Peter. He did not understand the necessity of our Lord's death and would have actually prevented His sacrifice on the cross. Here was *self-conceit* in Simon Peter. He thought he knew what was right and fitting for his Master better than his Master Himself, and actually undertook to show the Messiah a more excellent way. And last but not least, Simon Peter did it all with the *best intentions!* He meant well. His motives were pure. But zeal and earnestness are no excuse for error. A man may mean well and yet fall into tremendous mistakes.

Let us learn humility from the facts here recorded. Let us beware of being puffed up with our own spiritual attainments or exalted by the praise of others. Let us never think that we know everything and are not likely to err. We see that it is but a little step from making a good confession to being a *Satan* in Christ's way. Let us pray daily, "Hold me up, keep me, teach me, let me not err."

Lastly, let us learn charity towards others from the facts here recorded. Let us not be in a hurry to cast off our brother as graceless because of errors and mistakes. Let us remember that his heart may be right in the sight of God, like Peter's, though like Peter he may for a time turn aside. Rather, let us call to mind Paul's advice and act upon it. *If anyone is caught in any trespass, you who are spiritual, restore such a one in a spirit of gentleness; each one looking to yourself, so that you too will not be tempted* (Galatians 6:1).

Mark 8:34-38

And He summoned the crowd with His disciples, and said to them, "If anyone wishes to come after Me, he must deny himself, and take up his cross and follow Me. For whoever wishes to save his life will lose it, but whoever loses his life for My sake and the gospel's will save it. For what does it profit a man to gain the whole world, and forfeit his soul? For what will a man give in exchange for his soul? For whoever is ashamed of Me and My words in this adulterous and sinful generation, the Son of Man will also be ashamed of him when He comes in the glory of His Father with the holy angels."

The words of our Lord Jesus Christ in this passage are peculiarly weighty and solemn. They were spoken to correct the mistaken views of His disciples as to the nature of His kingdom. But they contain truths of the deepest importance to Christians in every age of the church. The whole passage is one which should often form the subject of private meditation.

We learn, for one thing from these verses, *the absolute necessity of self-denial if we would be Christ's disciples and be saved.* What says our Lord? *"If anyone wishes to come after Me, he must deny himself, and take up his cross and follow Me."*

Salvation is undoubtedly all of grace. It is offered freely in the gospel to the chief of sinners without money and without price. *For by grace you have been saved through faith; and that not of yourselves, it is the gift of God; not as a result of works, so that no one may boast* (Ephesians 2:8-9). But all who accept this great salvation must prove the reality of their faith by carrying the cross after Christ. They must not think to enter heaven without trouble, pain, suffering, and conflict on earth. They must be content to take up the cross of doctrine, and the cross of practice – the cross of holding a faith which the world despises, and the cross of living a life which the world ridicules as too strict and overly righteous. They must be willing to crucify the flesh, to mortify the deeds of the body, to fight daily with the devil, to come out from the world, and to lose their lives, if needful, for Christ's sake and the gospel's. These are hard sayings, but they admit of no evasion. The words of our Lord are plain and unmistakable. If we will not carry the cross, we shall never wear the crown.

Let us not be deterred from Christ's service by fear of the cross. Heavy as that cross may seem, Jesus will give us grace to bear it. *I can do all things through Him who strengthens me* (Philippians 4:13). Thousands and tens of thousands have borne it before us and have found Christ's yoke easy and Christ's burden light. Yet no good thing on earth was ever attained without trouble. We cannot surely expect that without trouble we can enter the kingdom of God. Let us go forward boldly and allow no difficulty to keep us back. The cross along the way is but for a few years. The glory at the end is forevermore.

Let us often ask ourselves whether our Christianity costs us anything. Does it entail any sacrifice? Has it the true stamp of heaven? Does it carry with it any cross? If not, we may well tremble and be afraid. We have everything to learn. A religion which costs nothing is worth nothing. It will do us no good in the life that now is. It will lead to no salvation in the life to come.

We learn, for another thing from these verses, *the unspeakable value of the soul.* What says our Lord? *"What does it profit a man to gain the whole world, and forfeit his soul?"* These words were meant to stir us up to exertion and self-denial. They ought to ring in our ears like a trumpet every morning when we rise from our beds and every night when we lie down. May they be deeply engraved in our memories and never effaced by the devil and the world!

We all have a soul that will live forevermore. Whether we know it or not, we all carry about with us something which will live on when our bodies are moldering in the grave. We all have a soul for which we shall have to give account to God. It is a solemn thought when we consider how little attention most men give to anything except this world. But it is true.

Any man may lose his own soul. He cannot save it. Christ alone can do that. But he can lose it, and lose it in many different ways. He may murder it by loving sin and cleaving to the world. He may poison it by choosing a religion of lies and believing man-made superstitions. He may starve it by neglecting church and refusing to receive into his heart the gospel. Many are the ways that lead to the pit. Whatever way a man takes, he, and he alone, is accountable for it. Weak, corrupt, fallen, and impotent as human nature is, man has a mighty power of destroying, ruining, and losing his own soul.

The whole world cannot make up to a man the loss of his soul. The possession of all the treasures that the world contains would not compensate for eternal ruin. They would not satisfy us and make us happy while we had them. They could only be enjoyed for a few years at best, and must then be left forevermore. Of all unprofitable and foolish bargains that man can make, the worst is that of giving up his soul's salvation for the sake of this present world. It is a bargain of which thousands, like Esau, who sold his birthright for a morsel of meat, have repented – but many, unfortunately, like Esau, have repented too late.

Let these sayings of our Lord sink deep into our hearts. Words are inadequate to express their importance. May we remember them in the hour of temptation, when the soul seems a small and unimportant thing, and the world seems very bright and great. May we remember them in the hour of persecution, when we are tried by the fear of man and half inclined to forsake Christ. In hours like these, let us call to mind this mighty question of our Lord and repeat it to ourselves, *"What does it profit a man to gain the whole world, and forfeit his soul?"*

We learn, in the last place from these verses, *the great danger of being ashamed of Christ.* What says our Lord? *"Whoever is ashamed of Me and My words in this adulterous and sinful generation, the Son of Man will also be ashamed of him when He comes in the glory of His Father with the holy angels."*

When can it be said of anyone that he is ashamed of Christ? We are guilty of it when we are ashamed of letting people see that we believe and love the doctrines of Christ, that we desire to live according to the commandments of Christ, and that we wish to be reckoned among the people of Christ. Christ's doctrine, laws, and people were never popular and never will be. The man who boldly confesses that he loves them is sure to bring on himself ridicule and persecution. Whoever shrinks from this confession from fear of this ridicule and persecution is ashamed of Christ and comes under the sentence of the passage before us.

Perhaps there are few of our Lord's sayings which are more condemning than this: *The fear of man brings a snare* (Proverbs 29:25). There are thousands of men who would face a lion or storm a breach, if duty called them, and fear nothing – and yet would be ashamed of being thought "religious" and would not dare to avow that they desired to please Christ rather than man. Amazing indeed is the power of ridicule! Incredible is the bondage in which men live to the opinion of the world!

Let us all pray daily for faith and courage to confess Christ before men. Of sin, or worldliness, or unbelief, we may well be ashamed. We ought never to be ashamed of Him who died for us on the cross. In spite of laughter, mockery, and hard words, let us boldly avow that we serve Christ. Let us often look forward to the day of His second coming and remember what He says in this place. Better a thousand times confess Christ now and be despised by man than be disowned by Christ before His Father in the day of judgment.

Mark Chapter 9

Mark 9:1-13

And Jesus was saying to them, "Truly I say to you, there are some of those who are standing here who will not taste death until they see the kingdom of God after it has come with power." Six days later, Jesus took with Him Peter and James and John, and brought them up on a high mountain by themselves. And He was transfigured before them; and His garments became radiant and exceedingly white, as no launderer on earth can whiten them. Elijah appeared to them along with Moses; and they were talking with Jesus. Peter said to Jesus, "Rabbi, it is good for us to be here; let us make three tabernacles, one for You, and one for Moses, and one for Elijah." For he did not know what to answer; for they became terrified. Then a cloud formed, overshadowing them, and a voice came out of the cloud, "This is My beloved Son, listen to Him!" All at once they looked around and saw no one with them anymore, except Jesus alone. As they were coming down from the mountain, He gave them orders not to relate to anyone what they had seen, until the Son of Man rose from the dead. They seized upon that statement, discussing with one another what rising from the dead meant. They asked Him, saying, "Why is it that the scribes say that Elijah must come first?" And He said to them, "Elijah does first come and restore all things. And yet how is it written of the Son of Man that He will suffer many things and be treated with contempt? But I say to you that Elijah has indeed come, and they did to him whatever they wished, just as it is written of him."

THE CONNECTION OF THIS PASSAGE with the end of the previous chapter ought never to be overlooked. Our Lord had been speaking of His own coming death and passion – of the necessity of self-denial, if men would be His disciples – of the need of losing our lives, if we would have them saved. But in the same breath He goes on to speak of His future kingdom and glory. He takes the edge off His "hard sayings" by promising a sight of that glory to some of those who heard Him. And in the history of the transfiguration, which is here recorded, we see that promise fulfilled.

The first thing which demands our notice in these verses is *the marvelous vision they contain of the glory which Christ and His people shall have at His second coming.*

There can be no doubt that this was one of the principal purposes of the transfiguration. It was meant to teach the disciples that though their Lord was lowly and poor in appearance now, He would one day appear in such royal majesty as became the Son of God. It was meant to teach them that when their Master came the second time, His saints like Moses and Elijah would appear with Him. It was meant to remind them that though reviled and persecuted now because they belonged to Christ, they would one day be clothed with honor and be partakers of their Master's glory.

We have reason to thank God for this vision. We are often tempted to give up Christ's service because of the cross and affliction which it entails. We see few with us and many against us. We find our names cast out as evil and all manner of evil said of us because we believe and love the gospel. Year after year we see our companions in Christ's service removed by death, and we feel as if we knew little about them except that they are gone to an unknown world and that we are left alone. All these things are grievous to flesh and blood. No wonder that the faith of believers sometimes languishes and their eyes fail while they look for their hope.

Let us see in the story of the transfiguration a remedy for such doubting thoughts as these. The vision of the holy mount is a gracious pledge that glorious things are in store for the people of God. Their crucified Savior shall come again in power and great glory. His saints shall all come with Him and are in safekeeping until that happy day. We may wait patiently. *When Christ, who is our life, is revealed, then you also will be revealed with Him in glory* (Colossians 3:4).

The second thing which demands our notice in this passage is *the strong expression of the apostle Peter when he saw his Lord transfigured.* "Rabbi," he said, "*it is good for us to be here.*"

No doubt there was much in this saying which cannot be commended. It showed an ignorance of the purpose for which Jesus came into the world to suffer and to die. It showed a forgetfulness of his brethren, who were not with him, and of the dark world which so much needed his Master's presence. Above all, the proposal which he made at the same time to *make three tabernacles* for Moses, Elijah, and Christ showed a low view of his Master's dignity and implied that he did not know that one greater than Moses and Elijah was there. In all these respects the apostle's exclamation is not to be praised but to be blamed.

But having said this, let us not fail to observe what joy and happiness this glorious vision conferred on this warmhearted disciple. Let us see in his fervent cry, *"It is good for us to be here,"* what comfort and consolation the sight of glory can give to a true believer. Let us look forward and try to form some idea of the pleasure which the saints shall experience when they shall at last meet the Lord Jesus at His second coming and meet to part no more. A vision of a few minutes was sufficient to warm and stir Peter's heart. The sight of two saints in glory was so cheering and quickening that he would gladly have enjoyed more of it. What then shall we say when we see our Lord appear at the last day with all His saints? What shall we say when we ourselves are allowed to share in His glory, and join the happy company, and feel that we shall go out no more from the joy of our Lord? These are questions that no man can answer. The happiness of that great day of gathering together is one that we cannot now conceive. The feelings of which Peter had a little foretaste will then be ours in full experience. We shall all say with one heart and one voice, when we see Christ and all His saints, "It is good for us to be here."

The last thing which demands our notice in this passage is *the distinct testimony which it bears to Christ's office and dignity as the promised*

Messiah. We see this testimony first in the appearance of Moses and Elijah, the representatives of the law and the prophets. They appear as witnesses that Jesus is He of whom they spoke in old times and of whom they wrote that He would come.[8] They disappear after a few minutes and leave Jesus alone, as though they would show that they were only witnesses, and that our Master having come, the servants resign to Him the chief place. We see this testimony, secondly, in the miraculous voice from heaven, saying, *"This is My beloved Son, listen to Him!"* The same voice of God the Father which was heard at our Lord's baptism was heard once more at His transfiguration. On both occasions there was the same solemn declaration, *"This is My beloved Son."* On this last occasion, there was an addition of three most important words: *"Listen to Him!"*

The whole conclusion of the vision was calculated to leave a lasting impression on the minds of the three disciples. It taught them in the most striking manner that their Lord was far above them and the prophets, as the master of the house is above the servants, and that they must in all things believe, follow, obey, trust, and listen to Him.

Finally, the last words of the voice from heaven are words that should be ever before the minds of all true Christians. They should "listen to Christ." He is the great Teacher – those who would be wise must learn of Him. He is the Light of the World – those who would not err must follow Him. He is the head of the church – those who would be living members of His mystical body must ever look to Him. The grand question that concerns us all is not so much what man says or ministers say, or what the church says or what councils say, but what says Christ? Him let us hear. In Him let us abide. On Him let us lean. To Him let us look. He and He only will never fail us, never disappoint us, and never lead us astray. Happy are they who know experimentally the meaning

---

8   The coming of Elijah, which forms the topic of conversation between our Lord and His disciples in the latter part of the passage now expounded, is a deep and mysterious subject. I believe that a literal appearing of Elijah the prophet before the second coming of Christ may be expected. Dark and incomprehensible as the subject is, the scriptural arguments in favor of this view appear to me unanswerable. Any other view seems to do violence to the plain meaning of the words of Malachi 4:5-6, Matthew 17:11, and John 1:21. There seems no reason why there should not be a double "coming of Elijah" – the first, *in spirit and power,* when John the Baptist preached – the second, literal and in person, when he shall come at the end of the world, immediately before the great and dreadful day of the Lord.

of the text, *"My sheep hear My voice, and I know them, and they follow Me; and I give eternal life to them, and they will never perish; and no one will snatch them out of My hand"* (John 10:27-28).

Mark 9:14-29

When they came back to the disciples, they saw a large crowd around them, and some scribes arguing with them. Immediately, when the entire crowd saw Him, they were amazed and began running up to greet Him. And He asked them, "What are you discussing with them?" And one of the crowd answered Him, "Teacher, I brought You my son, possessed with a spirit which makes him mute; and whenever it seizes him, it slams him to the ground and he foams at the mouth, and grinds his teeth and stiffens out. I told Your disciples to cast it out, and they could not do it." And He answered them and said, "O unbelieving generation, how long shall I be with you? How long shall I put up with you? Bring him to Me!" They brought the boy to Him. When he saw Him, immediately the spirit threw him into a convulsion, and falling to the ground, he began rolling around and foaming at the mouth. And He asked his father, "How long has this been happening to him?" And he said, "From childhood. It has often thrown him both into the fire and into the water to destroy him. But if You can do anything, take pity on us and help us!" And Jesus said to him, "'If You can?' All things are possible to him who believes." Immediately the boy's father cried out and said, "I do believe; help my unbelief." When Jesus saw that a crowd was rapidly gathering, He rebuked the unclean spirit, saying to it, "You deaf and mute spirit, I command you, come out of him and do not enter him again." After crying out and throwing him into terrible convulsions, it came out; and the boy became so much like a corpse that most of them said, "He is dead!" But Jesus took him by the hand and raised him; and he got up. When He came into the house, His disciples began questioning Him privately, "Why could we not drive it out?" And He said to them, "This kind cannot come out by anything but prayer."

The contrast between these verses and those which precede them in the chapter is very striking. We pass from the Mount of Transfiguration to a grievous history of the work of the devil. We come down from the vision of glory to a conflict with satanic possession. We change the blessed company of Moses and Elijah for crude interaction with unbelieving scribes. We leave the foretaste of millennial glory and the solemn voice of God the Father testifying to God the Son, and return once more to a scene of pain, weakness, and misery – a boy in agony of body, a father in deep distress, and a little band of feeble disciples restrained by Satan's power and unable to give relief. The contrast, we must all feel, is very great. Yet it is but a faint emblem of the change of scene that Jesus voluntarily undertook to witness when He first laid aside His glory and came into the world. And it is after all a vivid picture of the life of all true Christians. With them, as with their Master, work, conflict, and scenes of weakness and sorrow will always be the rule. With them too, visions of glory, foretastes of heaven, and seasons on the mount will always be the exception.

Let us learn from these verses *how dependent Christ's disciples are on the company and help of their Master.*

We see this truth brought out in a striking manner in the scene which meets our Lord's eyes when He came down from the mount. Like Moses when he came down from Mount Sinai, He finds His little flock in confusion. He sees His nine apostles beset by a party of malicious scribes and baffled in an attempt to heal one who had been brought to them possessed with a devil. The very same disciples who a short time before had done many miracles and *cast out many demons*, had now met with a case too hard for them. They were learning by humbling experience the great lesson: *"Apart from Me you can do nothing"* (John 15:5). It was a useful lesson, no doubt, and overruled to their spiritual good. It would probably be remembered all the days of their lives. The things that we learn by stinging experience abide in our memories, while truths heard with the ear are often forgotten. But we may be sure it was a bitter lesson at the time. We do not like to learn that we can do nothing without Christ.

We need not look far to see many illustrations of this truth in the history of Christ's people in every age. The very men who at one time have done great exploits for the cause of the gospel, at another time have failed entirely and proved weak and unstable as water. The temporary recantations of Cranmer and Jewell are striking examples. The holiest and best of Christians has nothing to glory in. His strength is not his own. He has nothing but what he has received. He has only to provoke the Lord to leave him for a season, and he will soon discover that his power is gone. Like Samson, when his hair was shorn, he is as weak as any other man.

Let us learn a lesson of humility from the failure of the disciples. Let us strive to realize every day our need of the grace and presence of Christ. With Him we may do all things. Without Him we can do nothing at all. With Him we may overcome the greatest temptations. Without Him the least may overcome us. Let our cry be every morning, "Leave us not to ourselves, for we know not what a day may bring forth. If Your presence does not go with us, we cannot go up."

Let us learn, in the second place from these verses, *how early in life we are liable to be injured by Satan.* We read a fearful description of the miseries inflicted by Satan on the young man whose case is here recorded. And we are told that he had been under this dreadful visitation from his very infancy. It had been happening to him *from childhood.*

There is a lesson of deep importance here which we must not overlook. We must labor to do good to our children even from their earliest years. If Satan begins so early to do them harm, we must not be behind him in diligence to lead them to God. How soon in life a child becomes responsible and accountable is a difficult question to answer. Perhaps it is far sooner than many of us suppose. One thing, at all events, is very clear – it is never too soon to strive and pray for the salvation of the souls of children and never too soon to speak to them as moral beings and tell them of God, and Christ, and right, and wrong. The devil, we may be quite sure, loses no time in endeavoring to influence the minds of young people. He begins with them even *from childhood.* Let us work

135

hard to counteract him. If young hearts can be filled by Satan, they can also be filled with the Spirit of God.

Let us learn, in the third place from these verses, *how faith and unbelief can be mixed together in the same heart.* The words of the child's father set this truth before us in a touching way. *"I do believe,"* he cried, *"help my unbelief."*

We see in those words a vivid picture of the heart of many a true Christian. Few indeed are to be found among believers in whom trust and doubt, hope and fear do not exist side by side. Nothing is perfect in a child of God so long as he is in the body. His knowledge, and love, and humility are all more or less defective and mingled with corruption. And as it is with his other graces, so it is with his faith. He believes and yet has about him a remainder of unbelief.

What shall we do with our faith? We must *use it.* Weak, trembling, doubting, and feeble as it may be, we must use it. We must not wait until it is great, perfect, and mighty, but like the man before us, turn it to account and hope that one day it will be more strong. "Lord," he said, *"I do believe."*

What shall we do with our unbelief? We must *resist it* and pray against it. We must not allow it to keep us back from Christ. We must take it to Christ as we take all other sins and infirmities and cry to Him for deliverance. Like the man before us, we must cry, *"Help my unbelief."*

These are experiential truths. Happy are they who know something of them. The world is ignorant of them. Faith and unbelief, doubts and fears are all foolishness to the natural man. But let the true Christian study these things well and thoroughly understand them. It is of the utmost importance to our comfort to know that a true believer may be known by his inward warfare as well as by his inward peace.

Let us learn, in the last place, *the complete dominion which our Lord exercises over Satan and all his agents.* The spirit who was too strong for the disciples is at once cast out by the Master. He speaks with mighty authority and Satan at once is obliged to obey. *"I command you, come out of him and do not enter him again."*

We may leave the passage with comfortable feelings. Greater is He that is for us than all those who are against us. Satan is strong, busy, active, and malicious. But Jesus is able to save to the uttermost all who come unto God by Him – from the devil, as well as from sin – from the devil, as well as from the world. Let us possess our souls in patience. Jesus still lives and will not let Satan pluck us out of His hand. Jesus still lives and will soon come again to deliver us entirely from the fiery darts of the wicked one. The great chain is prepared (Revelation 20:1). Satan shall one day be bound. *The God of peace will soon crush Satan under your feet* (Romans 16:20).

Mark 9:30-37

From there they went out and began to go through Galilee, and He did not want anyone to know about it. For He was teaching His disciples and telling them, "The Son of Man is to be delivered into the hands of men, and they will kill Him; and when He has been killed, He will rise three days later." But they did not understand this statement, and they were afraid to ask Him. They came to Capernaum; and when He was in the house, He began to question them, "What were you discussing on the way?" But they kept silent, for on the way they had discussed with one another which of them was the greatest. Sitting down, He called the twelve and said to them, "If anyone wants to be first, he shall be last of all and servant of all." Taking a child, He set him before them, and taking him in His arms, He said to them, "Whoever receives one child like this in My name receives Me; and whoever receives Me does not receive Me, but Him who sent Me."

Let us observe in these verses *our Lord's renewed announcement of His own coming death and resurrection. He was teaching His disciples and telling them, "The Son of Man is to be delivered into the hands of men, and they will kill Him; and when He has been killed, He will rise three days later."*

The dullness of the disciples in spiritual things appears once more as soon as this announcement is made. There was good in the tidings as well as seeming evil, sweet as well as bitter, life as well as death, and the resurrection as well as the cross. But it was all darkness to the bewildered twelve. *They did not understand this statement, and they were afraid to ask Him.* Their minds were still full of their mistaken ideas of their Master's reign upon earth. They thought that His earthly kingdom was immediately to appear. Never are we so slow to understand as when prejudice and preconceived notions darken our eyes.

The immense importance of our Lord's death and resurrection comes out strongly in this fresh announcement which He makes. It is not for nothing that He reminds us again that He must die. He would have us know that His death was the great end for which He came into the world. He would remind us that by that death the great problem was to be solved – how God could be just and yet justify sinners. He did not come upon earth merely to teach, and preach, and work miracles. He came to make satisfaction for sin by His own blood and suffering on the cross. Let us never forget this. The incarnation, and example, and words of Christ are all of deep importance. But the grand object which demands our notice in the history of His earthly ministry is His death on Calvary.

Let us observe, in the second place in these verses, *the ambition and love of preeminence which the apostles exhibited. On the way they had discussed with one another which of them was the greatest.*

How strange this sounds! Who would have thought that a few fishermen and publicans could have been overcome by envious rivalry and the desire of supremacy? Who would have expected that poor men, who had given up all for Christ's sake, would have been troubled by strife and dissension as to the place and precedence which each one deserved? Yet so it is. The fact is recorded for our learning. The Holy Spirit has caused it to be written down for the perpetual use of Christ's church. Let us take care that it is not written in vain.

It is a solemn fact, whether we like to allow it or not, that pride is one of the most common sins which beset human nature. We are all born Pharisees. We all naturally think far better of ourselves than we ought. We all naturally imagine that we deserve something better than we have. It is an old sin. It began in the garden of Eden when Adam and

Eve thought they had not gotten everything that their merits deserved. It is a subtle sin. It rules and reigns in many a heart without being detected and can even wear the garb of humility. It is a most soul-ruining sin. It prevents repentance, keeps men back from Christ, halts brotherly love, and nips in the bud spiritual desires. Let us watch against it and be on our guard. Of all garments, none is so graceful, none wears so well, and none is so rare as true humility.

Let us observe, in the third place, *the peculiar standard of true greatness which our Lord sets before His disciples.* He says to them, *"If anyone wants to be first, he shall be last of all and servant of all."*

These words are deeply instructive. They show us that the maxims of the world are directly contrary to the mind of Christ. The world's idea of greatness is to rule, but Christian greatness consists in serving. The world's ambition is to receive honor and attention, but the desire of the Christian should be to give rather than receive, and to attend on others rather than be attended on himself. In short, the man who lays himself out most to serve his fellow men and to be useful in his day and generation is the greatest man in the eyes of Christ.

Let us strive to make a practical use of this heart-searching maxim. Let us seek to do good to our fellow men and to mortify that self-pleasing and self-indulgence to which we are all so prone. Is there any service that we can render to our fellow Christians? Is there any kindness that we can show them to help them and promote their happiness? If there is, let us do it without delay. Well would it be for Christendom if empty boasts of churchmanship and orthodoxy were less frequent, and practical attention to our Lord's words in this passage more common. The men who are willing to be last of all and servants of all for Christ's sake are always few. Yet these are the men who do good, break down prejudices, convince infidels that Christianity is a reality, and shake the world.

Let us observe, in the last place, *what encouragement our Lord gives us to show kindness to the least and lowest who believe in His name.* He teaches this lesson in a very touching manner; He took a child in His arms and said to His disciples, *"Whoever receives one child like this in My name receives Me; and whoever receives Me does not receive Me, but Him who sent Me."*

The principle here laid down is a continuation of that which we have just considered. It is one which is foolishness to the natural man. Flesh and blood can see no other way to greatness than crowns, and rank, and wealth, and high position in the world. The Son of God declares that the way lies in devoting ourselves to the care of the weakest and lowest of His flock. He enforces His declaration by marvelous words which are often read and heard without thought. He tells us that to receive one child in His name is to receive Christ, and to receive Christ is to receive God.

There is rich encouragement here for all who devote themselves to the charitable work of doing good to neglected souls. There is encouragement for everyone who labors to restore the outcast to a place in society – to raise the fallen, to gather together the ragged children whom no man cares for, to pluck the worst of characters from a life of sin like brands from the burning, and to bring the wanderers home. Let all such take comfort when they read these words. Their work may often be hard and discouraging. They may be mocked, ridiculed, and held up to scorn by the world. But let them know that the Son of God observes all they do and is well pleased. Whatever the world may think, these are the ones whom Jesus will delight to honor at the last day.

Mark 9:38-50

John said to Him, "Teacher, we saw someone casting out demons in Your name, and we tried to prevent him because he was not following us." But Jesus said, "Do not hinder him, for there is no one who will perform a miracle in My name, and be able soon afterward to speak evil of Me. For he who is not against us is for us. For whoever gives you a cup of water to drink because of your name as followers of Christ, truly I say to you, he will not lose his reward. Whoever causes one of these little ones who believe to stumble, it would be better for him if, with a heavy millstone hung around his neck, he had been cast into the sea. If your hand causes you to stumble, cut it off; it is better for you to enter life crippled, than, having your two hands, to go into hell, into the unquenchable fire, [where their worm does not die, and the fire is not quenched.] If your foot causes you to stumble, cut it off; it is better for you to enter life lame, than, having your two feet, to be cast into hell, [where their worm does not die, and the fire is not quenched.] If your eye causes you to stumble, throw it out; it is better for you to enter the kingdom of God with one eye, than, having two eyes, to be cast into hell, where their worm does not die, and the fire is not quenched. "For everyone will be salted with fire. Salt is good; but if the salt becomes unsalty, with what will you make it salty again? Have salt in yourselves, and be at peace with one another."

We see in these verses *the mind of Christ on the great subject of toleration in religion.* The apostle John said to Jesus, *"Teacher, we saw someone casting out demons in Your name, and we tried to prevent him because he was not following us."*

The man was doing a good work without doubt. He was warring on the same side as the apostles beyond question. But this did not satisfy John. He did not work in the company of the apostles. He did not fight in line with them. And therefore John had opposed him. But let us hear now what the great head of the church declares! *"Do not hinder him,"* Jesus said, *"for there is no one who will perform a miracle in My name, and be able soon afterward to speak evil of Me. For he who is not against us is for us."*

Here is a golden rule indeed and one that human nature severely needs and has too often forgotten. Men of all branches of Christ's church are apt to think that no good can be done in the world unless it is done by their own party and denomination. They are so narrow-minded that they cannot conceive the possibility of working on any other pattern but that which they follow. They make an idol of their own peculiar ecclesiastical machinery and can see no merit in any other. They are like him who cried when Eldad and Medad prophesied in the camp, *"Moses, my lord, restrain them"* (Numbers 11:28).

To this intolerant spirit we owe some of the blackest pages of church history. Christians have repeatedly persecuted Christians for no better reason than that which is here given by John. They have practically proclaimed to their brethren, "You shall either follow us or not work for Christ at all."

Let us be on our guard against this feeling. It is only too near the surface of all our hearts. Let us study to realize that liberal and tolerant spirit which Jesus here recommends, and be thankful for good works wheresoever and by whomever done. Let us beware of the slightest inclination to stop and check others merely because they do not choose to adopt our plans or work by our side. We may think our fellow Christians mistaken in some points. We may fancy that more would be done for Christ if they would join us and if all worked in the same way. We may see many evils arising from religious dissensions and divisions. But all this must not prevent us from rejoicing if the works of the devil are destroyed and souls are saved.

Is our neighbor warring against Satan? Is he really trying to labor for Christ? This is the grand question. Better a thousand times that the work should be done by other hands than not done at all. Happy is he who knows something of the spirit of Moses when he said, *"Would that all the LORD's people were prophets, that the LORD would put His Spirit upon them!"* (Numbers 11:29); and of Paul when he says, *Christ is proclaimed; and in this I rejoice* (Philippians 1:18).

We see, for another thing in these verses, *the need of giving up anything that stands between us and the salvation of our souls.* The *hand* and the *foot* are to be cut off, and the *eye* to be plucked out, if they are occasions of falling. The things that are dear to us as eye, foot, or hand are to be cast off and given up if they injure our souls, whatever pain the sacrifice may cost us.

This is a rule that sounds stern and harsh at first sight. But our loving Master did not give the rule without cause. Compliance with it is absolutely necessary, since neglect of it is the sure way to hell. Our bodily senses are the channels through which many of our most formidable temptations approach us. Our bodily members are ready instruments of evil but slow to that which is good. The eye, the hand, and the foot are good servants, when under right direction. But they need daily watching, lest they lead us into sin.

Let us resolve by God's grace to make a practical use of our Lord's solemn injunction in this place. Let us regard it as the advice of a wise physician, the counsel of a tender father, and the warning of a faithful friend. However men may ridicule us for our strictness and preciseness, let us habitually *[crucify our] flesh with its passions and desires.* Let us deny ourselves any enjoyment rather than incur the peril of sinning against God. Let us walk in Job's steps when he says, *"I have made a covenant with my eyes"* (Job 31:1). Let us remember Paul when he says, *I discipline my body and make it my slave, so that, after I have preached to others, I myself will not be disqualified* (1 Corinthians 9:27).

We see, in the last place in these verses, *the reality, awfulness, and eternality of future punishment.* Three times the Lord Jesus speaks of hell. Three times He mentions that *their worm does not die.* Three times He says that *the fire is not quenched.*

These are dreadful expressions. They call for reflection rather than exposition. They should be pondered, considered, and remembered by all professing Christians. It matters little whether we regard them as figurative and emblematic. If they are so, one thing at least is very clear. The worm and the fire are emblems of real things. There is a real hell, and that hell is eternal.

There is no mercy in keeping back from men the subject of hell. Fearful and tremendous as it is, it ought to be pressed on all as one of the great truths of Christianity. Our loving Savior speaks frequently of it. The apostle John, in the book of Revelation, often describes it. The servants of God in these days must not be ashamed of confessing their belief in it. Were there no boundless mercy in Christ for all who believe in Him, we might well shrink from the dreadful topic. Were there no precious blood of Christ able to cleanse away all sin, we might well keep silent about the wrath to come. But there is mercy for all who ask in Christ's name. There is a fountain open for all sin. Let us then boldly and unhesitatingly maintain that there is a hell, and beseech men to flee from it before it be too late. *Knowing the fear of the Lord,* the worm, and the fire, let us *persuade men* (2 Corinthians 5:11). It is not possible to say too much about Christ. But it is quite possible to say too little about hell.

Let the concluding words of our Lord ring in our ears as we leave the passage: *"Have salt in yourselves, and be at peace with one another."* Let us make sure that we have in our hearts the saving grace of the Holy Spirit, sanctifying, purifying, and preserving from corruption our whole inward man. Let us watch the grace given to us with daily watchfulness, and pray to be kept from carelessness and sin, lest we be overtaken in faults and bring misery on our conscience and discredit on our profession. Above all let us live in peace one with another, not seeking great things or striving for the preeminence, but clothed with humility and loving all who love Christ in sincerity. These seem simple things. But in attending to them is great reward.

Mark Chapter 10

Mark 10:1-12

Getting up, He went from there to the region of Judea and beyond the Jordan; crowds gathered around Him again, and, according to His custom, He once more began to teach them. Some Pharisees came up to Jesus, testing Him, and began to question Him whether it was lawful for a man to divorce his wife. And He answered and said to them, "What did Moses command you?" They said, "Moses permitted a man to write a certificate of divorce and send her away." But Jesus said to them, "Because of your hardness of heart he wrote you this commandment. But from the beginning of creation, God made them male and female. For this reason a man shall leave his father and mother, and the two shall become one flesh; so they are no longer two, but one flesh. What therefore God has joined together, let no man separate." In the house the disciples began questioning Him about this again. And He said to them, "Whoever divorces his wife and marries another woman commits adultery against her; and if she herself divorces her husband and marries another man, she is committing adultery."

THE OPENING VERSE OF THIS PASSAGE shows us *the patient perseverance of our Lord Jesus Christ as a teacher.* We are told that *getting up, He went from there to the region of Judea and beyond the Jordan; crowds gathered around Him again, and, according to His custom, He once more began to teach them.*

Wherever our Lord went, He was always about His Father's business, preaching, teaching, and laboring to do good to souls. He threw away no opportunity. In the whole history of His earthly ministry, we never read of an idle day. Of Him it may be truly said that He *sow[ed] beside all waters* (Isaiah 32:20), and that in the morning He sowed His seed, and in the evening He was not idle (Ecclesiastes 11:6).

And yet our Lord knew the hearts of all men. He knew perfectly well that the great proportion of His hearers were hardened and unbelieving. He knew, as He spoke, that most of His words fell to the ground uncared for and unheeded, and that so far as concerned the salvation of souls, most of His labor was in vain. He knew all this, and yet He labored on.

Let us see in this fact a standing pattern for all who try to do good to others, whatever their office may be. Let it be remembered by every minister and every missionary, by every schoolmaster and every Sunday school teacher, by every district visitor and every lay agent, by every head of a house who has family prayers, and by every caretaker who has the charge of children. Let all such remember Christ's example and resolve to do likewise. We are not to give up teaching because we see no good done. We are not to relax our exertions because we see no fruit of our toil. We are to work on steadily, keeping before us the great principle that duty is ours and results are God's.

There must be ploughmen and sowers as well as reapers and binders of sheaves. The honest master pays his laborers according to the work they do and not according to the crops that grow on his land. Our Master in heaven will deal with all His servants at the last day in like manner. He knows that success is not in their hands. He knows that they cannot change hearts. He will reward them according to their labor and not according to the fruits which have resulted from their labor. It is not the good and *successful* servant but the good and *faithful* servant to whom He will say, *"Enter into the joy of your master"* (Matthew 25:21).

The greater portion of this passage is meant to show us *the dignity and importance of marriage*. It is plain that the prevailing opinions of the Jews upon this subject when our Lord was upon earth were lax and low in the extreme. The binding character of the marriage tie was not recognized. Divorce for slight and trivial causes was allowable and common. The duties of husbands towards wives and of wives towards husbands, as a natural consequence, were little understood. To correct this state of things, our Lord sets up a high and holy standard of principles. He refers to the original institution of marriage at the creation as the union of one man and one woman. He quotes and endorses the solemn words used at the marriage of Adam and Eve as words of perpetual significance: *"A man shall leave his father and mother, and the two shall become one flesh."* He adds a solemn comment to these words: *"What therefore God has joined together, let no man separate."* And finally, in reply to the inquiry of His disciples, He declares that divorce followed by remarriage, except for the cause of unfaithfulness, is a breach of the seventh commandment.

The importance of the whole subject on which our Lord here pronounces judgment can hardly be overrated. We ought to be very thankful that we have so clear and full an exposition of His mind upon it. The marriage relationship lies at the very root of the social system of nations. The public morality of a people and the private happiness of the families which compose a nation are deeply involved in the whole question of the law of marriage. The experience of all nations confirms the wisdom of our Lord's decision in this passage in the most striking manner. It is a fact clearly ascertained that polygamy and permission to obtain divorce on slight grounds have a direct tendency to promote immorality. In short, the nearer a nation's laws about marriage approach the law of Christ, the higher has the moral tone of that nation always proved to be.

It becomes all those who are married, or purpose to be married, to ponder well the teaching of our Lord Jesus Christ in this passage. Of all relations of life, none ought to be regarded with such reverence and none taken in hand so cautiously as the relation of husband and wife. In no relation is so much earthly happiness to be found if it be entered upon discreetly, advisedly, and in the fear of God. In none is so much misery seen to follow if it be taken in hand unadvisedly, lightly, wantonly, and without thought. From no step in life does so much benefit come to the soul if people marry *in the Lord.* From none does the soul take so much harm if fancy, passion, or any mere worldly motive is the only cause which produces the union. Solomon was the wisest of men.

Did not Solomon king of Israel sin regarding these things? Yet among the many nations there was no king like him, and he was loved by his God, and God made him king over all Israel; nevertheless the foreign women caused even him to sin (Nehemiah 13:26).

There is, unfortunately, only too much necessity for impressing these truths upon people. It is a mournful fact that few steps in life are generally taken with so much levity, self-will, and forgetfulness of God as marriage. Few are the young couples who think of inviting Christ to their wedding! It is a mournful fact that unhappy marriages are one great cause of the misery and sorrow of which there is so much in the world. People find out too late that they have made a mistake and go in bitterness all their days. Happy are they who in the matter of marriage observe three rules. The first is to marry only in the Lord and after prayer for God's approval and blessing. The second is not to expect too much from their spouse and to remember that marriage is, after all, the union of two sinners and not of two angels. The third rule is to strive first and foremost for one another's sanctification. The more holy married people are, the happier they are. *Christ also loved the church and gave Himself up for her, so that He might sanctify her, having cleansed her* (Ephesians 5:25-26).

Mark 10:13-16

And they were bringing children to Him so that He might touch them; but the disciples rebuked them. But when Jesus saw this, He was indignant and said to them, "Permit the children to come to Me; do not hinder them; for the kingdom of God belongs to such as these. Truly I say to you, whoever does not receive the kingdom of God like a child will not enter it at all." And He took them in His arms and began blessing them, laying His hands on them.

The scene brought before us in these four verses is deeply interesting. We see young children brought to Christ *so that He might touch them*, and the disciples rebuking those that brought them. We are told that when Jesus saw this, He was *indignant* and rebuked His disciples in words of a very remarkable tenor. And finally we are told that *He took them in His arms and began blessing them, laying His hands on them.*

Let us learn, for one thing from this passage, *how much attention the souls of children should receive from the church of Christ.* The great head of the church found time to take special notice of children. Although His time on earth was precious, and grown-up men and women were perishing on every side for lack of knowledge, He did not think little boys and girls of small importance. He had room in His mighty heart even for them. He declared by His outward gesture and deed His good will toward them. And not least, He has left on record words concerning them which His church should never forget: *"The kingdom of God belongs to such as these."*

We must never allow ourselves to suppose that little children's souls may be safely let alone. Their characters for life depend exceedingly on what they see and hear during their first seven years. They are never too young to learn evil and sin. They are never too young to receive religious impressions. They think in their childish way about God, and their souls, and a world to come far sooner and far more deeply than most people are aware. They are far more ready to respond to appeals to their feeling of right and wrong than many suppose. They have each a conscience. God has mercifully not left Himself without a witness in their hearts, fallen and corrupt as their natures are. They have each a soul which will live forever in heaven or in hell. We cannot begin too soon to endeavor to bring them to Christ.

These truths ought to be diligently considered by every branch of the church of Christ. It is the duty of every Christian congregation to make provision for the spiritual training of its children. The boys and girls of every family should be taught as soon as they can learn, they should be brought to public worship as soon as they can behave with propriety, and they should be regarded with affectionate interest as the future congregation which will fill our places when we are dead. We may confidently expect Christ's blessing on all attempts to do good to children. No church can be regarded as being in a healthy state which neglects its younger members and lazily excuses itself on the plea that "young people will be young," and that it is useless to try to do them good. Such a church shows plainly that it has not the mind of Christ. A congregation which consists of none but grown-up people, whose children are idling at home or running wild in the streets or fields, is a most deplorable and unsatisfactory sight. The members of such a congregation may pride themselves on their numbers and on the soundness of their own views. They may content themselves with loud assertions that they cannot change their children's hearts and that God will convert them some day if He thinks fit. But they have yet to learn that Christ regards them as neglecting a solemn duty, and that Christians who do not use every means to bring children to Christ are committing a great sin.

Mark 10:17-27

As He was setting out on a journey, a man ran up to Him and knelt before Him, and asked Him, "Good Teacher, what shall I do to inherit eternal life?" And Jesus said to him, "Why do you call Me good? No one is good except God alone. You know the commandments, 'Do not murder, Do not commit adultery, Do not steal, Do not bear false witness, Do not defraud, Honor your father and mother.'" And he said to Him, "Teacher, I have kept all these things from my youth up." Looking at him, Jesus felt a love for him and said to him, "One thing you lack: go and sell all you possess and give to the poor, and you will have treasure in heaven; and come, follow Me." But at these words he was saddened, and he went away grieving, for he was one who owned much property. And Jesus, looking around, said to His disciples, "How hard it will be for those who are wealthy to enter the kingdom of God!" The disciples were amazed at His words. But Jesus answered again and said to them, "Children, how hard it is to enter the kingdom of God! It is easier for a camel to go through the eye of a needle than for a rich man to enter the kingdom of God." They were even more astonished and said to Him, "Then who can be

*saved?" Looking at them, Jesus said, "With people it is impossible,
but not with God; for all things are possible with God."*

The story we have now read is recorded no less than three times in the
New Testament. Matthew, Mark, and Luke were all inspired by one
Spirit to write it for our learning. There is no doubt a wise purpose in
this threefold repetition of the same simple facts. It is intended to show
us that the lessons of the passage deserve particular notice from the
church of Christ.

Let us learn, for one thing from this passage, *the self-ignorance of man.*

We are told of one who *ran up* to our Lord and *knelt before Him, and
asked Him* the solemn question, *"What shall I do to inherit eternal life?"*
At first sight there was much that was promising in this man's case. He
showed anxiety about spiritual things, while most around him were
careless and indifferent. He showed a disposition to reverence our Lord
by kneeling before Him, while scribes and Pharisees despised Him. Yet
all this time this man was profoundly ignorant of his own heart. He
hears our Lord recite those commandments which make up our duty
to our neighbor and at once declares, *"I have kept all these things from
my youth up."* The searching nature of the moral law and its application to our thoughts and words as well as our actions are matters with
which he is utterly unacquainted.

The spiritual blindness here exhibited is unfortunately most common. Myriads of professing Christians at the present day have not an
idea of their own sinfulness and guilt in the sight of God. They flatter
themselves that they have never done anything very wicked. They have
never murdered, or stolen, or committed adultery, or borne false witness. They cannot surely be in much danger of missing heaven. They
forget the holy nature of that God with whom they have to do. They
forget how often they break His law in temper or imagination, even
when their outward conduct is correct. They never study such portions
of Scripture as the fifth chapter of Matthew, or at any rate they study it
with a thick veil over their hearts and do not apply it to themselves. The
result is that they are wrapped up in self-righteousness. Like the church
of Laodicea, they are *rich, and have become wealthy, and have need of*

nothing (Revelation 3:17). Self-satisfied they live, and self-satisfied too often they die.

Let us beware of this state of mind. So long as we think that we can keep the law of God, Christ profits us nothing. Let us pray for self-knowledge. Let us ask for the Holy Spirit to convince us of sin, to show us our own hearts, to show us God's holiness, and so to show us our need of Christ. Happy is he who has learned by experience the meaning of Paul's words, *I was once alive apart from the Law; but when the commandment came, sin became alive and I died* (Romans 7:9). Ignorance of the law and ignorance of the gospel will generally be found together. He whose eyes have really been opened to the spirituality of the commandments will never rest until he has found Christ.

Let us learn, for another thing from this passage, *the love of Christ towards sinners.*

This is a truth which is brought out in the expression used by Mark when, in his account of this man's story, he says that *looking at him, Jesus felt a love for him.* That love, beyond doubt, was a love of pity and compassion. Our Lord beheld with pity the strange mixture of earnestness and ignorance which the case before Him presented. He saw with compassion a soul struggling with all the weakness and infirmity entailed by the fall – the conscience ill at ease and sensible that it needed relief – the understanding sunk in darkness and blinded as to the first principles of spiritual religion. Just as we look with sorrow at some noble ruin, roofless and shattered and unfit for man's use, yet showing many a mark of the skill with which it was designed and raised at first, so may we suppose that Jesus looked with tender concern at this man's soul.

We must never forget that Jesus feels love and compassion for the souls of the ungodly. Without controversy He feels a distinguishing love for those who hear His voice and follow Him. They are His sheep, given to Him by the Father, and watched with a special care. They are His bride, joined to Him in an everlasting covenant, and dear to Him as part of Himself. But the heart of Jesus is a wide heart. He has abundance of pity, compassion, and tender concern even for those who are following sin and the world. He who wept over unbelieving Jerusalem is still the same. He would still gather into His bosom the ignorant and self-righteous, the faithless and impenitent, if they were only willing to be gathered (Matthew 23:37). We may boldly tell the chief of sinners that Christ loves him. Salvation is ready for the worst of men if they will only come to Christ. If men are lost, it is not because Jesus does not love them and is not ready to save. His own solemn words unravel the mystery: *Men loved the darkness rather than the Light* (John 3:19). *You are unwilling to come to Me so that you may have life* (John 5:40).

Let us learn, in the last place from this passage, *the immense danger of the love of money.* This is a lesson which is twice enforced on our notice. Once it comes out in the conduct of the man whose history is here related. With all his professed desire for eternal life, he loved his money better than his soul. *He went away grieving.* Once it comes out in the solemn words of our Lord to His disciples. *"How hard it will be for those who are wealthy to enter the kingdom of God!" "It is easier for a camel to go through the eye of a needle than for a rich man to enter the kingdom of God."* The last day alone will fully prove how true those words are.

Let us watch against the love of money. It is a snare to the poor as well as to the rich. It is not so much the having money as the trusting in it which ruins the soul. Let us pray for contentment with such things as we have. The highest wisdom is to be of one mind with Paul: *I have learned to be content in whatever circumstances I am* (Philippians 4:11).

Mark 10:28-34

Peter began to say to Him, "Behold, we have left everything and followed You." Jesus said, "Truly I say to you, there is no one who has left house or brothers or sisters or mother or father or children or farms, for My sake and for the gospel's sake, but that he will receive a hundred times as much now in the present age, houses and brothers and sisters and mothers and children and farms, along with persecutions; and in the age to come, eternal life. But many who are first will be last, and the last, first." They were on the road going up to Jerusalem, and Jesus was walking

on ahead of them; and they were amazed, and those who fol-
lowed were fearful. And again He took the twelve aside and
began to tell them what was going to happen to Him, saying,
"Behold, we are going up to Jerusalem, and the Son of Man will
be delivered to the chief priests and the scribes; and they will con-
demn Him to death and will hand Him over to the Gentiles. They
will mock Him and spit on Him, and scourge Him and kill Him,
and three days later He will rise again."

The first thing which demands our attention in these verses is *the glo-rious promise which they contain*. The Lord Jesus said to His apostles, *"Truly I say to you, there is no one who has left house or brothers or sisters or mother or father or children or farms, for My sake and for the gospel's sake, but that he will receive a hundred times as much now in the present age, houses and brothers and sisters and mothers and children and farms, along with persecutions; and in the age to come, eternal life."*

There are few wider promises than this in the Word of God. There is none certainly in the New Testament which holds out such encouragement for the life that now is. Let everyone who is fearful and faint-hearted in Christ's service look at this promise. Let all who are enduring hardness and tribulation for Christ's sake study this promise well and drink out of it comfort.

To all who make sacrifices on account of the gospel, Jesus promises *a hundred times as much now in the present age*. They shall have not only pardon and glory in the world to come. They shall also have even here upon earth hopes, and joys, and sensible comforts sufficient to make up for all that they lose. They shall find in the communion of saints new friends, new relations, and new companions more loving, faithful, and valuable than any they had before their conversion. Their introduction into the family of God shall be an abundant recompense for exclusion from the society of this world. This may sound startling and incredible to many ears. But thousands have found by experience that it is true.

To all who make sacrifices on account of the gospel, Jesus promises *in the age to come, eternal life*. As soon as they put off their earthly tabernacle, they shall enter upon a glorious existence, and in the morning of the resurrection shall receive such honor and joy as pass man's understanding. Their light afflictions for a few years shall end in an everlasting reward. Their fights and sorrows while in the body shall be exchanged for perfect rest and a conqueror's crown. They shall dwell in a world where there is no death, no sin, no devil, no cares, no weeping, and no parting, for the former things will have passed away. God has said it, and it shall all be found true.

Where is the saint who will dare to say in the face of these glorious promises that there is no encouragement to serve Christ? Where is the man or woman whose hands are beginning to hang down and whose knees are beginning to faint in the Christian race? Let all such ponder this passage and take fresh courage. The time is short. The end is sure. Heaviness may endure for a night, but joy comes in the morning. Let us wait patiently on the Lord.

The second thing which demands our attention in these verses is *the solemn warning which they contain.* The Lord Jesus saw the secret self-conceit of His apostles. He gives them a word in season to check their high thoughts. *"Many who are first will be last, and the last, first."*

How true were these words when applied to the twelve apostles! There stood among those who heard our Lord speak a man who at one time seemed likely to be one of the foremost of the twelve. He was one who appeared more careful and trustworthy than any. He had the charge of the money bag and kept what was put in it. And yet that man fell away and came to a disgraceful end. His name was Judas Iscariot.

Again, there did not stand among our Lord's hearers that day one who at a later period did more for Christ than any of the twelve. At the time when our Lord spoke, he was a young Pharisee, brought up at the feet of Gamaliel, and zealous for nothing so much as the law. And yet that young man in the end was converted to the faith of Christ, was not behind the chief apostles, and labored more abundantly than all. His name was Saul. Well might our Lord say, *"The first will be last, and the last, first."*

How true were these words when we apply them to the history of Christian churches! There was a time when Asia Minor, and Greece, and Northern Africa were full of professing Christians, while England

and America were heathen lands. Sixteen hundred years have made a mighty change. The churches of Africa and Asia have fallen into complete decay. Western churches are now laboring to spread the gospel over the world. Well might our Lord say, *"The first will be last, and the last, first."*

How true these words appear to believers when they look back over their own lives and remember all they have seen from the time of their own conversion! How many began to serve Christ at the same time with themselves and seemed to run well for a season. But where are they now? The world has got hold of one. False doctrine has beguiled another. A mistake in marriage has spoiled a third. Few indeed are the believers who cannot call to mind many such cases. Few have failed to discover by sorrowful experience that the last are often first, and the first last.

Let us learn to pray for humility when we read texts like this. It is not enough to begin well. We must persevere, and go on, and continue in well-doing. We must not be content with the fair blossoms of a few religious convictions, and joys, and sorrows, and hopes, and fears. We must bear the good fruit of settled habits of repentance, faith, and holiness. Happy is he who counts the cost and resolves, having once begun to walk in the narrow way, by God's grace never to turn aside.

The last thing that demands our attention in this passage is *our Lord's clear foreknowledge of His own suffering and death.* Calmly and deliberately He tells His disciples of His coming passion at Jerusalem. One after another He describes all the leading circumstances which will attend His death. Nothing is reserved. Nothing is kept back.

Let us closely observe this. There was nothing involuntary and unforeseen in our Lord's death. It was the result of His own free, determinate, and deliberate choice. From the beginning of His earthly ministry, He saw the cross before Him and went to it a willing sufferer. He knew that His death was the needful payment that must be made to reconcile God and man. That payment He had covenanted and engaged to make at the price of His own blood. And so when the appointed time came, like a faithful substitute, He kept His word and died for our sins on Calvary.

Let us ever bless God that the gospel sets before us such a Savior, so faithful to the terms of the covenant – so ready to suffer – so willing to be reckoned sin and a curse in our stead. Let us not doubt that He who fulfilled His engagement to suffer will also fulfill His engagement to save all who come to Him. Let us not only accept Him gladly as our Redeemer and Advocate, but also gladly give ourselves and all we have to His service. Surely, if Jesus cheerfully died for us, it is a small thing to require Christians to live for Him.

Mark 10:35-45

James and John, the two sons of Zebedee, came up to Jesus, saying, "Teacher, we want You to do for us whatever we ask of You." And He said to them, "What do you want Me to do for you?" They said to Him, 'Grant that we may sit, one on Your right and on Your left, in Your glory." But Jesus said to them, "You do not know what you are asking. Are you able to drink the cup that I drink, or to be baptized with the baptism with which I am baptized?" They said to Him, "We are able." And Jesus said to them, "The cup that I drink you shall drink; and you shall be baptized with the baptism with which I am baptized. But to sit on My right or on My left, this is not Mine to give; but it is for those for whom it has been prepared." Hearing this, the ten began to feel indignant with James and John. Calling them to Himself, Jesus said to them, "You know that those who are recognized as rulers of the Gentiles lord it over them; and their great men exercise authority over them. But it is not this way among you, but whoever wishes to become great among you shall be your servant; and whoever wishes to be first among you shall be slave of all. For even the Son of Man did not come to be served, but to serve, and to give His life a ransom for many."

Let us observe in this passage *the ignorance of our Lord's disciples.* We find James and John petitioning for the first places in the kingdom of glory. We find them confidently declaring their ability to drink of their Master's cup and be baptized with their Master's baptism.[9] In spite of

---

9   The manner in which our Lord uses the word *baptism* in the passage now expounded deserves careful notice. He says to two disciples who were already baptized with water,

all the plain warnings of our Lord, they clung obstinately to the belief that Christ's kingdom on earth was immediately going to appear. Notwithstanding their many shortcomings in Christ's service, they had no misgivings as to their power to endure anything which might come upon them. With all their faith, and grace, and love for Jesus, they knew neither their own hearts nor the nature of the path before them. They still dreamed of temporal crowns and earthly rewards. They still knew not what manner of men they were.

There are few true Christians who do not resemble James and John when they first begin the service of Christ. We are apt to expect far more present enjoyment from our religion than the gospel warrants us to expect. We are apt to forget the cross and the tribulation and to think only of the crown. We form an incorrect estimate of our own fortitude and power of endurance. We misjudge our own ability to withstand temptation and trial. And the result of all is that we often buy wisdom dearly by bitter experience, after many disappointments, and not a few falls.

Let the case before us teach us the importance of a solid and calm judgment in our religion. Like James and John, we are right in coveting the best gifts and in telling all our desires to Christ. Like them we are right in believing that Jesus is King of Kings and will one day reign upon the earth. But let us not, like them, forget that there is a cross to be borne by every Christian, and that *through many tribulations we must enter the kingdom of God* (Acts 14:22). Let us not, like them, be overconfident in our own strength and too forward in professing that we can do anything that Christ requires. Let us, in short, beware of a boastful spirit when we first begin to run the Christian course. If we remember this, it may save us many a humbling fall.

Let us observe, secondly in this passage, *what praise our Lord bestows*

"Are you able . . . to be baptized with the baptism with which I am baptized?" The expression is very remarkable. It is a clear proof that in the New Testament a sacramental dipping or sprinkling with water is not always necessarily implied by the word *baptism*. It establishes the fact that there is such a thing as being baptized, in a certain sense, without the use of any outward ordinance at all. This is a point that ought to be remembered in interpreting some of the passages in the Epistles where the words *baptism* and *baptized* are used. In such texts, for instance, as *baptism now saves you* (1 Peter 3:21), or *for all of you who have been baptized into Christ have clothed yourselves with Christ* (Galatians 3:27), it is clear that something more is contained than any mere outward ordinance.

on lowliness and devotion to the good of others. It seems that the ten were much displeased with James and John because of the petition which they made to their Master. Their ambition and love of preeminence were once more excited at the idea of anyone being placed above themselves. Our Lord saw their feelings and, like a wise physician, proceeded at once to supply a corrective medicine. He tells them that their ideas of greatness are built on a mistaken foundation. He repeats with renewed emphasis the lesson already laid down in the preceding chapter: *"Whoever wishes to be first among you shall be slave of all."* And He backs up all by the overwhelming argument of His own example: *"Even the Son of Man did not come to be served, but to serve."*

Let all who desire to please Christ watch and pray against self-esteem. It is a feeling which is deeply rooted in our hearts. Thousands have come out from the world, taken up the cross, professed to forsake their own righteousness and believe in Christ, and have felt irritated and annoyed when a brother has been more honored than themselves. These things ought not so to be. We ought often to ponder the words of Paul: *Do nothing from selfishness or empty conceit, but with humility of mind regard one another as more important than yourselves* (Philippians 2:3). Blessed is that man who can sincerely and gladly rejoice when others are exalted, though he himself is overlooked and passed by!

Above all, let all who desire to walk in Christ's steps labor to be useful to others. Let them lay themselves out to do good in their day and generation. There is always a vast field for doing it, if men have the will and inclination. Let them never forget that true greatness does not consist in being an admiral or a general, a statesman or an artist. It consists in devoting ourselves body, soul, and spirit to the blessed work of making our fellow men more holy and more happy. It is those who exert themselves by the use of scriptural means who lessen the sorrow and increase the joy of all around them – the Howards, the Wilberforces, the Martyns, the Judsons of a country – who are truly great in the sight of God. While they live, they are laughed at, mocked, ridiculed, and often persecuted. But their memorial is on high. Their names are written in heaven. Their praise endures forever. Let us remember these things and while we have time, do good unto all men and be servants of all for Christ's sake. Let us strive to leave the world better, holier, and happier than it was when we were born. A life spent in this way is truly Christlike and brings its own reward.

Let us observe lastly in this passage *the language which our Lord uses in speaking of His own death.* He says that the Son of Man came to *give His life a ransom for many.*

This is one of those expressions which ought to be carefully treasured up in the minds of all true Christians. It is one of the texts which prove incontrovertibly the atoning character of Christ's death. That death was no common death like the death of a martyr or of other holy men. It was the public payment by an almighty Representative of the debts of sinful man to a holy God. It was the ransom which a divine Surety undertook to provide in order to procure liberty for sinners, tied and bound by the chain of their sins. By that death Jesus made a full and complete satisfaction for man's countless transgressions. He bore our sins in His own body on the tree. The Lord laid on Him the iniquity of us all. When He died, He died for us. When He suffered, He suffered in our stead. When He hung on the cross, He hung there as our Substitute. When His blood flowed, it was the price of our souls.

Let all who trust in Christ take comfort in the thought that they build on a sure foundation. It is true that we are sinners, but Christ has borne our sins. It is true that we are poor helpless debtors, but Christ has paid our debts. It is true that we deserve to be shut up forever in the prison of hell. But thanks be to God, Christ has paid a full and complete ransom for us. The door is wide open. The prisoners may go free. May we all know this privilege by heartfelt experience and walk in the blessed liberty of the children of God.

Mark 10:46-52

Then they came to Jericho. And as He was leaving Jericho
with His disciples and a large crowd, a blind beggar named
Bartimaeus, the son of Timaeus, was siting by the road. When
he heard that it was Jesus the Nazarene, he began to cry out

and say, "Jesus, Son of David, have mercy on me!" Many were sternly telling him to be quiet, but he kept crying out all the more, "Son of David, have mercy on me!" And Jesus stopped and said, "Call him here." So they called the blind man, saying to him, "Take courage, stand up! He is calling for you." Throwing aside his cloak, he jumped up and came to Jesus. And answering him, Jesus said, "What do you want Me to do for you?" And the blind man said to Him, "Rabboni, I want to regain my sight!" And Jesus said to him, "Go; your faith has made you well." Immediately he regained his sight and began following Him on the road.

We read in these verses an account of one of our Lord's miracles. Let us see in it, as we read, a vivid emblem of spiritual things. We are not studying a history which concerns us personally any more than the exploits of Caesar or Alexander. We have before us a picture which ought to be deeply interesting to the soul of every Christian.

In the first place, we have here *an example of strong faith*. We are told that as Jesus went out of Jericho, a blind man named Bartimaeus *was sitting by the road. When he heard that it was Jesus the Nazarene, he began to cry out and say, "Jesus, Son of David, have mercy on me!"*

Bartimaeus was blind in body but not in soul. The eyes of his understanding were open. He saw things which Annas and Caiaphas and hosts of letter-learned scribes and Pharisees never saw at all. He saw that Jesus of Nazareth, as our Lord was contemptuously called – Jesus, who had lived for thirty years in an obscure Galilean village – this very Jesus was the Son of David and the Messiah of whom prophets had prophesied long ago. He had witnessed none of our Lord's mighty miracles. He had not had the opportunity of beholding dead people raised with a word and lepers healed by a touch. Of all these privileges, his blindness totally deprived him. But he had heard the report of our Lord's mighty works, and hearing, had believed. He was satisfied from mere hearsay that He of whom such wonderful things were reported must be the promised Savior and must be able to heal him. And so when our Lord drew near, he cried, *"Jesus, Son of David, have mercy on me!"*

Let us strive and pray that we may have like precious faith. Like Bartimaeus, we are not allowed to see Jesus with our bodily eyes. But we have the report of His power, and grace, and willingness to save in the Gospel. We have exceeding great promises from His own lips, written down for our encouragement. Let us trust those promises implicitly and commit our souls to Christ unhesitatingly. Let us not be afraid to place all our confidence on His own gracious words and to believe that what He has engaged to do for sinners, He will surely perform. What is the beginning of all saving faith but a soul's venture on Christ? What is the life of saving faith, when once begun, but a continual leaning on an unseen Savior's word? What is the first step of a Christian but a crying like Bartimaeus, "Jesus, have mercy on me!" What is the daily course of a Christian but keeping up the same spirit of faith? *Though you do not see Him now, but believe in Him, you greatly rejoice with joy inexpressible and full of glory* (1 Peter 1:8).

We have, in the second place in these verses, *an example of determined perseverance in the face of difficulties.* We are told that when Bartimaeus began to cry out, *"Jesus, Son of David, have mercy on me!"* he met with little encouragement from those who were near him. On the contrary, *many were sternly telling him to be quiet.* But he was not to be stopped. If others did not know the misery of blindness, he did. If others did not think it worthwhile to take such trouble in order to obtain relief, he, at any rate, knew better. He cared not for the rebukes of unfeeling bystanders. He heeded not the ridicule which his importunity probably brought on him. *He kept crying out all the more,* and so crying obtained his heart's desire and received his sight.

Let all who wish to be saved closely observe this conduct of Bartimaeus and walk diligently in his steps. Like him, we must care nothing about what others think and say of us when we seek the healing of our souls. There never will be a lack of people who will tell us that it is too soon or too late, that we are going too fast or too far, that we need not pray so much or read our Bibles so much or be so anxious about salvation. We must give no heed to such people. Like Bartimaeus, we must cry out *all the more,* "Jesus, have mercy on me!"

What is the reason that men are so halfhearted in seeking Christ?

Why are they so soon deterred, and checked, and discouraged in drawing near to God? The answer is short and simple. They do not feel sufficiently their own sins. They are not thoroughly convinced of the plague of their own hearts and the disease of their own souls. Once a man sees his own guilt as it really is, he will never rest until he has found pardon and peace in Christ. It is those who, like Bartimaeus, really know their own deplorable condition who persevere like Bartimaeus and are finally healed.

In the last place, we have in these verses *an example of the constraining influence which gratitude to Christ ought to have upon our souls.* Bartimaeus did not return home as soon as he was restored to sight. He would not leave Him from whom he had received such mercy. At once he devoted the new powers, which his cure gave him, to the Son of David who had worked the cure. His history concludes with the touching expression that he *began following Him on the road.*

Let us see in these simple words a lively emblem of the effect that the grace of Christ ought to have on everyone who tastes it. It ought to make him a follower of Jesus in his life and to draw him with mighty power into the way of holiness. Freely pardoned, he ought to give himself freely and willingly to Christ's service. Bought at so mighty a price as the blood of Christ, he ought to devote himself heartily and thoroughly to Him who redeemed him. Grace really experienced will make a man feel daily, What shall I render unto the Lord for all His benefits? It did so for the apostle Paul. He says, *The love of Christ controls us* (2 Corinthians 5:14). It will do so for all true Christians at the present day. The man who boasts of having a saving interest in Christ, while he does not follow Christ in his life, is a miserable self-deceiver and is ruining his own soul. *All who are being led by the Spirit of God, these*, and these only, *are the sons of God* (Romans 8:14).

Have we had our eyes opened by the Spirit of God? Have we yet been taught to see sin, and Christ, and holiness, and heaven in their true light? Can we say, *"One thing I do know, that though I was blind, now I see"* (John 9:25)? If so, we shall know the things of which we have been reading by experience. If not, we are yet in the broad way that leads to destruction and have everything to learn.

Mark Chapter 11

Mark 11:1-11

As they approached Jerusalem, at Bethphage and Bethany, near the Mount of Olives, He sent two of His disciples, and said to them, "Go into the village opposite you, and immediately as you enter it, you will find a colt tied there, on which no one has yet ever sat; untie it and bring it here. If anyone says to you, 'Why are you doing this?' you say, 'The Lord has need of it'; and immediately he will send it back here." They went away and found a colt tied at the door, outside in the street; and they untied it. Some of the bystanders were saying to them, "What are you doing, untying the colt?" They spoke to them just as Jesus had told them, and they gave them permission. They brought the colt to Jesus and put their coats on it; and He sat on it. Any many spread their coats in the road, and others spread leafy branches which they had cut from the fields. Those who went in front and those who followed were shouting:

> *"Hosanna!*
> *Blessed is He who comes in the name of the Lord;*
> *Blessed is the coming kingdom of our father David;*
> *Hosanna in the highest!"*

Jesus entered Jerusalem and came into the temple; and after looking around at everything, He left for Bethany with the twelve, since it was already late.

THE EVENT DESCRIBED IN THESE VERSES is a singular exception in the history of our Lord's earthly ministry. Generally speaking, we see Jesus withdrawing Himself from public notice, often passing His time in the remote parts of Galilee, not infrequently abiding in the wilderness, and so fulfilling the prophecy that *"He will not cry or raise His voice, nor make His voice heard in the street"* (Isaiah 42:2). Here, and here only, our Lord appears to drop His private character and of His own choice calls public attention to Himself. He deliberately makes a public entry into Jerusalem at the head of His disciples. He voluntarily rides into the Holy City, surrounded by a vast multitude crying, *"Hosanna!"* like King David returning to his palace in triumph (2 Samuel 19:40). All this too was done at a time when myriads of Jews were gathered out of every land to Jerusalem to keep the Passover. We may well believe that the Holy City rang with the tidings of our Lord's arrival. It is probable there was not a house in Jerusalem in which the entry of the prophet of Nazareth was not known and talked of that night.

These things should always be remembered in reading this portion of our Lord's history. It is not for nothing that this entry into Jerusalem is four times related in the New Testament. It is evident that it is a scene in the earthly life of Jesus which Christians are intended to study with special attention. Let us study it in that spirit and see what practical lessons we may learn from the passage for our own souls.

Let us observe, in the first place, *how public our Lord purposely made the last act of His life*. He came to Jerusalem to die, and He desired that all Jerusalem should know it. When He taught the deep things of the Spirit, He often spoke to none but His apostles. When He delivered His parables, He often addressed none but a multitude of poor and ignorant Galileans. When He worked His miracles, He was generally at Capernaum or in the land of Zebulon and Naphtali. But when the time came that He should die, He made a public entry into Jerusalem. He drew the attention of rulers, and priests, and elders, and scribes, and Greeks, and Romans to Himself. He knew that the most wonderful event that ever happened in this world was about to take place. The eternal Son of God was about to suffer in the place of sinful men as the great sacrifice for sin about to be offered up, the great Passover Lamb about to be slain, and the great atonement for the world's sin about to be made. He therefore ordered it so that His death was eminently a public death. He overruled things in such a way that the eyes of all Jerusalem were fixed upon Him, and when He died, He died before many witnesses.

Let us see here one more proof of the unspeakable importance of the death of Christ. Let us treasure up His gracious sayings. Let us strive to walk in the steps of His holy life. Let us prize His intercession. Let us long for His second coming. But never let us forget that the crowning fact in all we know of Jesus Christ is His death upon the cross. From that death flows all our hopes. Without that death we would have nothing solid beneath our feet. May we prize that death more and more every year we live; and in all our thoughts about Christ, may we rejoice in nothing so much as the great fact that He died for us!

Let us observe, in the second place in this passage, *the voluntary poverty which our Lord underwent when He was upon earth*. How did He enter Jerusalem when He came to it on this remarkable occasion? Did He come in a royal chariot with horses, soldiers, and attendants around Him like the kings of this world? We are told nothing of the kind. We read that He borrowed the colt of a donkey for the occasion and sat upon the garments of His disciples for lack of a saddle. This was in perfect keeping with all the tenor of His ministry. He never had any of the riches of this world. When He crossed the Sea of Galilee, it was in a borrowed boat. When He rode into the Holy City, it was on a borrowed beast. When He was buried, it was in a borrowed tomb.

We have in this simple fact an instance of that marvelous union of weakness and power, riches and poverty, the Godhead and the manhood, which may be so often traced in the history of our blessed Lord. Who that reads the Gospels carefully can fail to observe that He who could feed thousands with a few loaves was Himself sometimes hungry, and He who could heal the sick and infirm was Himself sometimes weary, that He who could cast out devils with a word was Himself tempted, and He who could raise the dead could Himself submit to die?

We see the very same thing in the passage before us. We see the power of our Lord in His bending the wills of a vast multitude to conduct Him into Jerusalem in triumph. We see the poverty of our Lord in His borrowing a donkey to carry Him when He made His triumphal entry. It is all wonderful, but there is a fitness in it all. It is appropriate and right that we should never forget the union of the divine and human natures in our Lord's person. If we saw His divine acts only, we might forget that He was man. If we saw His seasons of poverty and weakness only, we might forget that He was God. But we are intended to see in Jesus divine strength and human weakness united in one person. We cannot explain the mystery, but we may take comfort in the thought that this is our Savior, this is our Christ – one able to sympathize, because He is man, but one almighty to save, because He is God.

Finally, let us see in the simple fact that our Lord rode on a borrowed donkey one more proof that *poverty is in itself no sin.* The causes which occasion much of the poverty there is around us are undoubtedly very sinful. Drunkenness, extravagance, immorality, dishonesty, and idleness, which produce so much of the destitution in the world, are unquestionably wrong in the sight of God. But to be born a poor man and to inherit nothing from our parents – to work with our own hands for our bread and to have no land of our own – all this is not sinful at all. The honest poor man is as honorable in the sight of God as the richest king. The Lord Jesus Christ Himself was poor. Silver and gold He had none. He had often nowhere to lay His head. Though He was rich, yet for our sakes He became poor. To be like Him in circumstances cannot be in itself wrong. Let us do our duty in that state of life to which God has called us, and if He thinks fit to keep us poor, let us not be ashamed. The Savior of sinners cares for us as well as for others. The Savior of sinners knows what it is to be poor.

Mark 11:12-21

On the next day, when they had left Bethany, He became hungry. Seeing at a distance a fig tree in leaf, He went to see if perhaps He would find anything on it; and when He came to it, He found nothing but leaves, for it was not the season for figs. He said to it, "May no one ever eat fruit from you again!" And His disciples

were listening. Then they came to Jerusalem. And He entered the
temple and began to drive out those who were buying and selling
in the temple, and overturned the tables of the money changers
and the seats of those who were selling doves; and He would not
permit anyone to carry merchandise through the temple. And
He began to teach and say to them, "Is it not written, 'My house
shall be called a house of prayer for all the nations'? But you have
made it a robbers' den." The chief priests and the scribes heard
this, and began seeking how to destroy Him; for they were afraid
of Him, for the whole crowd was astonished at His teaching.
When evening came, they would go out of the city. As they were
passing by in the morning, they saw the fig tree withered from the
roots up. Being reminded, Peter said to Him, "Rabbi, look, the fig
tree which You cursed has withered."

We see in the beginning of this passage *one of the many proofs that our Lord Jesus Christ was really man.* We read that *He became hungry.* He had a nature and bodily constitution like our own in all things, sin only excepted. He could weep, and rejoice, and suffer pain. He could be weary and need rest. He could be thirsty and need drink. He could be hungry and need food.

Expressions like this should teach us the condescension of Christ. How wonderful they are when we reflect upon them! He who is the eternal God, He who made the world and all that it contains, He from whose hand the fruits of the earth, the fish of the sea, the fowls of the air, and the beasts of the field all had their beginning – He, even He, was pleased to suffer hunger when He came into the world to save sinners. This is a great mystery. Kindness and love like this pass man's understanding. No wonder that Paul speaks of *the unfathomable riches of Christ* (Ephesians 3:8).

Expressions like this should teach us Christ's power to sympathize with His believing people on earth. He knows their sorrows by experience. He can be touched with the feeling of their infirmities. He has had experience of a body and its daily needs. He has allowed Himself the severe sufferings that the body of man is liable to. He has tasted pain, and weakness, and weariness, and hunger, and thirst. When we tell Him of these things in our prayers, He knows what we mean and is no stranger to our troubles. Surely this is just the Savior and Friend that poor, aching, groaning human nature requires!

We learn, in the second place from these verses, *the great danger of unfruitfulness and formality in religion.* This is a lesson which our Lord teaches in a remarkable typical action. We are told that coming to a fig tree in search of fruit and finding on it *nothing but leaves,* He pronounced on it the solemn sentence: *"May no one ever eat fruit from you again!"* And we are told that the next day the fig tree was found *withered from the roots up.* We cannot doubt for a moment that this whole transaction was an emblem of spiritual things. It was a parable in deeds, as full of meaning as any of our Lord's parables in words.

But who were they to whom this withered fig tree was intended to speak? It was a sermon of threefold application, a sermon that ought to speak loudly to the consciences of all professing Christians. Though withered and dried up, that fig tree yet speaks. There was a voice in it for the Jewish Church. Rich in the leaves of a formal religion but barren of all fruits of the Spirit, that church was in fearful danger at the very time when this withering took place. Well would it have been for the Jewish Church if it had had eyes to see its peril!

There was a voice in the fig tree for all the branches of Christ's visible church in every age and every part of the world. There was a warning against an empty profession of Christianity unaccompanied by sound doctrine and holy living, which some of those branches would have done well to lay to heart.

But above all there was a voice in that withered fig tree for all carnal, hypocritical, and falsehearted Christians. Well would it be for all who are content with a name to live while in reality they are dead, if they would only see their own faces in the looking glass of this passage.

Let us take care that we each individually learn the lesson that this fig tree conveys. Let us always remember that baptism, and church membership, and reception of the Lord's Supper, and a diligent use of the outward forms of Christianity are not sufficient to save our souls. They are leaves, nothing but leaves, and without fruit they will add to our condemnation. Like the fig leaves of which Adam and Eve made themselves garments, they will not hide the nakedness of our souls from the eye of an all-seeing God or give us boldness when we stand before Him at the last day. No! We must bear fruit or be lost forever. There must be fruit in our hearts and fruit in our lives, the fruit of repentance toward God, faith toward our Lord Jesus Christ, and true holiness in our conversation. Without such fruits as these, a profession of Christianity will only sink us lower into hell.

We learn, in the last place from this passage, *how reverently we ought to use places which are set apart for public worship.* This is a truth which is taught us in a striking manner by our Lord Jesus Christ's conduct when He went into the temple. We are told that *He entered the temple and began to drive out those who were buying and selling in the temple, and overturned the tables of the money changers and the seats of those who were selling doves.* And we are told that He enforced this action by warrant of Scripture, saying, *"Is it not written, 'My house shall be called a house of prayer for all the nations'? But you have made it a robbers' den."*

We need not doubt that there was a deep meaning in this action of our Lord on this occasion. Like the cursing of the fig tree, the whole transaction was eminently typical. But in saying this, we must not allow ourselves to lose sight of one simple and obvious lesson which lies on the surface of the passage. That lesson is the sinfulness of careless and irreverent behavior in the use of buildings set apart for the public service of God. It was not so much as the house of sacrifice but as the *house of prayer* that our Lord purified the temple. His action clearly indicates the feeling with which every *house of prayer* should be regarded. A Christian place of worship no doubt is in no sense so sacred as the Jewish tabernacle, or temple. Its arrangements have no typical meaning. It is not built after a divine model and intended to serve as an example of heavenly things. But it does not follow because these things are so that a Christian place of worship is to be used with no more reverence than a private dwelling, or a shop, or an inn. There is surely a decent reverence which is due to a place where Christ and His people regularly meet together and public prayer is offered up – a reverence which it is foolish and unwise to brand as superstitious and confound with Roman Catholicism. There is a certain feeling of sanctity and solemnity which ought to belong to all places where Christ is preached and souls are born again, a feeling which does not depend on any consecration of man and ought to be encouraged rather than checked. At all events the mind of the Lord Jesus in this passage seems very plain. He takes notice of men's behavior in places of worship, and all irreverence or profanity is an offense in His sight.

Let us remember these verses whenever we go to the house of God and take heed that we go in a serious frame of mind and do not offer the sacrifice of fools. Let us call to mind where we are, what we are doing, what business we are about, and in whose presence we are engaged. Let us beware of giving God a mere formal service while our hearts are full of the world. Let us leave our business and money at home and not carry them with us to church. Let us beware of allowing any buying and selling in our hearts in the midst of our religious assemblies. The Lord still lives, who cast out buyers and sellers from the temple, and when He sees such conduct, He is much displeased.

Mark 11:22-26

And Jesus answered saying to them, "Have faith in God. Truly I say to you, whoever says to this mountain, 'Be taken up and cast into the sea,' and does not doubt in his heart, but believes that what he says is going to happen, it will be granted him. Therefore I say to you, all things for which you pray and ask, believe that you receive them, and they will be granted you. Whenever you stand praying, forgive, if you have anything against anyone, so that your Father who is in heaven will also forgive you your transgressions. [But if you do not forgive, neither will your Father who is in heaven forgive your transgressions."][10]

Let us learn from these words of our Lord Jesus Christ *the immense importance of faith.*

10   Altered to closer match the King James Version.

This is a lesson which our Lord teaches first by a proverbial saying. Faith shall enable a man to accomplish works and overcome difficulties as great and formidable as the removing of a mountain and casting it into the sea. Afterwards, the lesson is impressed upon us still further by a general exhortation to exercise faith when we pray. *"All things for which you pray and ask, believe that you receive them, and they will be granted you."* This promise must of course be taken with a reasonable qualification. It assumes that a believer will ask things which are not sinful and which are in accordance with the will of God. When He asks such things, he may confidently believe that his prayer will be answered. To use the words of James, *He must ask in faith without any doubting* (James 1:6).

The faith here commended must be distinguished from that faith which is essential to justification. In principle, undoubtedly, all true faith is one and the same. It is always trust or belief. But in the object and operations of faith, there are diversities, which it is useful to understand. Justifying faith is that act of the soul by which a man lays hold on Christ and has peace with God. Its special object is the atonement for sin which Jesus made on the cross. The faith spoken of in the passage now before us is a grace of more general significance, the fruit and companion of justifying faith but still not to be confused with it. It is rather a general confidence in God's power, wisdom, and goodwill towards believers. And its special objects are the promises, the word, and the character of God in Christ.

Confidence in God's power and will to help every believer in Christ and in the truth of every word that God has spoken is the grand secret of success and prosperity in our religion. In fact, it is the very root of saving Christianity. *By it the men of old gained approval* (Hebrews 11:2). *He who comes to God must believe that He is and that He is a rewarder of those who seek Him* (Hebrews 11:6). To know the full worth of it in the sight of God, we should often study the eleventh chapter of the epistle to the Hebrews.

Do we desire to grow in grace and in the knowledge of our Lord Jesus Christ? Do we wish to make progress in our religion and become strong Christians and not mere babes in spiritual things? Then let us pray daily for more faith and watch our faith with most jealous watchfulness. Here is the cornerstone of our religion. A flaw or weakness here will affect the whole condition of our inner man. According to our faith will be the degree of our peace, our hope, our joy, our decision in Christ's service, our boldness in confession, our strength in work, our patience in trial, our resignation in trouble, and our sensible comfort in prayer. All, all will hinge on the proportion of our faith. Happy are they who know how to rest their whole weight continually on a covenant God and to walk by faith, not by sight. *He who believes in it will not be disturbed* (Isaiah 28:16).

Let us learn, for another thing from these verses, *the absolute necessity of a forgiving spirit towards others.* This lesson is here taught us in a striking way. There is no immediate connection between the importance of faith, of which our Lord had just been speaking, and the subject of forgiving injuries. But the connecting link is prayer. First we are told that faith is essential to the success of our prayers. But then it is added that no prayers can be heard which do not come from a forgiving heart. *Whenever you stand praying, forgive, if you have anything against anyone, so that your Father who is in heaven will also forgive you your transgressions.*

The value of our prayers, we can all understand, depends exceedingly on the state of mind in which we offer them. But the point before us is one which receives far less attention than it deserves. Our prayers must not only be earnest, fervent, sincere, and in the name of Christ. They must contain one more ingredient besides. They must come from a forgiving heart. We have no right to look for mercy if we are not ready to extend mercy to our brethren. We cannot really feel the sinfulness of the sins we ask to have pardoned if we cherish malice towards our fellow men. We must have the heart of a brother toward our neighbor on earth if we wish God to be our Father in heaven. We must not flatter ourselves that we have the Spirit of adoption if we cannot bear and forbear.

This is a heart-searching subject. The quantity of malice, bitterness, and party spirit among Christians is fearfully great. No wonder that so many prayers seem to be thrown away and unheard. It is a subject which ought to come home to all classes of Christians. All have not equal gifts of knowledge and utterance in their approaches to God. But all can forgive their fellow men. It is a subject which our Lord Jesus Christ has taken special pains to impress on our minds. He has given it a prominent place in that pattern of prayers, the Lord's Prayer. We are all familiar from our infancy with the words, *If you forgive others for their transgressions, your heavenly Father will also forgive you* (Matthew 6:14). Well would it be for many, if they would consider what those words mean!

Let us leave the passage with serious self-inquiry. Do we know what it is to be of a forgiving spirit? Can we forgive the injuries that we receive from time to time in this evil world? Can we pass over a transgression and pardon an offense? If not, where is our Christianity? If not, why should we wonder that our souls do not prosper? Let us resolve to amend our ways in this matter. Let us determine by God's grace to forgive even as we hope to be forgiven. This is the nearest approach we can make to the mind of Christ Jesus. This is the character which is most suitable to a poor sinful child of Adam. God's free forgiveness of sins is our highest privilege in this world. God's free forgiveness will be our only title to eternal life in the world to come. Then let us be forgiving during the few years that we are here upon earth.

Mark 11:27-33

They came again to Jerusalem. And as He was walking in the temple, the chief priests and the scribes and the elders came to Him, and began saying to Him, "By what authority are You doing these things, or who gave You this authority to do these things?" And Jesus said to them, "I will ask you one question, and you answer Me, and then I will tell you by what authority I do these things. Was the baptism of John from heaven, or from men? Answer Me." They began reasoning among themselves, saying, "If we say, 'From heaven,' He will say, 'Then why did you not believe him?' But shall we say, 'From men'?"—they were afraid of the people, for everyone considered John to have been a real prophet. Answering Jesus, they said, "We do not know." And Jesus said to them, "Nor will I tell you by what authority I do these things."

Let us observe in these verses *how much spiritual blindness may be in the hearts of those who hold high ecclesiastical office.* We see *the chief priests and the scribes and the elders* coming to our Lord Jesus and raising difficulties and objections in the way of His work.

These men, we know, were the accredited teachers and rulers of the Jewish Church. They were regarded by the Jews as the fountain and springhead of religious knowledge. They were, most of them, regularly ordained to the position they held and could trace their orders by regular descent from Aaron. And yet we find these very men, at the time when they ought to have been instructors of others, full of prejudice against the truth and bitter enemies of the Messiah!

These things are written to show Christians that they must beware of depending too much on ordained men. They must not look up to ministers as popes or regard them as infallible. The orders of no church confer infallibility, whether they be Episcopal, Presbyterian, or Independent. Bishops, priests, and deacons, at their best, are only flesh and blood, and may err, both in doctrine and practice, as well as the chief priests and elders of the Jews. Their acts and teaching must always be tested by the Word of God. They must be followed so far as they follow Scripture and no further. There is only one priest and bishop of souls who makes no mistakes. That one is the Lord Jesus Christ. In Him alone is no weakness, no failure, no shadow of infirmity. Let us learn to lean more entirely on Him. Let us *not call anyone on earth [our] father* (Matthew 23:9). So doing, we shall never be disappointed.

Let us observe, in the second place, *how envy and unbelief make men throw discredit on the commission of those who work for God.* These chief priests and elders could not deny the reality of our Lord's miracles of mercy. They could not say that His teaching was contrary to Holy Scripture or that His life was sinful. What then did they do? They attacked His claim to attention and demanded to know His authority – *"By what authority are You doing these things, or who gave You this authority?"*

There can be no doubt whatsoever that as a general principle, all who undertake to teach others should be regularly appointed to the work. Paul himself declares that this was the case with our Lord in the matter of the priestly office – *No one takes the honor to himself, but receives it when he is called by God, even as Aaron was* (Hebrews 5:4). And even now when the office of the sacrificing priest no longer exists, the words of the twenty-third Article of the Church of England are wise and scriptural: "It is not lawful for any man to take upon him the office of public preaching, or ministering the sacraments in the congregation, before he be lawfully called and sent to execute the same." But it is one thing to maintain the lawfulness of an outward call to minister in sacred things and quite another to assert that it is the one thing needful without which no work for God can be done. This is the point on which the Jews evidently erred in the time of our Lord's earthly ministry and on which many have unfortunately followed them down to the present day.

Let us beware of this narrow spirit and especially in these last ages of the world. Unquestionably, we must not undervalue order and discipline in the church. It is just as valuable there as it is in an army. But we must not suppose that God is absolutely tied to the use of ordained men. We must not forget that there may be an inward call of the Holy Spirit without any outward call of man, no less than an outward call of man without any inward call of the Holy Spirit. The first question after all is this: Is a man for Christ or against Him? What does he teach? How does he live? Is he doing good? If questions like these can be answered satisfactorily, let us thank God and be content. We must remember that a physician is useless, however high his degree and diploma, if he cannot cure diseases, and a soldier useless, however well dressed and drilled, if he will not face the enemy in the day of battle. The best doctor is the man who can cure, and the best soldier the man who can fight.

Let us observe, in the last place, *what dishonesty and equivocation unbelievers may be led into by prejudice against the truth.* The chief priests and elders dared not answer our Lord's question about John's baptism. They dared not say it was *from men*, because they feared the people. They dared not confess that it was *from heaven*, because they knew our Lord would say, *"Then why did you not believe him?"* "He *has testified of Me."* What then did they do? They told a direct lie. They said, *"We do not know."*

It is a sad fact that dishonesty like this is far from being uncommon among unconverted people. There are thousands who evade appeals to their conscience by answers which are not true. When pressed to attend to their souls, they say things which they know are not correct. They love the world and their own way, and like our Lord's enemies, are determined not to give them up, but like them also, are ashamed to say the truth. And so they answer exhortations to repentance and decision by false excuses. One man pretends that he "cannot understand" the doctrines of the gospel. Another assures us that he really "tries" to serve God but makes no progress. A third declares that he has every wish to serve Christ but "has no time." All these are often nothing better than miserable equivocations. As a general rule, they are as worthless as the chief priest's answer, *"We do not know."*

The plain truth is that we ought to be very slow to give credit to the unconverted man's professed reasons for not serving Christ. We may be tolerably sure that when he says, "I cannot," the real meaning of his heart is "I will not." A really honest spirit in religious matters is a mighty blessing. Once a man is willing to live up to his light and act up to his knowledge, he will soon know of the doctrine of Christ and come out from the world (John 7:17). The ruin of thousands is simply this – that they deal dishonestly with their own souls. They allege pretended difficulties as the cause of their not serving Christ, while in reality they *[love] the darkness rather than the Light* and have no honest desire to change (John 3:19).

Mark Chapter 12

Mark 12:1-12

And He began to speak to them in parables: "A man planted a vineyard and put a wall around it, and dug a vat under the wine press and built a tower, and rented it out to vine-growers and went on a journey. At the harvest time he sent a slave to the vine-growers, in order to receive some of the produce of the vineyard from the vine-growers. They took him, and beat him and sent him away empty-handed. Again he sent them another slave, and they wounded him in the head, and treated him shamefully. And he sent another, and that one they killed; and so with many others, beating some and killing others. He had one more to send, a beloved son; he sent him last of all to them, saying, 'They will respect my son.' But those vine-growers said to one another, 'This is the heir; come, let us kill him, and the inheritance will be ours!' They took him, and killed him and threw him out of the vineyard. What will the owner of the vineyard do? He will come and destroy the vine-growers, and will give the vineyard to others. Have you not even read this Scripture:

> *'The stone which the builders rejected,*
> *This became the chief corner stone;*
> *This came about from the Lord,*
> *And it is marvelous in our eyes'?"*

And they were seeking to seize Him, and yet they feared the people, for they understood that He spoke the parable against them. And so they left Him and went away.

THE VERSES BEFORE US CONTAIN A HISTORICAL PARABLE. The history of the Jewish nation from the day that Israel left Egypt down to the time of the destruction of Jerusalem is here set before us as in a mirror. Under the figure of the vineyard and the husbandmen, the Lord Jesus tells the story of God's dealings with His people for fifteen hundred years. Let us study it attentively and apply it to ourselves.

Let us observe, in the first place, *God's special kindness to the Jewish Church and nation*. He gave to them peculiar privileges. He dealt with them as a man deals with a piece of land which he separates and hedges in for *a vineyard*. He gave them good laws and ordinances. He planted them in a goodly land and cast out seven nations before them. He passed by greater and mightier nations to show them favor. He let alone Egypt, and Assyria, and Greece, and Rome, and showered down mercies on a few million people in Palestine. The vineyard of the Lord was the house of Israel. No family under heaven ever received so many signal and distinguishing privileges as the family of Abraham.

And we too, who live in Great Britain, can we say that we have received no special mercies from God? We cannot say so. Why are we not a heathen country like China? Why are we not a land of idolaters like India? We owe it all to the distinguishing favor of God. It is not for our goodness and worthiness, but of God's free grace that our country is what our country is among the nations of the earth. Let us be thankful for our mercies and know the hand from which they come. Let us not be high-minded, but humble, lest we provoke God to take our mercies away. If Israel had peculiar national privileges, so do we. Let us observe this and take heed lest that which happened to Israel should happen also to them.

Let us observe, in the second place, *God's patience towards the Jewish nation*. What is their whole history as recorded in the Old Testament but a long record of repeated provocations and repeated pardons. Over and over again we read of prophets being sent to them and warnings being delivered, but too often entirely in vain. One servant after another came to the vineyard of Israel and asked for fruit. One servant after another was *sent away empty-handed* by the Jewish husbandmen and no fruit borne by the nation to the glory of God. *They continually mocked the messengers of God, despised His words and scoffed at His prophets* (2 Chronicles 36:16). Yet hundreds of years passed away before *the wrath of the* LORD *arose against His people, until there was no remedy.* Never was there a people so patiently dealt with as Israel.

And we too, who dwell in Great Britain, have we no patience of God to be thankful for? Beyond doubt, we have abundant cause to say that our Lord is patient. He does not deal with us according to our sins or reward us according to our iniquities. We have often provoked Him to take our candlestick away and to deal with us as He has dealt with Tyre, and Babylon, and Rome. Yet His patience and loving-kindness continue still. Let us beware that we do not presume on His goodness too far. Let us hear in His mercies a loud call to us to bear fruit, and let us strive to abound in that righteousness which alone exalts a nation (Proverbs 14:34). Let every family in the land feel their responsibility to God, and then the whole nation will be seen showing forth His praise.

Let us observe, in the third place, *the hardness and wickedness of human nature as exemplified in the history of the Jewish people.*

It is difficult to imagine a more striking proof of this truth than the summary of Israel's dealings with God's messengers which our Lord sketches in this parable. Prophet after prophet was sent to them in vain. Miracle after miracle was wrought among them without any lasting effect. The Son of God Himself, the well-beloved, at last came down to them and was not believed. God Himself was manifest in the flesh, dwelling among them, and *they took him, and killed him.*

There is no truth so little realized and believed as the desperate wickedness of the human heart. Let the parable before us this day be always reckoned among the standing proofs of it. Let us see in it what men and women can do in the full blaze of religious privileges – in the midst of prophecies and miracles – in the presence of the Son of God Himself. *The mind set on the flesh is hostile against God* (Romans 8:7). Men never saw God face to face but once, when Jesus became a man and lived upon earth. They saw Him holy, harmless, undefiled, going about doing good. Yet they would not have Him, rebelled against Him, and at last killed Him. Let us dismiss from our minds the idea that there is any innate goodness or natural rectitude in our hearts. Let us put away the common notion that seeing and knowing what is good is enough to make a man a Christian. The great experiment has been made in the instance of the Jewish nation. We too, like Israel, might have among us miracles, prophets, and the company of Christ Himself in the flesh and yet, like Israel, have them in vain. Nothing but the Spirit of God can change the heart. We *must be born again* (John 3:7).

Let us observe, in the last place, that *men's consciences may be pierced, and yet they may continue impenitent.* The Jews to whom our Lord addressed the solemn historical parable which we have been reading saw clearly that it applied to themselves. They felt that they and their forefathers were the husbandmen to whom the vineyard was leased and who ought to have rendered fruit to God. They felt that they and their forefathers were the wicked laborers who had refused to give the Master of the vineyard His dues and had shamefully treated His servants, *beating some and killing others.* Above all, they felt that they themselves were planning the last crowning act of wickedness which the parable described. They were about to kill the well-beloved Son, and *[throw] him out of the vineyard.* All this they knew perfectly well. *They understood that He spoke the parable against them.* Yet though they knew it, they would not repent. Though convicted by their own consciences, they were hardened in sin.

Let us learn from this dreadful fact that knowledge and conviction alone save no man's soul. It is quite possible to know that we are wrong and be unable to deny it and yet cleave to our sins obstinately and perish miserably in hell. The thing that we all need is a change of heart and will. For this let us pray earnestly. Until we have this, let us never rest. Without this, we shall never be real Christians and reach heaven. Without it we may live all our lives like the Jews, knowing inwardly that we are wrong and yet, like the Jews, persevere in our own way and die in our sins.

Mark 12:13-17

Then they sent some of the Pharisees and Herodians to Him in order to trap him in a statement. They came and said to Him, "Teacher, we know that You are truthful and defer to no one; for You are not partial to any, but teach the way of God in truth. Is it lawful to pay a poll-tax to Caesar, or not? Shall we pay or shall we not pay?" But He, knowing their hypocrisy, said to them, "Why are you testing Me? Bring Me a denarius to look at." They brought one. And He said to them, "Whose likeness and inscription is this?" And they said to Him, "Caesar's." And Jesus said to them, "Render to Caesar the things that are Caesar's, and to God the things that are God's." And they were amazed at Him.

Let us observe in the beginning of this passage *how men of different religious opinions can unite in opposing Christ.* We read of *Pharisees and Herodians* coming together to *trap Him in a statement* and perplex Him with a hard question. The Pharisee was a superstitious formalist who cared for nothing but the outward ceremonies of religion. The Herodian was a mere man of the world who despised all religion and cared more for pleasing men than God. Yet when there came among them a mighty teacher who assailed the ruling passions of both alike and spared neither formalist nor worldling, we see them making common cause and uniting in a common effort to stop His mouth.

It has always been so from the beginning of the world. We may see the same thing going on at the present day. Worldly men and formalists have little real sympathy for one another. They dislike one another's principles and despise one another's ways. But there is one thing which they both dislike even more, and that is the pure gospel of Jesus Christ. And hence, whenever there is a chance of opposing the gospel, we shall always see the worldly man and the formalist combine and act together. We must expect no mercy from them – they will show none. We must never reckon on their divisions – they will always patch up an alliance to resist Christ.

Let us observe, for another thing in this passage, *the exceeding subtlety of the question propounded to our Lord.* His enemies asked Him, *"Is it lawful to pay a poll-tax to Caesar, or not? Shall we pay or shall we not pay?"* Here was a question which it seemed at first sight impossible to answer without peril. If our Lord had replied, "Pay," the Pharisees would have accused Him before the priests as one who regarded the Jewish nation as under subjection to Rome. If our Lord had replied, "Do not pay," the Herodians would have accused Him before Pilate as a seditious person who taught rebellion against the Roman government. The trap was indeed well planned. Surely we may see in it the cunning hand of one greater than man. That old serpent the devil was there.

We shall do well to remember that of all questions which have perplexed Christians, none have ever proved so intricate and puzzling as the class of questions which the Pharisees and Herodians here propounded. What are the dues of Caesar, and what are the dues of God? Where do the rights of the church end, and where do the rights of the state begin? What are lawful civil claims, and what are lawful spiritual claims? All these are hard knots and deep problems which Christians have often found it difficult to untie and almost impossible to solve. Let us pray to be delivered from them. Never does the cause of Christ suffer so much as when the devil succeeds in bringing churches into collisions and lawsuits with the civil powers. In such collisions precious time is wasted, energies are misapplied, ministers are drawn off from their proper work, the souls of people suffer, and a church's victory often proves only one degree better than a defeat. "Give peace in our time, O Lord," is a prayer of wide meaning and one that should often be on a Christian's lips.

Let us observe, in the last place, *the marvelous wisdom which our Lord showed in His answer to His enemies.*

Their flattering words did not deceive Him. He *[knew] their hypocrisy.* His all-seeing eye detected the *earthen vessel[s] overlaid with silver dross* which stood before Him (Proverbs 26:23). He was not imposed upon, as too many of His people are, by glowing language and fine speeches.

He made the daily practice of His own enemies supply Him with an answer to their cunning questions. He tells them to bring Him a denarius, a common coin which they themselves were in the habit of using. He asks them, *"Whose likeness and inscription is this?"* stamped upon that coin. They are obliged to reply, *"Caesar's."* They were themselves using a Roman coin issued and circulated by the Roman government. By their own confession they were in some way under the power of the Romans, or this Roman money would not have been current among them. At once our Lord silences them by the memorable words, *"Render to Caesar the things that are Caesar's, and to God the things that are God's."* He bids them pay tribute to the Roman government in temporal things, for by using its money they bound themselves to do so. Yet He bids them give obedience to God in spiritual things and not to suppose that duty to an earthly sovereign and a heavenly sovereign are incapable of being reconciled one with the other. In short, He bids the proud Pharisee not to refuse his dues to Caesar and the worldly Herodian not to refuse his dues to God.

Let us learn from this masterly decision the great principle that true Christianity was never meant to interfere with a man's obedience to the civil powers. So far from this being the case, it ought to make him a quiet, loyal, and faithful subject. He ought to regard the powers that be as ordained of God, and to submit to their rules and regulations so long as the law is enforced, though he may not thoroughly approve of them. If the law of the land and the law of God come into collision, no doubt his course is clear – he must obey God rather than man. Like the three young men, though he serves a heathen king, he must not bow down to an idol. Like Daniel, though he submits to a tyrannical government, he must not give over praying in order to please the ruling powers.

Let us often pray for a larger measure of that spirit of wisdom which dwelt so abundantly in our blessed Lord. Many are the evils which have arisen in the church of Christ from a morbid and distorted view of the relative positions of the civil government and of God. Many are the rents and divisions which have been occasioned by lack of sound judgment as to their comparative claims. Happy is he who remembers our Lord's decision in this passage, understands it rightly, and makes a practical application of it to his own times.

Mark 12:18-27

Some Sadducees (who say that there is no resurrection) came to Jesus, and began questioning Him, saying, "Teacher, Moses wrote for us that if a man's brother dies and leaves behind a wife and leaves no child, his brother should marry the wife and raise up children to his brother. There were seven brothers; and the first took a wife, and died leaving no children. The second one married her, and died leaving behind no children; and the third likewise; and so all seven left no children. Last of all the woman died also. In the resurrection, when they rise again, which one's wife will she be? For all seven had married her." Jesus said to them, "Is this not the reason you are mistaken, that you do not understand the Scriptures or the power of God? For when they rise from the dead, they neither marry nor are given in marriage, but are like angels in heaven. But regarding the fact that the dead rise again, have you not read in the book of Moses, in the passage about the burning bush, how God spoke to him, saying, 'I am the God of Abraham, and the God of Isaac, and the God of Jacob'? He is not the God of the dead, but of the living; you are greatly mistaken."

These verses relate a conversation between our Lord Jesus Christ and the Sadducees. The religion of these men, we know, was little better than infidelity. They said there was *no resurrection*. They too, like the Pharisees, thought to entangle and perplex our Lord with hard questions. The church of Christ must not expect to fare better than its Master. Formalism on one side and infidelity on another are two enemies for whose attacks we must always be prepared.

We learn from this passage *how much unfairness may often be detected in the arguments of infidels.*

The question propounded by the Sadducees is a striking illustration of this. They tell him of a woman who married seven brothers in succession, had no children, and outlived her seven husbands. They ask *which one's wife* of all the seven would the woman be *in the resurrection*. It may well be surmised that the case was a supposed one and not a real one. On the face of it, there is the strongest appearance of improbability. The chances against such a case occurring in reality are almost infinite. But that was nothing to the Sadducees. All they cared for was to raise a difficulty and if possible to put our Lord to silence. The doctrine of the resurrection they had not the face manfully to deny. The possible consequences of the doctrine were the ground which they chose to take up. There are three things which we shall do well to remember if unfortunately we have at any time to argue with infidels.

For one thing, let us remember that an infidel will always try to press us with the difficulties and deep things of religion and especially with those which are connected with the world to come. We must avoid this mode of argument as far as possible. It is leaving the open field to fight in a jungle. We must endeavor, as far as we can, to make our discussion turn on the great plain facts and evidences of Christianity.

For another thing, let us remember that we must be on our guard against unfairness and dishonesty in argument. It may seem hard and uncharitable to say this. But experience proves that it is needful. Thousands of professed infidels have confessed in their latter days that they had never studied the Bible which they pretended to deny, and though well read in the works of unbelievers and skeptics, had never calmly examined the foundations of Christianity.

Above all, let us remember that every infidel has a conscience. To this we may always appeal confidently. The very men who talk most loudly and disdainfully against religion are often feeling conscious, even while they talk, that they are wrong. The very arguments which they have sneered at and ridiculed will often prove at last not to have been thrown away.

We learn, in the second place from this passage, *how much of religious error may be traced to ignorance of the Bible.* Our Lord's first words in reply to the Sadducees declare this plainly. He says, *"Is this not the reason you are mistaken, that you do not understand the Scriptures?"*

The truth of the principle here laid down is proved by facts in almost every age of church history. The reformation in Josiah's day was closely connected with the discovery of the book of the law. The false doctrines of the Jews in our Lord's time were the result of neglecting the Scriptures. The dark ages of Christendom were times when the Bible was kept back from the people. The Protestant Reformation was mainly effected by translating and circulating the Bible. The churches which are most flourishing at this day are churches which honor the Bible. The nations which enjoy most moral light are nations in which the Bible is most known. The parishes in our land where there is most true religion are those in which the Bible is most studied. The godliest families are Bible-reading families. The holiest men and women are Bible-reading people. These are simple facts which cannot be denied.

Let these things sink deeply into our hearts and bear fruit in our lives. Let us not be ignorant of the Bible, lest we fall into some deadly error. Let us rather read it diligently and make it our rule of faith and practice. Let us labor to spread the Bible over the world. The more the Book is known, the better the world will be. Not least, let us teach our children to value the Bible. The very best portion we can give them is a knowledge of the Scriptures.

We learn, in the last place from this passage, *how different will be the state of things after the resurrection from the state in which we live now.* Our Lord tells us that *when they rise from the dead, they neither marry nor are given in marriage, but are like angels in heaven.*

It would be foolish to deny that there are many difficulties connected with the doctrine of the life to come. It must needs be so. The world beyond the grave is a world unseen by mortal eyes and therefore unknown. The conditions of existence there are necessarily hidden from us, and if more were told, we would probably not understand it. Let it suffice us to know that the bodies of the saints shall be raised and, though glorified, shall be like their bodies on earth – so like them, that those who knew them once shall know them again. But though raised with a real body, the risen saint will be completely freed from everything which is now an evidence of weakness and infirmity. There shall be nothing like Mahomet's gross and sensual Paradise in the Christian's future existence. Hunger and thirst being no more – there shall be no need of food. Weariness and fatigue being no more – there shall be no need of sleep. Death being no more – there shall be no need of births to supply the place of those who are removed. Enjoying the full presence of God and His Christ – men and women shall no more need the marriage union in order to help one another. Able to serve God without weariness and attend to Him without distraction, doing His will perfectly and seeing His face continually, clothed in a glorious body – they shall be *like angels in heaven.*

There is comfort in all this for the true Christian. In the body that he now has, he often *groan[s], being burdened* from a daily sense of weakness and imperfection (2 Corinthians 5:4). He is now tried by many cares about this world – what to eat, and what to drink, and what to put on – how to manage his affairs, where to live, and what company to choose. In the world to come, all shall be changed. Nothing shall be lacking to make his happiness complete.

One thing only we must carefully bear in mind. Let us take heed that we rise again in the *resurrection of life* and not in the *resurrection of judgment* (John 5:29). To the believer in the Lord Jesus, the resurrection will be the greatest of blessings. To the worldly, the godless, and the profane, the resurrection will be a misery and a curse. Let us never rest until we are one with Christ and Christ in us, and then we may look forward with joy to a life to come.

Mark 12:28-34

One of the scribes came and heard them arguing, and recognizing that He had answered them well, asked Him, "What commandment is the foremost of all?" Jesus answered, "The foremost is, 'Hear, O Israel! The Lord our God is one Lord; and you shall love the Lord your God with all your heart, and with all your soul, and with all your mind, and with all your strength.' The second is this, 'You shall love your neighbor as yourself.' There is no other commandment greater than these." The scribe said to Him, "Right, Teacher; You have truly stated that He is One, and there is no one else besides Him; and to love Him with all the heart and with all the understanding and with all the strength, and to love one's neighbor as himself, is much more than all burnt offerings and sacrifices." When Jesus saw that he had answered intelligently, He said to him, "You are not far from the kingdom of God." After that, no one would venture to ask Him any more questions.

These verses contain a conversation between our Lord Jesus Christ and *one of the scribes*. For the third time in one day, we see our Lord tried by a hard question. Having put to silence the Pharisees and Sadducees, He is asked to decide a point on which much difference of opinion prevailed among the Jews: *"What commandment is the foremost of all?"* We have reason to bless God that so many hard questions were propounded to our Lord. Without them the marvelous words of wisdom which His three answers contain might never have been spoken at all. Here, as in many other cases, we see how God can bring good out of evil. He can make the most malicious assaults of His enemies work around to the good of His church and redound to His own praise. He can make the enmity of Pharisees and Sadducees and scribes minister instruction to His people. Little did the three questioners in this chapter think what benefit their crafty questions would confer on all Christendom. *"Out of the eater came something to eat"* (Judges 14:14).

Let us observe in these verses *how high is our Lord Jesus Christ's standard of duty to God and man.*

The question that the scribe propounded was a very wide one: *"What commandment is the foremost of all?"* The answer he received was probably very unlike what he expected. At any rate, if he thought that our Lord would commend to him the observance of some outward form or ceremony, he was mistaken. He hears these solemn words: *"'You shall love the Lord your God with all your heart, and with all your soul, and with all your mind, and with all your strength.' The second is this, 'You shall love your neighbor as yourself.'"*

How striking is our Lord's description of the *feeling* with which we ought to regard both God and our neighbor! We are not merely to obey the one or to abstain from injuring the other. In both cases we are to give far more than this. We are to give love, the strongest of all affections and the most comprehensive. A rule like this includes everything.

It makes all petty details unnecessary. Nothing will be intentionally lacking where there is love.

How striking again is our Lord's description of the *measure* in which we should love God and our neighbor! We are to love God better than ourselves with all the powers of our inward man. We cannot love Him too much. We are to love our neighbor as ourselves and to deal with him in all respects as we would like him to deal with us. The marvelous wisdom of this distinction is clear and plain. We may easily err in our affections toward others, either by thinking too little or too much of them. We therefore need the rule to love them as ourselves, neither more nor less. We cannot err in our affection toward God in the matter of excess. He is worthy of all we can give Him. We are therefore to love Him with all our heart.

Let us keep these two grand rules continually before our minds and use them daily in our journey through life. Let us see in them a summary of all that we ought to aim at in our practice, both as regards God and man. By them let us try every difficulty of conscience that may happen to beset us as to right and wrong. Happy is that man who strives to frame his life according to these rules.

Let us learn from this brief exposition of the true standard of duty how great is the need in which we all naturally stand of the atonement and mediation of our Lord Jesus Christ. Where are the men or women who can say with truth that they have perfectly loved God and perfectly loved man? Where is the person on earth who must not plead "guilty" when tried by such a law as this? No wonder that the Scripture says, *"There is none righteous, not even one"* (Romans 3:10). *By the works of the Law no flesh will be justified* (Romans 3:20). It is only gross ignorance of the requirements of God's law which makes people undervalue the gospel. The man who has the clearest view of the moral law will always be the man who has the highest sense of the value of Christ's atoning blood.

Let us observe, for another thing in these verses, *how far a man may go in religion and yet not be a true disciple of Christ.*

The scribe in the passage now before us was evidently a man of more knowledge than most of his equals. He saw things which many scribes and Pharisees never saw at all. His own words are a strong proof of this.

"*There is no one else besides Him; and to love Him with all the heart and with all the understanding and with all the strength, and to love one's neighbor as himself, is much more than all burnt offerings and sacrifices.*" These words are remarkable in themselves, and doubly remarkable when we remember who the speaker was and the generation among whom he lived. No wonder that we read next that our Lord said, "*You are not far from the kingdom of God.*"

But we must not shut our eyes to the fact that we are nowhere told that this man became one of our Lord's disciples. On this point there is a mournful silence. The parallel passage in Matthew throws not a gleam of light on his case. The other parts of the New Testament tell us nothing about him. We are left to draw the painful conclusion that, like the rich young man, he could not make up his mind to give up all and follow Christ, or that, like the chief rulers elsewhere mentioned, he *loved the approval of men rather than the approval of God* (John 12:43). In short, though *not far from the kingdom of God*, he probably never entered into it and died outside.

Cases like that of this scribe are unfortunately far from being uncommon. There are thousands on every side who, like him, see much and know much of religious truth and yet live and die undecided. There are few things which are so much overlooked as the length to which people may go in religious attainments and yet never be converted and never saved. May we all take note of this man's case and take heed!

Let us beware of resting our hopes of salvation on mere intellectual knowledge. We live in days when there is great danger of doing so. Education makes children acquainted with many things in religion of which their parents were once utterly ignorant. But education alone will never make a Christian in the sight of God. We must not only know the leading doctrines of the gospel with our heads but also receive them into our hearts and be guided by them in our lives. May we never rest until we are inside the kingdom of God, until we have truly repented, really believed, and have been made new creatures in Christ Jesus. If we rest satisfied with being *not far from the kingdom*, we shall find at last that we are shut out forevermore.

Mark 12:35-44

And Jesus began to say, as He taught in the temple, "How is it that the scribes say that the Christ is the son of David? David himself said in the Holy Spirit,

> *'The Lord said to my Lord,*
> *"Sit at My right hand,*
> *Until I put Your enemies beneath Your feet."'*

David himself calls Him 'Lord'; so in what sense is He his son?" And the large crowd enjoyed listening to Him. In His teaching He was saying: "Beware of the scribes who like to walk around in long robes, and like respectful greetings in the market places, and chief seats in the synagogues and places of honor at banquets, who devour widows' houses, and for appearance's sake offer long prayers; these will receive greater condemnation." And He sat down opposite the treasury, and began observing how the people were putting money into the treasury; and many rich people were putting in large sums. A poor widow came and put in two small copper coins, which amount to a cent. Calling His disciples to Him, He said to them, "Truly I say to you, this poor widow put in more than all the contributors to the treasury; for they all put in out of their surplus, but she, out of her poverty, put in all she owned, all she had to live on."

We have seen in the earlier part of this chapter how the enemies of our Lord endeavored to *trap Him in a statement.* We have seen how the Pharisees, the Sadducees, and the scribes successively propounded to Him hard questions – questions we can hardly fail to observe as more likely to administer strife than edification. The passage before us begins with a question of a very different character. Our Lord Himself propounds it. He asks His enemies about Christ and the meaning of Holy Scripture. Such questions are always truly profitable. Well would it be for the church if theological discussions were less about trifles and more about weighty matters and things necessary to salvation.

Let us learn, in the first place from these verses, *how much there is about Christ in the Old Testament Scriptures*. Our Lord desires to expose the ignorance of the Jewish teachers about the true nature of the Messiah. He does it by referring to a passage in the book of Psalms and showing that the scribes did not rightly understand it. And in so doing He shows us that one subject, about which David was inspired by the Holy Spirit to write, was Christ.

We know, from our Lord's own words in another place, that the Old Testament Scriptures *testify about [Christ]* (John 5:39). They were intended to teach men about Christ by types, and figures, and prophecy until He Himself should appear on earth. We should always keep this in mind in reading the Old Testament, but never so much as in reading the Psalms. Christ is undoubtedly to be found in every part of the Law and the Prophets, but nowhere is He so much to be found as in the book of Psalms. His experience and sufferings at His first coming into the world – His future glory and His final triumph at His second coming – are the chief subjects of many a passage in that wonderful part of God's Word. It is a true saying that we should look for Christ quite as much as David in reading the Psalms.

Let us beware of undervaluing or despising the Old Testament. In its place and proportion, the Old Testament is just as valuable as the New. There are probably many rich passages in that part of the Bible which have never yet been fully explored. There are deep things about Jesus in it which many walk over like hidden gold mines and know not the treasures beneath their feet. Let us reverence all of the Bible. All is given by inspiration, and all is profitable. One part throws light upon another, and no part can ever be neglected without loss and damage to our souls. A boastful contempt for the Old Testament Scriptures has often proved the first step towards infidelity.

Let us learn, in the second place from these verses, *how odious is the sin of hypocrisy in the sight of Christ*. This is a lesson which is taught us by our Lord's warning against the scribes. He exposes some of their notorious practices: their ostentatious manner of dressing; their love of the honor and praise of man rather than God; their love of money, disguised under a pretended concern for widows; and their long-protracted public devotions intended to make men think them eminently godly. And He winds up all by the solemn declaration, *"These will receive greater condemnation."*

Of all the sins into which men can fall, none seem so exceedingly sinful as false profession and hypocrisy. At all events, none have drawn from our Lord's mouth such strong language and such heavy denunciations. It is bad enough to be led away captive by open sin and to serve diverse lusts and pleasures. But it is even worse to pretend to have a religion while in reality we serve the world. Let us beware of falling into this abominable sin. Whatever we do in religion, let us never wear a cloak. Let us be real, honest, thorough, and sincere in our Christianity. We cannot deceive an all-seeing God. We may take in poor shortsighted man by a little talk and profession, and a few lively phrases, and an affectation of devoutness. But God is not mocked. He is a discerner of the thoughts and intents of the heart. His all-seeing eye pierces through the paint, and varnish, and tinsel which cover the unsound heart. The day of judgment will soon be here. *"The joy of the godless [is] momentary"* (Job 20:5). His end will be shame and everlasting contempt.

One thing, however, must never be forgotten in connection with the subject of hypocrisy. Let us not flatter ourselves that because some make a false profession of religion, others need not make any profession at all. This is a common delusion and one against which we must carefully guard. It does not follow – because some bring Christianity into contempt by professing what they do not really believe and feel – that we should run unto the other extreme and bring it into contempt by a cowardly silence and by keeping our religion out of sight. Let us rather be doubly careful to adorn our doctrine by our lives. Let us prove our sincerity by the consistency of our lives. Let us show the world that there is a true coin as well as a counterfeit coin, and that the visible church contains Christians who can witness a good confession as well as Pharisees and scribes. Let us confess our Master modestly and humbly but firmly and decidedly, and show the world that although some men may be hypocrites, there are others who are honest and true.

Let us learn, in the last place from these verses, *how pleasing to Christ is self-denying liberality in giving.* This is a lesson which is taught us in a striking manner by our Lord's commendation of a certain poor widow. We are told that He *began observing how the people were putting* their voluntary contributions for God's service into the public collection box or *treasury.* He saw that *many rich people were putting in large sums.* At last he saw this poor widow cast in all that she had for her daily maintenance. And then we hear Him pronounce the solemn words, *"This poor widow put in more than all the contributors to the treasury,"* more in the sight of Him who looks not merely at the amount given, but at the ability of the giver – not merely at the quantity contributed, but at the motive and heart of the contributor.

There are few of our Lord's sayings so much overlooked as this. There are thousands who remember all His doctrinal discourses and yet contrive to forget this little incident in His earthly ministry. The proof of this is to be seen in the meager and sparing contributions which are yearly made by Christ's church to do good in the world. The proof is to be seen in the miserably small incomes of all the missionary societies in proportion to the wealth of the churches. The proof is to be seen in the long annual lists of self-complacent guinea subscribers, of whom many could easily give hundreds of pounds. The stinginess of professing Christians in all matters which concern God and religion is one of the crying sins of the day and one of the worst signs of the times. The givers to Christ's cause are but a small section of the visible church. Not one baptized person in twenty probably knows anything of being *rich toward God* (Luke 12:21). The vast majority spend pounds on themselves and give not even pennies to Christ. Let us mourn over this state of things and pray God to amend it. Let us pray Him to open men's eyes, and awaken men's hearts, and stir up a spirit of liberality. Above all, let us each do our own duty and give liberally and gladly to every Christian object while we can. There will be no giving when we are dead. Let us give as those who remember that the eyes of Christ are upon us. He still sees exactly what each gives and knows exactly how much is left behind. Above all, let us give as the disciples of a crucified Savior who gave Himself for us body and soul on the cross. Freely we have received. Let us freely give.

Mark Chapter 13

Mark 13:1-8

As He was going out of the temple, one of His disciples said to Him, "Teacher, behold what wonderful stones and what wonderful buildings!" And Jesus said to him, "Do you see these great buildings? Not one stone will be left upon another which will not be torn down." As He was sitting on the Mount of Olives opposite the temple, Peter and James and John and Andrew were questioning Him privately, "Tell us, when will these things be, and what will be the sign when all these things are going to be fulfilled?" And Jesus began to say to them, "See to it that no one misleads you. Many will come in My name, saying, 'I am He!' and will mislead many. When you hear of wars and rumors of wars, do not be frightened; those things must take place; but that is not yet the end. For nation will rise up against nation, and kingdom against kingdom; there will be earthquakes in various places; there will also be famines. These things are merely the beginning of birth pangs."

THE CHAPTER WE HAVE NOW BEGUN IS FULL OF PROPHECY – prophecy of which part has been fulfilled and part remains to be accomplished. Two great events form the subject of this prophecy. One is the destruction of Jerusalem and the consequent end of the Jewish dispensation. The other is the second coming of our Lord Jesus Christ and the winding up of the state of things under which we now live. The destruction of Jerusalem was an event which happened only forty years after our Lord was crucified. The second coming of Christ is an event which is yet to come, and we may yet live to see it with our own eyes.[11]

Chapters like this ought to be deeply interesting to every true Christian. No history ought to receive so much of our attention as the past and future history of the church of Christ. The rise and fall of worldly empires are events of comparatively small importance in the sight of God. Babylon, and Greece, and Rome, and France, and England are as nothing in His eyes by the side of the mystical body of Christ. The march of armies and the victories of conquerors are mere trifles in comparison with the progress of the gospel and the final triumph of the Prince of Peace. May we remember this in reading prophetical Scripture! *Blessed is he who reads* (Revelation 1:3).

The first thing that demands our attention in the verses before us is *the prediction of our Lord concerning the temple at Jerusalem.*

The disciples, with the natural pride of Jews, had called their Master's attention to the architectural splendor of the temple. *"Behold,"* they said, *"what wonderful stones and what wonderful buildings!"* They received an answer from the Lord very different from what they expected, a heart-saddening answer and one well calculated to stir up inquisitive thoughts in their minds. No word of admiration falls from His lips. He expresses no commendation of the design or workmanship of the gorgeous structure before Him. He appears to lose sight of the form and

---

11   I believe that in the prophecy now under consideration, our Lord had in view a second siege of Jerusalem and a second tribulation accompanying that siege, as well as the first siege and tribulation when the city was taken by Titus. That such a siege is to be expected, the fourteenth chapter of Zechariah appears to me to be unanswerable proof. I see no other way of explaining the close connection which appears in the prophecy between the *tribulation* here foretold and *the Son of Man coming in clouds with great power and glory.* To interpret that *Son of Man coming* as the coming of the Roman army in judgment on the Jews appears to me positive trifling with Scripture.

The view that our Lord is prophesying of two sieges of Jerusalem and two tremendous tribulations which would fall especially on the Jews, and of His own second coming as an event which would immediately follow the second siege makes the whole chapter plain and intelligible. All these events ought to be deeply interesting to believers and would be especially so to Jewish believers like the apostles in whose time the temple was yet standing, the Jewish dispensation not yet put aside, and Jerusalem not yet destroyed.

It may be well to remark that the temple here spoken of was in a certain sense the third temple which had been built at Jerusalem. The first was built by Solomon and destroyed by Nebuchadnezzar. The second was built by Ezra and Nehemiah. The third, if it may be so called, was enlarged and almost rebuilt about the time of our Lord Jesus Christ's birth, by Herod. The enormous size of the stones used in building it and the general magnificence of the whole fabric are attested not only by Josephus but also by the heathen writers.

loveliness of the material building in His concern for the wickedness of the nation to which it belonged. *"Do you see these great buildings?"* He replies. *"Not one stone will be left upon another which will not be torn down."*

Let us learn from this solemn saying that the true glory of a church does not consist in its buildings for public worship but in the faith and godliness of its members. The eyes of our Lord Jesus Christ could find no pleasure in looking at the very temple which contained the holy of holies, and the golden candlestick, and the altar of burnt offering. Much less, may we suppose, can He find pleasure in the most splendid places of worship among professing Christians if His Word and His Spirit are not honored in it.

We shall all do well to remember this. We are naturally inclined to judge things by the outward appearance like children who value poppies more than corn. We are too apt to suppose that where there is a stately ecclesiastical building and a magnificent ceremonial – carved stone and painted glass – fine music and gorgeously dressed ministers, there must be some real religion. And yet there may be no religion at all. It may be all form and show and appeal to the senses. There may be nothing to satisfy the conscience – nothing to cure the heart. It may prove on inquiry that Christ is not preached in that stately building and the Word of God is not expounded. The ministers may perhaps be utterly ignorant of the gospel, and the worshipers may be dead in trespasses and sins. We need not doubt that God sees no beauty in such a building as this. We need not doubt the Parthenon had no glory in God's sight compared to the dens and caves where the early Christians worshiped, or that the lowest room where Christ is preached at this day is more honorable in His eyes than St. Peter's Cathedral at Rome.

Let us, however, not run into the absurd extreme of supposing that it matters not what kind of building we set apart for God's service. There is no popery in making a church handsome. There is no true religion in having a dirty, mean, shabby, and disorderly place of worship. *All things must be done properly and in an orderly manner* (1 Corinthians 14:40). But let it be a settled principle in our religion, however beautiful we make our churches, to regard pure doctrine and holy practice as their principal ornaments. *Without* these two things, the noblest ecclesiastical edifice is radically defective. It has no glory if God is not there. *With* these two things, the humblest brick cottage where the gospel is preached is lovely and beautiful. It is consecrated by Christ's own presence and the Holy Spirit's own blessing.

The second thing that demands our attention in these verses is *the remarkable manner in which our Lord commences the great prophecy of this chapter.*

We are told that four of His disciples, aroused no doubt by His warning prediction about the temple, applied to Him for further information. *"Tell us,"* they said, *"when will these things be, and what will be the sign when all these things are going to be fulfilled?"*

The answer which our Lord gives to these questions begins at once with a prediction of coming false doctrine and coming wars. If His disciples thought He would promise them immediate success and temporal prosperity in this world, they were soon undeceived. So far from bidding them expect a speedy victory of truth, He tells them to look out for the rise of error. *"See to it that no one misleads you. Many will come in My name, saying, 'I am He!'"* So far from bidding them expect a general reign of peace and quietness, He tells them to prepare for wars and troubles. *"Nation will rise up against nation, and kingdom against kingdom; there will be earthquakes in various places; there will also be famines. These things are merely the beginning of birth pangs."*

There is something deeply instructive in this opening of our Lord' prophetical discourse. It seems like the keynote of what His church is to expect between His first and second advents. It looks as if it were specially intended to correct the mistaken views not only of His apostles but also of the vast body of professing Christians in every age. It looks as if our Lord knew well that man is always catching at the idea of a "good time coming" and as if He would give us plain notice that there will be no "good time" until He returns. It may not be pleasant to us to hear such tidings. But it is in strict accordance with what we read in the prophet Jeremiah: *"The prophets who were before me and before you from ancient times prophesied against many lands and against great kingdoms, of war and of calamity and of pestilence. The prophet who prophesies of peace, when the word of the prophet comes to pass, then that prophet will be known as one whom the* LORD *has truly sent"* (Jeremiah 28:8-9).

Let us learn from our Lord's opening prediction to be moderate in our expectations. Nothing has created so much disappointment in the church of Christ as the extravagant expectations in which many of its members have indulged. Let us not be carried away by the common idea that the world will be converted before the Lord Jesus returns and the earth filled with the knowledge of the Lord. It will not be so. There is nothing in Scripture to justify such expectations. Let us cease to expect a reign of peace. Let us rather look for wars. Let us cease to expect all men to be made holy by any existing instrumentality – schools, missions, preaching, or anything of the kind. Let us rather look for the rise of Antichrist himself. Let us understand that we live in a day of election and not of universal conversion. There will be no universal peace until the Prince of Peace appears. There will be no universal holiness until Satan is bound. It may cost us much to hold such opinions as these. But there is not a church or congregation on earth whose state does not show that these opinions are true and that *many are called, but few are chosen.* It may bring on us the unkind remarks and the unfavorable judgment of many. But the end will prove who is right and who is wrong. For that end let us wait patiently. Let us labor, and teach, and work, and pray. But let it not surprise us if we find our Lord's word strictly true – *"The way is narrow that leads to life, and there are few who find it"* (Matthew 7:14).

Mark 13:9-13

"But be on your guard; for they will deliver you to the courts, and you will be flogged in the synagogues, and you will stand before governors and kings for My sake, as a testimony to them. The gospel must first be preached to all the nations. When they arrest you and hand you over, do not worry beforehand about what you are to say, but say whatever is given you in that hour; for it

is not you who speak, but it is the Holy Spirit. Brother will betray brother to death, and a father his child; and children will rise up against parents and have them put to death. You will be hated by all because of My name, but the one who endures to the end, he will be saved."

In reading the prophecies of the Bible concerning Christ's church, we shall generally find judgment and mercy blended together. They are seldom all bitter without any sweet – seldom all darkness without any light. The Lord knows our weakness and readiness to faint, and He has taken care to mingle consolations with threatenings – kind words with hard words, like warp and woof in a garment. We may take note of this throughout the book of Revelation. We may see it all through the prophecy we are now considering. We may note it in the few verses which we have just read.

Let us observe, in the first place, *what troubles our Lord bids His people expect between the time of His first and second comings.* Trouble, no doubt, is the portion of all men since the day that Adam fell. It came in with the thorns and thistles. *Man is born for trouble, as sparks fly upward* (Job 5:7). But there are special troubles to which believers in Jesus Christ are liable, and of these our Lord gives them plain warning.

They must expect trouble *from the world.* They must not look for the help of *governors and kings.* They will find their ways and their doctrines bring them no favor in high places. On the contrary, they will often be imprisoned, beaten, and brought before judgment seats as malefactors for no other reason than their adherence to the gospel of Christ.

They must expect trouble *from their own families. Brother will betray brother to death, and a father his child.* Their own flesh and blood will often forget to love them due to their hatred toward their religion. They will find sometimes that the enmity of the carnal mind against God is stronger than even the ties of family and blood.

We shall do well to lay these things to heart and to count the cost of being a Christian. We must think it no strange thing if our religion brings with it some bitter things. Our lot, no doubt, is cast in favorable times. The lines of most Christians are fallen in pleasant places.

We have no reason to be afraid of death or imprisonment if we serve Christ. But, for all that, we must make up our minds to endure a certain proportion of hardship if we are real, thorough, and decided Christians. We must be content to put up with laughter, ridicule, mockery, slander, and petty persecution. We must even bear hard words and unkindness from our nearest and dearest relations. The *stumbling block of the cross* has not ceased. *A natural man does not accept the things of the Spirit of God* (1 Corinthians 2:14). Those who are *born according to the flesh* will persecute those who are *born according to the Spirit* (Galatians 4:29). The utmost consistency of life will not prevent it. If we are converted, we must never be surprised to find that we are hated for Christ's sake.

Let us observe, in the second place, *what rich encouragement the Lord Jesus holds out to His persecuted people.* He sets before them three rich cordials to cheer their souls.

For one thing, He tells us that *the gospel must first be preached to all the nations.* It must be and it shall be. In spite of men and devils, the story of the cross of Christ shall be told in every part of the world. The gates of hell shall not prevail against it. Notwithstanding persecution, imprisonment, and death, there never shall be lacking a succession of faithful men who shall proclaim the glad tidings of salvation by grace. Few may believe them. Many of their hearers may continue hardened in sin. But nothing shall prevent the gospel from being preached. The Word shall never be bound, even though those who preach it may be imprisoned and slain (2 Timothy 2:9).

For another thing, our Lord tells us that those who are placed in special trial for the gospel's sake shall have special help in their time of need. The Holy Spirit shall assist them in making their defense. They shall have a mouth and wisdom which their adversaries shall not be able to refute or resist. As it was with Peter and John and Paul when they were brought before Jewish and Roman councils, so shall it be with all truehearted disciples. How thoroughly this promise has been fulfilled the histories of Huss, and Luther, and Latimer, and Ridley, and Baxter abundantly prove. Christ has been faithful to His Word.

For another thing, our Lord tells us that patient perseverance shall result in final salvation. *"The one who endures to the end, he will be saved.*" Not one of those who endure tribulation shall miss his reward. All shall at length reap a rich harvest. Though they sow in tears, they shall reap in joy. Their light affliction, which is but for a moment, shall lead to an eternal weight of glory.

Let us gather comfort from these comfortable promises for all true-hearted servants of Christ. Persecuted, vexed, and mocked as they are now, they shall find at length that they are on the victorious side. Beset, perplexed, and tried as they sometimes are, they shall never find themselves entirely forsaken. Though cast down, they shall not be destroyed. Let them possess their souls in patience. The end of all that they see going on around them is certain, fixed, and sure. The kingdoms of this world shall yet become the kingdoms of their God and of His Christ. And when the scoffers and ungodly who so often insulted them are put to shame, believers shall receive a crown of glory that fades not away.

Mark 13:14-23

"But when you see the abomination of desolation standing where it should not be (let the reader understand), then those who are in Judea must flee to the mountains. The one who is on the housetop must not go down, or go in to get anything out of his house; and the one who is in the field must not turn back to get his coat. But woe to those who are pregnant and to those who are nursing babies in those days! But pray that it may not happen in the winter. For those days will be a time of tribulation such as has not occurred since the beginning of the creation which God created until now, and never will. Unless the Lord had shortened those days, no life would have been saved; but for sake of the elect, whom He chose, He shortened the days. And then if anyone says to you, 'Behold, here is the Christ'; or, 'Behold, He is there'; do not believe him; for false Christs and false prophets will arise, and will show signs and wonders, in order to lead astray, if possible, the elect. But take heed; behold, I have told you everything in advance."

We are taught in these verses *the lawfulness of using means to provide for our own personal safety.* The language of our Lord Jesus Christ on the subject is clear and unmistakable – *"Those who are in Judea must flee to the mountains. The one who is on the housetop must not go down, or go in to . . . his house; and the one who is in the field must not turn back . . . pray that it may not happen in the winter."*[12] Not a word is said to make us suppose that flight from danger in certain circumstances is unworthy of a Christian. As to the time prophesied of in the passage before us, men may differ widely. But as to the lawfulness of taking measures to avoid peril, the teaching of the passage is plain.

The lesson is one of wide application and of much usefulness. A Christian is not to neglect the use of means, because he is a Christian, in the things of this life any more than in the things of the life to come. A believer is not to suppose that God will take care of him and provide for his needs if he does not make use of means and the common sense which God has given him as well as other people. Beyond doubt he may expect the special help of his Father in heaven in every time of need. But he must expect it in the diligent use of lawful means. To profess to trust God while we idly sit still and do nothing is nothing better than fanaticism and brings religion into contempt.

The Word of God contains several instructive examples on this subject to which we shall do well to take heed. The conduct of Jacob when he went to meet his brother Esau is a striking case in point. He first prays a most touching prayer and then sends his brother a carefully arranged present (Genesis 32:9-13). The conduct of Hezekiah when Sennacherib came against Jerusalem is another case. *"With us,"* he tells the people, *"is the LORD our God to help us and to fight our battles"* (2 Chronicles 32:8). And yet, at the same time, he built up the walls of

---

12   The meaning of the *abomination of desolation* in this passage has always perplexed the commentator. The most common view undoubtedly is that it signifies the Roman armies who executed God's judgment on the Jewish nation. It may be questioned whether this interpretation completely fulfills the prophecy. I venture, though with much diffidence, to suggest that a more complete and literal accomplishment yet remains to come. The remarkable words of Paul to the Thessalonians appear to me scarcely to have received yet a complete fulfillment: *He takes his seat in the temple of God, displaying himself as being God* (2 Thessalonians 2:4). I own that it seems to me by no means improbable that a personal Antichrist, yet to be revealed at Jerusalem, may prove the final accomplishment of these words. I desire to avoid dogmatism on the subject. I only suggest it as a possible and probable thing.

the city and made darts and shields (2 Chronicles 32:5). The conduct of Paul is another case. Frequently we read of his fleeing from one place to another to preserve his life. Once we see him let down from the walls of Damascus by a basket. Once we hear him telling the soldiers on board the Alexandrian ship, *"Unless these men remain in the ship, you yourselves cannot be saved"* (Acts 27:31). We know the great apostle's faith and confidence. We know his courage and reliance on his Master. And yet we see that even he never despised the use of means. Let us not be ashamed to do likewise.

One thing only let us bear in mind. Let us not rest upon means while we use them. Let us look far beyond them to the blessing of God. It is a great sin to be like Asa and look not to the Lord but to the physicians. To use all means diligently and then leave the whole event in the hand of God is the mark at which a true believer ought to aim.

We are taught, for another thing in these verses, *the great privileges of God's elect.* Twice in the passage our Lord uses a remarkable expression about them. He says of the great tribulation, *"Unless the Lord had shortened those days, no life would have been saved; but for the sake of the elect, whom He chose, He shortened the days."* He says again of the false Christs and false prophets that they *"will show signs and wonders, in order to lead astray, if possible, the elect."*

It is plain from this and other passages in the Bible that God has an elect people in the world. They are those, according to the seventeenth Article of our church, whom "He has decreed by His counsel, secret to us, to deliver from curse and damnation; those whom He has chosen in Christ out of mankind, and decreed to bring by Christ to everlasting salvation, as vessels made to honor." To them, and them only, belong the great privileges of justification, sanctification, and final glory. They, and they only, are "called by the Spirit in due season." They, and they only, "obey the calling. They are made sons of God by adoption. They are made like the image of God's only begotten Son, Jesus Christ. They walk religiously in good works, and at length, by God's mercy, attain to everlasting felicity." To them belong the precious promises of the gospel. They are the bride, the Lamb's wife. They are the body of Christ. They are those whom God especially cares for in the world. Kings, princes, noblemen, and rich men are all nothing in God's eyes compared to His elect. These things are plainly revealed in Scripture. The pride of man may not like them. But they cannot be refuted.

The subject of election is, no doubt, deep and mysterious. Unquestionably it has been often sadly perverted and abused. But the misuse of truths must not prevent us from using them. Rightly used and fenced with proper cautions, election is a doctrine full of sweet, pleasant, and unspeakable comfort. Before we leave the subject, let us see what these cautions are.

For one thing, we must never forget that God's election does not destroy man's responsibility and accountability for his own soul. The same Bible which speaks of election always addresses men as free agents and calls on them to repent, to believe, to seek, to pray, to strive, and to labor. "In our doings," most wisely says the seventeenth Article, "that will of God is to be followed, which we have expressly declared unto us in the word of God."

For another thing, let us never forget that the great thing we have to do is repent and believe the gospel. We have no right to take any comfort from God's election unless we can show plain evidence of repentance and faith. We are not to stand still, troubling ourselves with anxious speculations as to whether we are elect or not, when God commands us plainly to repent and believe (Acts 17:30; 1 John 3:23). Let us cease to do evil. Let us learn to do well. Let us break off from sin. Let us lay hold on Christ. Let us draw near to God in prayer. So doing, we shall soon know and feel whether we are God's elect. To use the words of an old divine, we must begin at the grammar school of repentance and faith before we go to the university of election. It was when Paul remembered the faith, and hope, and love of the Thessalonians that he said, *"Knowing . . . His choice of you"* (1 Thessalonians 1:4).

Mark 13:24-31

"But in those days, after that tribulation, the sun will be darkened and the moon will not give its light, and the stars will be

falling from heaven, and the powers that are in the heavens will be shaken. Then they will see the Son of Man coming in clouds with great power and glory. And then He will send forth the angels, and will gather together His elect from the four winds, from the farthest end of the earth to the farthest end of heaven. "Now learn the parable from the fig tree: when its branch has already become tender and puts forth its leaves, you know that summer is near. Even so, you too, when you see these things happening, recognize that He is near, right at the door. Truly I say to you, this generation will not pass away until all these things take place. Heaven and earth will pass away, but My words will not pass away."

This part of our Lord's prophecy on the Mount of Olives is entirely unfulfilled. The events described in it are all yet to take place. They may possibly take place in our own day. The passage therefore is one which we ought always to read with peculiar interest.

Let us observe, in the first place, *what solemn majesty will attend our Lord Jesus Christ's second coming to this world.* The language that is used about the sun, moon, and stars conveys the idea of some universal convulsion of the universe at the close of the present dispensation. It reminds us of the apostle Peter's words, *The heavens will pass away with a roar and the elements will be destroyed with intense heat* (2 Peter 3:10). At such a time as this, amid terror and confusion exceeding all that even earthquakes or hurricanes are known to produce, men *will see the Son of Man coming in clouds with great power and glory.*

The second coming of Christ shall be utterly unlike the first. He came the first time in weakness, a tender infant, born of a poor woman in the manger at Bethlehem, unnoticed, unhonored, and scarcely known. He shall come the second time in royal dignity with the armies of heaven around Him, to be known, recognized, and feared by all the tribes of the earth. He came the first time to suffer, to bear our sins, to be reckoned a curse, and to be despised, rejected, unjustly condemned, and slain. He shall come the second time to reign, to put down every enemy beneath

His feet, to take the kingdoms of this world for His inheritance, to rule them with righteousness, to judge all men, and to live forevermore.

How vast the difference! How mighty the contrast! How startling the comparison between the second advent and the first! How solemn the thoughts that the subject ought to stir up in our minds! Here are *comforting* thoughts for Christ's friends. Their own King will soon be here. They shall reap according as they have sown. They shall receive a rich reward for all that they have endured for Christ's sake. They shall exchange their cross for a crown.

Here are *confounding* thoughts for Christ's foes. That same Jesus of Nazareth, whom they have so long despised and rejected, shall at length have the preeminence. That very Christ, whose gospel they have refused to believe, shall appear as their judge, and helpless, hopeless, and speechless, they will have to stand before His bar. May we all lay these things to heart and learn wisdom!

Let us observe, in the next place, *that the first event after the Lord's second coming shall be the gathering of His elect. "He will send forth the angels, and will gather together His elect from the four winds."*

The safety of the Lord's people shall be provided for when judgment falls upon the earth. He will do nothing until He has placed them beyond the reach of harm. The flood did not begin until Noah was safe in the ark. The fire did not fall on Sodom until Lot was safe within the walls of Zoar. The wrath of God on unbelievers shall not be let loose until believers are hidden and secure.

The true Christian may look forward to the advent of Christ without fear. However dreadful the things that shall come upon the earth, his Master will take care that no harm comes to him. He may well bear patiently the partings and separations of this present time. He shall have a joyful meeting, by and by, with all his brethren in the faith of every age, and country, and people, and tongue. Those who meet in that day shall meet to part no more. The great gathering is yet to come (2 Thessalonians 2:1).

Let us observe, in the next place, *how important it is to note the signs of our own times.* Our Lord bids His disciples *learn the parable from the fig tree.* Just as its budding leaves tell men that summer is near, so

209

the fulfillment of events in the world around us should teach us that the Lord's coming *is near, right at the door.*

It becomes all true Christians to observe carefully the public events of their own day. It is not only a duty to do this but also a sin to neglect it. Our Lord reproved the Jews for *not discern[ing] the signs of the times* (Matthew 16:3). They did not see that the scepter was passing away from Judah, and the weeks of Daniel were running out. Let us beware of falling into their error. Let us rather open our eyes and look at the world around us. Let us take note of how the previously strong Turkish power has now dried up and also note the increase of missionary work in the world. Let us take note of the revival of popery and the rise of new and subtle forms of infidelity. Let us observe the rapid spread of lawlessness and contempt for authority. What are these things but the budding of the fig tree? They show us that this world is wearing out and needs a new and better dynasty. It needs its rightful King, even Jesus. May we watch, and keep our garments, and live ready to meet our Lord (Revelation 16:15)!

Let us observe lastly in these verses *how carefully our Lord asserts the certainty of His predictions being fulfilled.* He speaks as though He foresaw the incredulity and skepticism of these latter days. He warns us emphatically against it – *"Heaven and earth will pass away, but My words will not pass away."*[13]

We ought never to allow ourselves to suppose that any prophecy is improbable or unlikely to be fulfilled merely because it is contrary to past experience. Let us not say, Where is the likelihood of Christ coming again? Where is the likelihood of the world being burned up? We have nothing to do with "likely" or "unlikely" in such matters. The only question is, What is written in God's Word? The words of Peter should never be forgotten: *In the last days mockers will come with their mocking,*

---

13   I take this opportunity of expressing my decided opinion that the word *generation* in the verse *"this generation will not pass away"* can only mean "this nation or people – the Jewish nation – shall not pass away." The view that it means "the generation of men which is alive now while I am speaking" would make our Lord to say that which was not true. His words were in no sense completely fulfilled when the generation to which He spoke had passed away. The view that it means "the same generation which is alive when these things begin shall also see them accomplished" appears to me untenable for one simple reason: it is not the natural meaning of the Greek words from which our translation is made.

following after their own lusts, and saying, "Where is the promise of His coming?" (2 Peter 3:3-4).

We shall do well to ask ourselves what we would have thought if we had lived on earth two thousand years ago. Would we have thought it more probable that the Son of God would come on earth as a poor man and die, or that He would come on earth as a king and reign? Would we not have said at once that if He came at all, He would come to reign and not to die? Yet we know that He did come as *a man of sorrows* and died on the cross. Then let us not doubt that He will come the second time in glory and reign as King forevermore.

Let us leave the passage with a thorough conviction of the truth of every jot of its predictions. Let us believe that every word of it shall prove at last to have been fully accomplished. Above all, let us strive to live under an abiding sense of its truth, like good servants ready to meet their master. Then, whatever be the fulfillment of it, or however soon, we shall be safe.

Mark 13:32-37

But of that day or hour no one knows, not even the angels in heaven, not the Son, but the Father alone. "Take heed, keep on the alert; for you do not know when the appointed time will come. It is like a man away on a journey, who upon leaving his house and putting his slaves in charge, assigning to each one his task, also commanded the doorkeeper to stay on the alert. Therefore, be on the alert—for you do not know when the master of the house is coming, whether in the evening, at midnight, or when the rooster crows, or in the morning—in case he should come suddenly and find you asleep. What I say to you I say to all, 'Be on the alert!'"

These verses conclude Mark's report of our Lord's prophecy on the Mount of Olives. They ought to form a personal application of the whole discourse to our consciences.

We learn from these verses that *the exact time of our Lord Jesus Christ's second advent is purposely withheld from His church.* The event is certain. The precise day and hour are not revealed. *"Of that day or hour no one knows, not even the angels in heaven."*

There is deep wisdom and mercy in this intentional silence. We have reason to thank God that the thing has been hidden from us. Uncertainty about the date of the Lord's return is calculated to keep believers in an attitude of constant expectation and to preserve them from despondency. What a dreary prospect the early church would have had before it if it had known for certain that Christ would not return to earth for at least fifteen hundred years! The hearts of men like Athanasius, Chrysostom, and Augustine might well have sunk within them if they had been aware of the centuries of darkness through which the world would pass before their Master came back to take the kingdom. What a quickening motive, on the other hand, true Christians have perpetually had for a close walk with God! They have never known, in any age, that their Master might not come suddenly to take account of His servants. This very uncertainty has supplied them with a reason for living always ready to meet Him.

There is one caution connected with the subject which must not be overlooked. We must not allow the uncertainty of the time of our Lord's second advent to prevent our giving attention to the unfulfilled prophecies of Scripture. This is a great delusion, but one into which, unfortunately, many Christians fall. There is a wide distinction to be drawn between dogmatical and positive assertions about dates, and a humble, prayerful searching into the good things yet to come. Against dogmatism about times and seasons, our Lord's words in this place are a standing caution. But as to the general profitableness of studying prophecy, we can have no plainer authority than the apostle Peter's words – *You do well to pay attention* to prophecy (2 Peter 1:19), and the apostle John's words in Revelation – *Blessed is he who reads* (Revelation 1:3).

We learn, in the second place from these verses, *what are the practical duties of all true believers in the prospect of the second coming of Jesus Christ.* Our Lord mentions three things to which His people should attend. He tells them plainly that He is coming again one day in power and great glory. He tells them at the same time that the precise hour and date of that coming are not known. What then are His people to do? In what position of mind are they to live? They are to watch. They are to pray. They are to work.

We are to *watch*. We are to live always on our guard. We are to keep our souls in a wakeful, lively state, prepared at any time to meet our Master. We are to beware of anything like spiritual lethargy, dullness, deadness, and apathy. The company, the employment of time, the society which induces us to forget Christ and His second advent should be observed, noted, and avoided. *"Let us not sleep as do others,"* says the apostle, *"but let us be alert and sober"* (1 Thessalonians 5:6).

We are to *pray*. We are to keep up habits of regular communion with God. We are to allow no coldness to come in between us and our Father in heaven, but to speak with Him daily, so that we may be ready at any moment to see Him face to face. Moreover, we are to make special prayer about the Lord's coming that we may *be found by Him in peace, spotless and blameless* (2 Peter 3:14), and that our hearts may at no time be overcharged with the cares of this life, and so the day come upon us suddenly (Luke 21:34).

Finally, we are to *work*. We are to realize that we are all servants of a great Master who has given to every man his work and expects that work to be done. We are to labor to glorify God, each in our particular sphere and relation. There is always something for everyone to do. We are to strive each of us to shine as a light, to be the salt of our own times, to be faithful witnesses for our Master, and to honor Him by conscientiousness and consistency in our daily lives. Our great desire must be to be found not idle and sleeping, but working and doing.

Such are the simple injunctions to which our Lord would have us attend. They ought to stir up in the hearts of all professing Christians great self-examination. Are we looking for our Savior's return? Do we long for His appearing? Can we say with sincerity, *"Come, Lord Jesus"*? Do we live as if we expected Christ to come again? These are questions which demand serious consideration. May we give them the attention which they deserve!

Does our Lord require us to neglect any of the duties of life in the expectation of His return? He requires nothing of the kind. He does not bid the farmer neglect his land, or the laborer his work, the merchant his business, or the lawyer his calling. All He asks is that baptized people should live up to the faith into which they were baptized, live as penitent people, live as believing people, and live as people who know that without holiness no man can see the Lord. So living, we are ready to meet our Master. Not living in this way, we are neither fit for death, judgment, nor eternity. To live in this way is to be truly happy, because it is to be truly prepared for anything that may come upon the earth. Let us never be content with a lower standard of practical Christianity than this. The last words of the prophecy are peculiarly solemn: *"What I say to you I say to all, 'Be on the alert!'"*

Mark Chapter 14

Mark 14:1-9

*Now the Passover and Unleavened Bread were two days away;
and the chief priests and the scribes were seeking how to seize
Him by stealth and kill Him; for they were saying, "Not during
the festival, otherwise there might be a riot of the people." While
He was in Bethany at the home of Simon the leper, and reclining
at the table, there came a woman with an alabaster vial of very
costly perfume of pure nard; and she broke the vial and poured
it over His head. But some were indignantly remarking to one
another, "Why has this perfume been wasted? For this perfume
might have been sold for over three hundred denarii, and the
money given to the poor." And they were scolding her. But Jesus
said, "Let her alone; why do you bother her? She has done a good
deed to Me. For you always have the poor with you, and whenever you wish you can do good to them; but you do not always
have Me. She has done what she could; she has anointed My body
beforehand for the burial. Truly I say to you, wherever the gospel
is preached in the whole world, what this woman has done will
also be spoken of in memory of her."*

THIS CHAPTER BEGINS THAT PART OF MARK'S GOSPEL which
describes our Lord's sufferings and death. Hitherto we have chiefly
seen our Savior as our prophet and teacher. We have now to see Him
as our High Priest. Hitherto we have had to consider His miracles and
sayings. We have now to consider His vicarious sacrifice on the cross.

Let us first observe in these verses *how God can disappoint the designs of wicked men and overrule them to His own glory.*

It is plain from Mark's words and the parallel passage in Matthew that our Lord's enemies did not intend to make His death a public transaction. They *were seeking how to seize Him by stealth. They were saying, "Not during the festival, otherwise there might be a riot of the people."* In short, it would appear that their original plan was to do nothing until the feast of the Passover was over and the Passover worshipers had returned to their own homes.

The overruling providence of God completely defeated this political design. The betrayal of our Lord took place at an earlier time than the chief priests had expected. The death of our Lord took place on the very day when Jerusalem was most full of people and the Passover Feast was at its height. In every way the counsel of these wicked men was turned to foolishness. They thought they were going to put an end forever to Christ's spiritual kingdom; in reality, they were helping to establish it. They thought to have made Him vile and contemptible by the crucifixion; in reality, they made Him glorious. They thought to have put Him to death secretly and without observation; instead, they were compelled to crucify Him publicly and before the whole nation of the Jews. They thought to have silenced His disciples and stopped their teaching; instead, they supplied them with a text and a subject forevermore. So easy is it for God to cause the wrath of man to praise Him (Psalm 76:10).

There is comfort in all this for true Christians. We live in a troubled world and are often tossed to and fro by anxiety about public events. Let us rest ourselves in the thought that everything is ordered for good by an all-wise God. Let us not doubt that all things in the world around us are working together for our Father's glory. Let us call to mind the words of the second psalm: *The kings of the earth take their stand and the rulers take counsel together against the* LORD (Psalm 2:2). And yet it goes on: *He who sits in the heavens laughs, the Lord scoffs at them* (Psalm 2:4). It has been so in time past. It will be so in time to come.

Let us observe secondly in these verses *how good works are sometimes undervalued and misunderstood.* We are told of the good work of a certain woman in pouring ointment on our Lord's head in a house at Bethany. She did it, no doubt, as a mark of honor and respect and in token of her own gratitude and love towards Him. Yet this act of hers was blamed by some. Their cold hearts could not understand such costly liberality. They called it *waste*. They were indignant. *They were scolding her.*

The spirit of these narrow-minded faultfinders is unfortunately only too common. Their followers and successors are to be found in every part of Christ's visible church. There is never lacking a generation of people who depreciate what they call "extremes" in religion and are incessantly recommending what they term "moderation" in the service of Christ. If a man devotes his time, money, and affections to the pursuit of worldly things, they do not blame him. If he gives himself up to the service of money, pleasure, or politics, they find no fault. But if the same man devotes himself and all he has to Christ, they can scarcely find words to express their sense of his folly. "He is beside himself." "He is out of his mind." "He is a fanatic." "He is an enthusiast." "He is righteous over-much." "He is an extreme man." In short, they regard it as *waste*.

Let charges like these not disturb us if we hear them made against us because we strive to serve Christ. Let us bear them patiently and remember that they are as old as Christianity itself. Let us pity those who make such charges against believers. They show plainly that they have no sense of obligation to Christ. A cold heart makes a slow hand. If a man once understands the sinfulness of sin and the mercy of Christ in dying for him, he will never think anything too good or too costly to give to Christ. He will rather feel, *What shall I render to the LORD for all His benefits toward me?* (Psalm 116:12). He will fear wasting time, talents, money, and affections on the things of this world. He will not be afraid of lavishing them on his Savior. He will fear going into extremes about business, money, politics, or pleasure, but he will not be afraid of doing too much for Christ.

Let us observe, in the last place, *how highly our Lord Jesus Christ esteems any service done to Himself.* Nowhere, perhaps, in the Gospels do we find such strong praises bestowed on any person as this woman here receives. Three points in particular stand out prominently in our

Lord's words to which many who now ridicule and blame others for their religion's sake would do well to take heed.

For one thing, our Lord says, *"Why do you bother her?"* A heart-searching question that, and one which all who persecute others because of their religion would find it hard to answer! What cause can they show? What reason can they assign for their conduct? None! None at all. They trouble others out of envy, malice, ignorance, and dislike of the true gospel.

For another thing, our Lord says, *"She has done a good deed to Me."* How great and marvelous is that praise from the lips of the King of Kings! Money is often given to the church or bestowed on charitable institutions from showiness or other false motives. But it is the person who loves and honors Jesus Himself who really does good deeds.

For another thing, our Lord says, *"She has done what she could."* No stronger word of commendation than that could possibly have been used. Thousands live and die without grace and are lost eternally, who are always saying, "I try all I can. I do all I can." And yet in saying so, they tell as great a lie as Ananias and Sapphira. Few, it may be feared, are to be found like this woman and really deserve to have it said of them that they "do what they can."

Let us leave the passage with practical self-application. Let us, like this holy woman whose conduct we have just heard described, devote ourselves and all we have to Christ's glory. Our position in the world may be lowly, and our means of usefulness few. But let us, like her, do what we can.

Finally, let us see in this passage *a sweet foretaste of things yet to come in the day of judgment.* Let us believe that the same Jesus who here pleaded the cause of His loving servant when she was scolded, will one day plead for all who have been His servants in this world. Let us work on, remembering that His eye is upon us, and that all we do is noted in His book. Let us not heed what men say or think of us because of our religion. The praise of Christ at the last day will more than compensate for all we suffer in this world from unkind tongues.

Mark 14:10-16

Then Judas Iscariot, who was one of the twelve, went off to the chief priests in order to betray Him to them. They were glad when they heard this, and promised to give him money. And he began seeking how to betray Him at an opportune time. On the first day of Unleavened Bread, when the Passover lamb was being sacrificed, His disciples said to Him, "Where do You want us to go and prepare for You to eat the Passover?" And He sent two of His disciples and said to them, "Go into the city, and a man will meet you carrying a pitcher of water; follow him; and wherever he enters, say to the owner of the house, 'The Teacher says, "Where is My guest room in which I may eat the Passover with My disciples?"' And he himself will show you a large upper room furnished and ready; prepare for us there." The disciples went out and came to the city, and found it just as He had told them; and they prepared the Passover.

In these verses, Mark tells us how our Lord was delivered into the hands of His enemies. It came to pass through the treachery of one of His own twelve disciples. The false apostle, Judas Iscariot, betrayed Him.

We ought to observe, firstly in this passage, *to what lengths a man may go in a false profession of religion.*

It is impossible to conceive a more striking proof of this painful truth than the history of Judas Iscariot. If ever there was a man who at one time looked like a true disciple of Christ and seemed likely to reach heaven, that man was Judas. He was chosen by the Lord Jesus Himself to be an apostle. He was privileged to be a companion of the Messiah and an eyewitness of His mighty works throughout His earthly ministry. He was an associate of Peter, James, and John. He was sent forth to preach the kingdom of God and to work miracles in Christ's name. He was regarded by all the eleven apostles as one of themselves. He was so like his fellow disciples that they did not suspect him of being a traitor. And yet this very man turns out at last a falsehearted child of the devil, departs entirely from the faith, assists our Lord's deadliest enemies, and leaves the world with a worse reputation than anyone since the days of Cain. Never was there such a fall, such an apostasy, such a miserable end to a fair beginning – such a total eclipse of a soul!

And how can this amazing conduct of Judas be accounted for? There is only one answer to that question. The love of money was the cause of this unhappy man's ruin. That same groveling covetousness which enslaved the heart of Balaam and brought on Gehazi a leprosy was the destruction of Iscariot's soul. No other explanation of his behavior will satisfy the plain statements of Scripture. His act was an act of base covetousness without a redeeming feature about it. The Holy Spirit declares plainly that *he was a thief* (John 12:6). And his case stands before the world as an eternal comment on the solemn words, *The love of money is a root of all sorts of evil* (1 Timothy 6:10).

Let us learn from this sad history of Judas to *clothe [our]selves with humility* and to be content with nothing short of the grace of the Holy Spirit in our hearts. Knowledge, gifts, profession, privileges, church membership, power of preaching, praying, and talking about religion are all useless things if our hearts are not converted. They are all no better than sounding brass and a tinkling cymbal if we have not put off the old man and put on the new. They will not deliver us from hell. Above all, let us remember our Lord's caution to *beware, and be on your guard against every form of greed* (Luke 12:15). It is a sin that eats like a canker, and once admitted into our hearts, may lead us finally into every wickedness. Let us pray to be *content with what [we] have* (Hebrews 13:5). The possession of money is not the one thing needful. Riches entail great peril on the souls of those who have them. The true Christian ought to be far more afraid of being rich than of being poor.

We ought to observe, secondly in this passage, *the intentional connection between the time of the Jewish Passover and the time of Christ's death*. We cannot doubt for a moment that it was not by chance but by God's providential appointment that our Lord was crucified in the Passover week and on the very day that the Passover lamb was slain. It was meant to draw the attention of the Jewish nation to Him as the true Lamb of God. It was meant to bring to their minds the true object and purpose of His death. Every sacrifice, no doubt, was intended to point the Jew onward to the one great sacrifice for sin which Christ offered. But none certainly was so striking a figure and type of our Lord's sacrifice as the slaying of the Passover lamb. It was preeminently an ordinance which was a *tutor to lead us to Christ* (Galatians 3:24). Never was there a type so full of meaning in the whole circle of Jewish ceremonies as the Passover was at its original institution.

Did the Passover remind the Jew of the marvelous deliverance of his forefathers out of the land of Egypt when God slew the firstborn? No doubt it did. But it was also meant to be a sign to him of the far greater redemption and deliverance from the bondage of sin which was to be brought in by our Lord Jesus Christ.

Did the Passover remind the Jew that by the death of an innocent lamb the families of his forefathers were once exempted from the death of their firstborn? No doubt it did. But it was also meant to teach him the far higher truth that the death of Christ on the cross was to be the life of the world.

Did the Passover remind the Jew that the sprinkling of blood on the doorposts of his forefathers' houses preserved them from the sword of the destroying angel? No doubt it did. But it was also meant to show him the far more important doctrine that Christ's blood sprinkled on man's conscience cleanses it from all stain of guilt and makes him safe from the wrath to come.

Did the Passover remind the Jew that none of his forefathers were safe from the destroying angel in the night when he slew the firstborn unless he actually ate of the slain lamb? No doubt it did. But it was meant to guide his mind to the far higher lesson that all who would receive benefit from Christ's atonement must actually feed upon Him by faith and receive Him into their hearts.

Let us call these things to mind and weigh them well. We shall then see a peculiar fitness and beauty in the time appointed by God for our Lord Jesus Christ's death on the cross. It happened at the very season when the mind of all Israel was being directed to the deliverance from Egypt and to the events of that wondrous night when it took place. The lamb slain and eaten by every member of the family – the destroying angel – the safety within the blood-sprinkled door would have been talked over and considered in every Jewish household the very week that our blessed Lord was slain. It would be strange indeed if such a remarkable death as His, at such a time, did not set many minds thinking and open many eyes. To what extent we shall never know until the last day.

Let it be a rule with us, in the reading of our Bibles, to study the types and ordinances of the Mosaic law with prayerful attention. They are all full of Christ. The altar, the scapegoat, the daily burnt offering, and the day of atonement are all so many signposts pointing to the great sacrifice offered by our Lord on Calvary. Those who neglect to study the Jewish ordinances as dark, dull, and uninteresting parts of the Bible only show their own ignorance and miss great advantages. Those who examine them with Christ as the key to their meaning will find them full of gospel light and comfortable truth.

Mark 14:17-25

When it was evening He came with the twelve. As they were reclining at the table and eating, Jesus said, "Truly I say to you that one of you will betray Me—one who is eating with Me." They began to be grieved and to say to Him one by one, "Surely not I?" And He said to them, "It is one of the twelve, who dips with Me in the bowl. For the Son of Man is to go just as it is written of Him; but woe to that man by whom the Son of Man is betrayed! It would have been good for that man if he had not been born." While they were eating, He took some bread, and after a blessing He broke it, and gave it to them, and said, "Take it; this is My body." And when He had taken a cup and given thanks, He gave it to them, and they all drank from it. And He said to them, "This is My blood of the covenant, which is poured out for many. Truly I say to you, I will never again drink of the fruit of the vine until that day when I drink it new in the kingdom of God."

These verses contain Mark's account of the institution of the Lord's Supper. The simplicity of the description deserves special observation.

Well would it have been for the church if men had not departed from the simple statements of Scripture about this blessed sacrament! It is a mournful fact that it has been corrupted by false explanations and superstitious additions until its real meaning, in many parts of Christendom, is utterly unknown. Let us, however, at present, dismiss from our minds all matters of controversy and study the words of Mark with a view to our own personal edification.

Let us learn from the passage before us *that self-examination should precede the reception of the Lord's Supper.* We cannot doubt that this was one object of our Lord's solemn warning, *"One of you will betray Me—one who is eating with Me."* He meant to stir up in the minds of His disciples those very searchings of heart which are here so touchingly recorded – *They began to be grieved and to say to Him one by one, "Surely not I?"* He meant to teach His whole church throughout the world that the time of drawing near to the Lord's Table should be a time for diligent self-inquiry.

The benefit of the Lord's Supper depends entirely on the spirit and frame of mind in which we receive it. The bread which we there eat and the wine which we there drink have no power to do good to our souls as medicine does good to our bodies without the cooperation of our hearts and wills. They will not convey any blessing to us by virtue of the minister's consecration if we do not receive them rightly, worthily, and with faith. To assert, as some do, that the Lord's Supper must do good to all those in the church whatever be the state of mind in which they receive it, is a monstrous and unscriptural figment of imagination and has given rise to gross and wicked superstition.

The state of mind which we should look for in ourselves before going to the Lord's Table is well described in the Catechism of the Church of England. We ought to "examine ourselves whether we repent truly of our former sins – whether we steadfastly purpose to lead a new life – whether we have a lively faith in God's mercy through Christ – and a thankful remembrance of His death – and whether we are in charity with all men." If our conscience can answer these questions satisfactorily, we may receive the Lord's Supper without fear. More than this

God does not require of anyone in a church. Less than this ought never to content us.

Let us take heed to ourselves in the matter of the Lord's Supper. It is easy to err about it on either side. On the one hand, we are not to be content with staying away from the Lord's Table under the vague plea of unfitness. As long as we so stay away, we are disobeying a plain command of Christ and are living in sin. But, on the other hand, we are not to go to the Lord's Table as a mere form and without thought. As long as we receive the sacrament in that state of mind, we derive no good from it and are guilty of a great transgression. It is a dreadful thing to be unfit for the sacrament, for this is to be unfit to die. It is a no less dreadful thing to receive it unworthily, for this is most provoking to God. The only safe course is to be a decided servant of Christ and to live the life of faith in Him. Then we may draw near with boldness and take the sacrament to our comfort.

Let us learn, in the second place from these verses, that *the principal object of our Lord's Supper is to remind us of Christ's sacrifice for us on the cross*. The bread is intended to bring to our recollection the body of Christ which was wounded for our transgressions. The wine is intended to bring to our recollection the blood of Christ which was shed to cleanse us from all sin. The atonement and propitiation which our Lord effected by His death as our Surety and Substitute stand out prominently in the whole ordinance. The false doctrine which some teach that His death was nothing more than the death of a very holy man who left us an example of how to die, turns the Lord's Supper into a meaningless ordinance and cannot possibly be reconciled with our Lord's words at its institution.

A clear understanding of this point is of great importance. It will place us in the right position of mind and teach us how we ought to feel in drawing near to the Lord's Table. It will produce in us true *humility* of spirit. The bread and wine will remind us of how sinful sin must be, when nothing but Christ's death could atone for it. It will produce in us *hopefulness* about our souls. The bread and wine will remind us that though our sins are great, a great price has been paid for our redemption. Not least, it will produce in us *gratitude*. The bread and wine will remind us of how great is our debt to Christ and how deeply bound we are to glorify Him in our lives. May these be the feelings that we experience whenever we receive the Lord's Supper!

Finally, we learn from these verses *the nature of the spiritual benefits which the Lord's Supper is intended to convey and the persons who have a right to expect them.* We may gather this lesson from the significant actions which are used in receiving this sacrament. Our Lord commands us to *eat* bread and to *drink* wine. Now eating and drinking are the acts of a living person. The object of eating and drinking is to be strengthened and refreshed. The conclusion we are meant to draw is manifestly that the Lord's Supper is appointed for the strengthening and refreshing of our souls, and that those who ought to partake of it are those who are lively, real Christians. All such will find this sacrament a means of grace. It will assist them to rest in Christ more simply and to trust in Him more entirely. The visible symbols of bread and wine will aid, quicken, and confirm their faith.

A right view of this point is of the utmost importance in these latter days. We must always beware of thinking that there is any way of eating Christ's body and drinking Christ's blood but by faith – or that receiving the Lord's Supper will give any man a different interest in Christ's sacrifice on the cross from that which faith gives. Faith is the one grand means of communication between the soul and Christ. The Lord's Supper can aid, quicken, and confirm faith, but it can never supersede it or supply its absence. Let this never be forgotten. Error on this point is a most fatal delusion and leads to many superstitions.

Let it be a settled principle in our Christianity that no unbeliever ought to go to the Lord's Table, and that the sacrament will not do our souls the slightest good if we do not receive it with repentance and faith. The Lord's Supper is not a converting or justifying ordinance, and those who come to it unconverted and unjustified will go away no better than they came, but rather worse. It is an ordinance for believers and not for unbelievers, for the living and not for the dead. It is meant to sustain life, but not to impart it – to strengthen and increase grace, but not to give it – to help faith to grow, but not to sow or plant it. Let these things sink down into our hearts and never be forgotten.

Are we alive unto God? This is the great question. If we are, let us go to the Lord's Supper and receive it thankfully and never turn our backs on the Lord's Table. If we do not go, we commit a great sin.

Are we yet dead in sin and worldliness? If we are, we have no business at the Communion table. We are on the broad way that leads to destruction. We must repent. We must be born again. We must be joined to Christ by faith. Then, and not until then, we are fit to be partakers of the Lord's Supper.

Mark 14:26-31

After singing a hymn, they went out to the Mount of Olives. And Jesus said to them, "You will all fall away, because it is written, 'I will strike down the shepherd, and the sheep shall be scattered.' But after I have been raised, I will go ahead of you to Galilee." But Peter said to Him, "Even though all may fall away, yet I will not." And Jesus sad to him, "Truly I say to you, that this very night, before a rooster crows twice, you yourself will deny Me three times." But Peter kept saying insistently, "Even if I have to die with You, I will not deny You!" And they all were saying the same thing also.

We see in these verses *how well our Lord foreknew the weakness and infirmity of His disciples.* He tells them plainly what they were going to do: *"You will all fall away."* He tells Peter in particular of the astounding sin which he was about to commit: *"This very night, before a rooster crows twice, you yourself will deny Me three times."*

Yet our Lord's foreknowledge did not prevent His choosing these twelve disciples to be His apostles. He allowed them to be His intimate friends and companions, knowing perfectly well what they would one day do. With a clear foresight of the sad weakness and lack of faith which they would exhibit at the end of His ministry, He granted them the mighty privilege of being continually with Him and hearing His voice. This is a remarkable fact and deserves to be held in continual remembrance.

Let us take comfort in the thought that the Lord Jesus does not cast off His believing people because of failures and imperfections. He knows what they are. He takes them as the husband takes the wife – with all their blemishes and defects; and once joined to Him by faith, He will never leave them. He is a merciful and compassionate High Priest. It is His glory to pass over the transgressions of His people and to cover their many sins. He knew what they were before conversion – wicked, guilty, and defiled; yet He loved them. He knows what they will be after conversion – weak, erring, and frail; yet He loves them. He has undertaken to save them, notwithstanding all their shortcomings, and what He has undertaken He will perform.

Let us learn to pass a charitable judgment on the conduct of professing believers. Let us not set them down in a low place and say they have no grace because we see much weakness and corruption in them. Let us remember that our Master in heaven bears with their infirmities, and let us try to bear with them too.

The church is little better than a great hospital. We ourselves are all more or less weak, and we all daily need the skillful treatment of the heavenly physician. There will be no complete cures until the resurrection day.

We see, in the second place in these verses, *how much comfort professing Christians may miss by carelessness and inattention.* Our Lord spoke plainly of His resurrection – *"After I have been raised, I will go ahead of you to Galilee."* Yet His words appear to have been thrown away and spoken in vain. Not one of His disciples seems to have noticed them or treasured them up in his heart. When He was betrayed, they forsook Him. When He was crucified, they were almost in despair. And when He rose again on the third day, they would not believe that it was true. They had heard of it frequently with the hearing of the ear, but it had never made any impression on their hearts.

What an exact picture we have here of human nature! How often we see the very same thing among professing Christians in the present day! How many truths we read yearly in the Bible, and yet remember them no more than if we had never read them at all! How many words of wisdom we hear in sermons heedlessly and thoughtlessly and live on as if we had never heard them! The days of darkness and affliction come upon us by and by, and then we prove unarmed and unprepared. On sick beds and in mourning, we see a meaning in texts and passages which we at one time heard listlessly and unconcernedly. Things flash across our minds at such seasons and make us feel ashamed that we had not noticed them before. We then remember to have read them, and heard them, and seen them, but they made no impression upon us. Like Hagar's well in the wilderness, they were close at hand, but, like Hagar, we never saw them (Genesis 21:19).

Let us pray for a quick understanding in hearing and reading God's Word. Let us search into every part of it and not lose any precious truth in it for lack of care. So doing, we shall lay up a good foundation against the time to come, and in sorrow and sickness be found armed.

Let us observe how little reason ministers have to be surprised if the words that they preach in sermons are often unnoticed and unheeded. They only drink of the same cup with their Master. Even He said many things which were not noticed when first spoken. And yet we know that *never has a man spoken the way this man [spoke]* (John 7:46). *A disciple is not above his teacher, nor a slave above his master* (Matthew 10:24). We have need of patience. Truths that seem neglected at first often bear fruit after many days.

We see, in the last place in these verses, *how much ignorant self-confidence may sometimes be found in the hearts of professing Christians.* The apostle Peter could not think it possible that he could ever deny his Lord. *"Even if I have to die with You,"* he says, *"I will not deny You!"* And he did not stand alone in his confidence. The other disciples were of the same mind. *And they all were saying the same thing also.* Yet what did all this confident boasting come to? Twelve hours did not pass away before all the disciples forsook our Lord and fled. Their loud professions were all forgotten. The present danger swept all their promises of fidelity clean away. So little do we know how we shall act in any particular situation until we are placed in it! So much do present circumstances alter our feelings!

Let us learn to pray for humility. *Pride goes before destruction, and a haughty spirit before stumbling* (Proverbs 16:18). There is far more wickedness in all our hearts than we know. We never can tell how far we might fall if once placed in temptation. There is no degree of sin into which the greatest saint may not run if he is not held up by the grace of God, and if he does not watch and pray. The seeds of every wickedness lie hidden in our hearts. They only need the convenient season to spring forth into a mischievous vitality. *Therefore let him who thinks he stands take heed that he does not fall* (1 Corinthians 10:12). *He who trusts in his own heart is a fool* (Proverbs 28:26). Let our daily prayer be, *Uphold me that I may be safe.*

Mark 14:32-42

They came to a place named Gethsemane; and He said to His disciples, "Sit here until I have prayed." And He took with Him Peter and James and John, and began to be very distressed and troubled. And He said to them, "My soul is deeply grieved to the point of death; remain here and keep watch." And He went a little beyond them, and fell to the ground and began to pray that if it were possible, the hour might pass Him by. And He was saying, "Abba! Father! All things are possible for You; remove this cup from Me; yet not what I will, but what You will." And He came and found them sleeping, and said to Peter, "Simon, are you asleep? Could you not keep watch for one hour? Keep watching and praying that you may not come into temptation; the spirit is willing, but the flesh is weak." Again He went away and prayed, saying the same words. And again He came and found them sleeping, for their eyes were very heavy; and they did not know what to answer Him. And He came the third time, and said to them, "Are you still sleeping and resting? It is enough; the hour has come; behold, the Son of Man is being betrayed into the hands of sinners. Get up, let us be going; behold, the one who betrays Me is at hand!"

EXPOSITORY THOUGHTS ON THE GOSPEL OF MARK

The history of our Lord's agony in the garden of Gethsemane is a deep and mysterious passage of Scripture. It contains things which the wisest preachers cannot fully explain. Yet it has upon its surface plain truths of most momentous importance.

Let us observe, in the first place, *how keenly our Lord felt the burden of the world's sin*. It is written that He began to be filled with horror and deep distress. He told them, *"My soul is deeply grieved to the point of death,"* and He *fell to the ground and began to pray that if it were possible, the hour might pass Him by.* There is only one reasonable explanation for these expressions. It was no mere fear of the physical suffering of death which drew them from our Lord's lips. It was a sense of the enormous load of human guilt which began at that time to press upon Him in a peculiar way. It was a sense of the unutterable weight of our sins and transgressions which were then specially laid upon Him. He was *becom[ing] a curse for us* (Galatians 3:13). He was bearing our griefs and carrying our sorrows according to the covenant He came on earth to fulfill. His Father *made Him who knew no sin to be sin on our behalf* (2 Corinthians 5:21). His holy nature felt acutely the hideous burden laid upon Him. These were the reasons for His extraordinary sorrow.

We ought to see in our Lord's agony in Gethsemane the exceeding sinfulness of sin. It is a subject on which the thoughts of professing Christians are far below what they should be. The careless, light way in which such sins as swearing, Sabbath-breaking, lying, and the like are often spoken of is painful evidence of the low condition of men's moral feelings. Let the recollection of Gethsemane have a sanctifying effect upon us. Whatever others do, let us never mock at sin.

Let us observe, in the second place, *what an example our Lord gives us of the importance of prayer in time of trouble*. In the hour of His distress, we find Him employing this great remedy. Twice we are told that when His soul was *deeply grieved*, He *began to pray* and *He went away and prayed*.

We shall never find a better formula than this for the patient bearing of affliction. The first person to whom we should turn in our trouble is God. The first expression of grief we should make should be in the form of a prayer. The reply may not be given immediately. The relief we need may not be granted at once. The thing that tries us may never be removed and taken away. But the mere act of pouring out our hearts and unbosoming ourselves at a throne of grace will do us good. The advice of James is wise and weighty – *Is anyone among you suffering? Then he must pray* (James 5:13).

Let us observe, in the third place, *what a striking example our Lord gives us of submission of will to the will of God.* Deeply as His human nature felt the pressure of the world's guilt, He still prayed that *if it were possible, the hour might pass Him by. "Remove this cup from Me; yet not what I will, but what You will."*

We can imagine no higher degree of perfection than that which is here set before us. To take patiently whatever God sends, to like nothing but what God likes, to wish nothing but what God approves, to prefer pain if it pleases God to send it, to forego ease if God does not think fit to bestow it, to lie passive under God's hand and know no will but His – this is the highest standard at which we can aim, and of this our Lord's conduct in Gethsemane is a perfect pattern.

Let us strive and labor to have *the mind of Christ* in this matter. Let us daily pray and endeavor to be enabled to mortify our self-will. It is for our happiness to do so. Nothing brings us so much misery on earth as having our own way. It is the best proof of real grace to do so. Knowledge, and gifts, and convictions, and feelings, and wishes are all very uncertain evidences. They are often to be found in unconverted people. But a continually increasing disposition to submit our own wills to the will of God is a far more healthy symptom. It is a sign that we are really *grow[ing] in the grace and the knowledge of our Lord and Savior Jesus Christ.*

Let us observe lastly in these verses *how much infirmity may be found even in the best Christians.* We have a painful illustration of this truth in the conduct of Peter, James, and John. They slept when they ought to have watched and prayed. Though invited by our Lord to watch with Him, they slept. Though warned a short time before that danger was at hand and their faith likely to fail, they slept. Though fresh from the Lord's Table with all its touching solemnities, they slept. Never was

231

there a more striking proof that the best of men are but men, and that so long as saints are in the body, they are compassed with infirmity.

These things are written for our learning. Let us take heed that they are not written in vain. Let us ever be on our guard against the slothful, indolent, and lazy spirit in religion which is natural to us all and especially in the matter of our private prayers. When we feel that spirit creeping over us, let us remember Peter, James, and John in the garden and take care.

The solemn counsel which our Lord addresses to His disciples should often ring in our ears: *"Keep watching and praying that you may not come into temptation; the spirit is willing, but the flesh is weak."* It should be the Christian's daily motto from the time of his conversion to the hour of his death.

Are we true Christians? And would we keep our souls awake? Let us not forget that we have within us a double nature – a ready *spirit* and a weak *flesh*, a carnal nature inclined to evil and a spiritual nature inclined to good. These two are contrary one to the other (Galatians 5:17). Sin and the devil will always find helpers in our hearts. If we do not crucify and rule over the flesh, it will often rule over us and bring us to shame.

Are we true Christians? And would we keep our souls awake? Then let us never forget to *keep watching and praying.* We must watch like soldiers – we are upon enemy ground. We must always be on our guard. We must fight a daily fight and war a daily warfare. The Christian's rest is yet to come. We must pray without ceasing, regularly, habitually, carefully, and at stated times. We must pray as well as watch, and watch as well as pray. Watching without praying is self-confidence and self-conceit. Praying without watching is enthusiasm and fanaticism. The man who knows his own weakness, and knowing it both watches and prays, is the man that will be held up and not allowed to fall.

Mark 14:43-52

Immediately while He was still speaking, Judas, one of the twelve, came up accompanied by a crowd with swords and clubs, who were from the chief priests and the scribes and the elders. Now he who was betraying Him had given them a signal, saying, "Whomever I kiss, He is the one; seize Him and lead Him away under guard." After coming, Judas immediately went to Him, saying, "Rabbi!" and kissed Him. They laid hands on Him and seized Him. But one of those who stood by drew his sword, and struck the slave of the high priest and cut off his ear. And Jesus said to them, "Have you come out with swords and clubs to arrest Me, as you would against a robber? Every day I was with you in the temple teaching, and you did not seize Me; but this has taken place to fulfill the Scriptures." And they all left Him and fled. A young man was following Him, wearing nothing but a linen sheet over his naked body; and they seized him. But he pulled free of the linen sheet and escaped naked.

Let us notice in these verses *how little our Lord's enemies understood the nature of His kingdom.* We read that Judas came to take Him *accompanied by a crowd with swords and clubs.* It was evidently expected that our Lord would be vigorously defended by His disciples and that He would not be taken prisoner without fighting. The chief priests and scribes clung obstinately to the idea that our Lord's kingdom was a worldly kingdom and therefore supposed that it would be upheld by worldly means. They had yet to learn the solemn lesson contained in our Lord's words to Pilate: *"My kingdom is not of this world"* (John 18:36).

We shall do well to remember this in all our endeavors to extend the kingdom of true religion. It is not to be propagated by violence or by an arm of flesh.

The weapons of our warfare are not of the flesh (2 Corinthians 10:4). *'Not by might nor by power, but by My Spirit,' says the* LORD *of hosts* (Zechariah 4:6). The cause of truth does not need force to maintain it. False religions, like Islam, have often been spread by the sword. False

Christianity, like that of the Roman Catholic Church, has often been enforced on men by bloody persecutions. But the real gospel of Christ requires no such aids as these. It stands by the power of the Holy Spirit. It grows by the hidden influence of the Holy Spirit on men's hearts and consciences. There is no clearer sign of a bad cause in religion than a readiness to appeal to the sword.

Let us notice secondly in these verses *how all things in our Lord's passion happened according to God's Word.* His own address to those who took Him exhibits this in a striking manner: *"This has taken place to fulfill the Scriptures."*

There was no accident or chance in any part of the close of our Lord's earthly ministry. The steps in which He walked from Gethsemane to Calvary were all marked out hundreds of years before. The twenty-second psalm and the fifty-third chapter of Isaiah were literally fulfilled. The wrath of His enemies, His rejection by His own people, His being dealt with as a malefactor, His being condemned by the assembly of the wicked – all had been foreknown and all foretold. All that took place was only the working out of God's great design to provide an atonement for the world's sin. The armed men whom Judas brought to lay hands on Jesus were, like Nebuchadnezzar and Sennacherib, unconscious instruments in carrying God's purposes into effect.

Let us rest our souls on the thought that all around us is ordered and overruled by God's almighty wisdom. The course of this world may often be contrary to our wishes. The position of the church may often be very unlike what we desire. The wickedness of worldly men and the inconsistencies of believers may often afflict our souls. But there is a hand above us moving the vast machine of this universe and making all things work together for His glory. The Scriptures are being yearly fulfilled. Not one jot or tittle in them shall ever fail to be accomplished. The kings of the earth may take counsel together, and the rulers of the nations may set themselves against Christ (Psalm 2:2), but the resurrection morning shall prove that even at the darkest time all things were being done according to the will of God.

Let us notice lastly in these verses *how much the faith of true believers may give way.* We are told that when Judas and his company laid hands on our Lord, and He quietly submitted to be taken prisoner, the eleven disciples *all left Him and fled.* Perhaps up to that moment they were buoyed up by the hope that our Lord would work a miracle and set Himself free. But when they saw no miracle worked, their courage failed them entirely. Their former protestations were all forgotten. Their promises to die with their Master rather than deny Him were all cast to the winds. The fear of present danger got the better of faith. The sense of immediate peril drove every other feeling out of their minds. They *all left Him and fled.*

There is something deeply instructive in this incident. It deserves the attentive study of all professing Christians. Happy is he who observes the conduct of our Lord's disciples and gathers from it wisdom!

Let us learn from the flight of these eleven disciples not to be over-confident in our own strength. The fear of man does indeed bring a snare. We never know what we may do if we are tempted, or to what extent our faith may give way. Let us be clothed with humility.

Let us learn to be charitable in our judgment of other Christians. Let us not expect too much from them or set them down as having no grace at all if we see them overtaken in a fault. Let us not forget that even our Lord's chosen apostles forsook Him in His time of need. Yet they rose again by repentance and became pillars of the church of Christ.

Finally, let us leave the passage with a deep sense of our Lord's ability to sympathize with His believing people. If there is one trial greater than another, it is the trial of being disappointed in those we love. It is a bitter cup which all true Christians have frequently to drink. Ministers fail them. Relatives fail them. Friends fail them. One cistern after another proves to be broken and to hold no water. But let them take comfort in the thought that there is one unfailing Friend, even Jesus, who can be touched with the feeling of their infirmities and has tasted of all their sorrows. Jesus knows what it is to see friends and disciples failing Him in the hour of need. Yet He bore it patiently and loved them notwithstanding all. He is never weary of forgiving. Let us strive to do likewise. Jesus, at any rate, will never fail us. It is written, *His compassions never fail* (Lamentations 3:22).

Mark 14:53-65

*They led Jesus away to the high priest; and all the chief priests
and the elders and the scribes gathered together. Peter had followed Him at a distance, right into the courtyard of the high
priest; and he was sitting with the officers and warming himself
at the fire. Now the chief priests and the whole Council kept trying to obtain testimony against Jesus to put Him to death, and
they were not finding any. For many were giving false testimony
against Him, but their testimony was not consistent. Some stood
up and began to give false testimony against Him, saying, "We
heard Him say, 'I will destroy this temple made with hands, and
in three days I will build another made without hands.'" Not even
in this respect was their testimony consistent. The high priest
stood up and came forward and questioned Jesus, saying "Do
You not answer? What is it that these men are testifying against
You?" But He kept silent and did not answer. Again the high
priest was questioning Him, and saying to Him, "Are You the
Christ, the Son of the Blessed One?" And Jesus said, "I am; and
you shall see the Son of Man sitting at the right hand of Power,
and coming with the clouds of heaven." Tearing his clothes, the
high priest said, "What further need do we have of witnesses?
You have heard the blasphemy; how does it seem to you?" And
they all condemned Him to be deserving of death. Some began
to spit at Him, and to blindfold Him, and to beat Him with their
fists, and to say to Him, "Prophesy!" And the officers received
Him with slaps in the face.*

Solomon tells us in the book of Ecclesiastes that one evil he has seen
under the sun is when *folly is set in many exalted places while rich men
sit in humble places* (Ecclesiastes 10:6). We can imagine no more complete illustration of his words than the state of things we have recorded
in the passage before us. We see the Son of God, *in whom are hidden
all the treasures of wisdom and knowledge* (Colossians 2:3), arraigned
as a malefactor before *all the chief priests and elders and the scribes.* We

see the heads of the Jewish nation combining together to kill their own Messiah and judging Him who will one day come in glory to judge them and all mankind. These things sound astonishing, but they are true.

Let us observe in these verses *how foolishly Christians sometimes thrust themselves into temptation.* We are told that when our Lord was led away prisoner, *Peter had followed Him at a distance, right into the courtyard of the high priest; and he was sitting with the officers and warming himself at the fire.* There was no wisdom in this act. Having once forsaken his Master and fled, he ought to have remembered his own weakness and not to have ventured into danger again. It was an act of rashness and presumption. It brought on him fresh trials of faith for which he was utterly unprepared. It threw him into bad company where he was not likely to get good, but harm. It paved the way for his last and greatest transgression – his thrice-repeated denial of his Master.

But it is an experimental truth that ought never to be overlooked, that when a believer has once begun to backslide and leave his first faith, he seldom stops short at his first mistake. He seldom makes only one stumble. He seldom commits only one fault. A blindness seems to come over his understanding. He appears to cast overboard his common sense and discretion. Like a stone rolling downhill, the further he goes on in sinning, the faster and more decided is his course. Like David, he may begin with idleness and end with committing every possible crime. Like Peter, he may begin with cowardice, go on to foolish trifling with temptation, and then end with denying Christ.

If we know anything of true saving religion, let us ever beware of the beginnings of backsliding. It is like the letting out of water, first a drop and then a torrent. Once out of the way of holiness, there is no saying to what we may come. Once giving way to petty inconsistencies, we may find ourselves one day committing every sort of wickedness. Let us keep far from the brink of evil. Let us not play with fire. Let us never fear being too particular, too strict, and too precise. No petition in the Lord's Prayer is more important than the last one: *Do not lead us into temptation.*

Let us observe, in the second place in these verses, *how much our Lord Jesus Christ had to endure from lying lips when tried before the chief priests.* We are told that *many were giving false testimony against Him, but their testimony was not consistent.*

We can easily conceive that this was not the least heavy part of our blessed Savior's passion. To be seized unjustly as a malefactor and put on trial as a criminal, when innocent, is a severe affliction. But to hear men inventing false charges against us and coining slanders – to listen to all the malignant virulence of unscrupulous tongues let loose against our character and know that it is all untrue – this is a cross indeed! *The words of a whisperer,* says Solomon, *are like dainty morsels* (Proverbs 18:8). *Deliver my soul, O LORD,* says David, *from lying lips, from a deceitful tongue* (Psalm 120:2). All this was a part of the cup which Jesus drank for our sakes. Great indeed was the price at which our souls were redeemed!

Let it never surprise true Christians if they are slandered and misrepresented in this world. They must not expect to fare better than their Lord. Let them rather look forward to it as a matter of course and see in it a part of the cross which all must bear after conversion. Lies and false reports are among Satan's choicest weapons. When he cannot deter men from serving Christ, he labors to harass them and make Christ's service uncomfortable. Let us bear it patiently and not count it a strange thing. The words of the Lord Jesus should often come to our minds: *Woe to you when all men speak well of you* (Luke 6:26). *Blessed are you when people insult you and persecute you, and falsely say all kinds of evil against you because of Me* (Matthew 5:11).

Let us observe lastly in these verses *what distinct testimony our Lord bore to His own messiahship and second advent in glory.* The high priest asks Him the solemn question, *"Are You the Christ, the Son of the Blessed One?"* He receives at once the emphatic reply, *"I am; and you shall see the Son of Man sitting at the right hand of power, and coming with the clouds of heaven."*

These words of our Lord ought always to be held in remembrance. The Jews could never say after these words that they were not clearly told that Jesus of Nazareth was the Christ of God. Before the great councils of their priests and elders, He declared, *"I am the Christ."* The Jews could never say after these words that He was so lowly and poor a person that

He was not worthy to be believed. He warned them plainly that His glory and greatness was all yet to come. They were only deferred and postponed until His second advent. They would yet see Him in royal power and majesty, *sitting at the right hand of power,* coming in the clouds of heaven, a judge, a conqueror, and a king. If Israel was unbelieving, it was not because Israel was not told what to believe.

Let us leave the passage with a deep sense of the reality and certainty of our Lord Jesus Christ's second coming. Once more at the very end of His ministry and in the face of His deadly enemies, we find Him asserting the mighty truth that He will come again to judge the world. Let it be one of the leading truths in our own personal Christianity. Let us live in the daily recollection that our Savior is one day coming back to this world. Let the Christ in whom we believe be not only the Christ who died for us and rose again – the Christ who lives for us and intercedes – but the Christ who will also one day return in glory to gather together and reward His people and to punish fearfully all His enemies.

Mark 14:66-72

As Peter was below in the courtyard, one of the servant-girls of the high priest came, and seeing Peter warming himself, she looked at him and said, "You also were with Jesus the Nazarene." But he denied it, saying, "I neither know nor understand what you are talking about." And he went out onto the porch. The servant-girl saw him, and began once more to say to the bystanders, "This is one of them!" But again he denied it. And after a little while the bystanders were again saying to Peter, "Surely you are one of them, for you are a Galilean too." But he began to curse and swear, "I do not know this man you are talking about!" Immediately a rooster crowed a second time. And Peter remembered how Jesus had made the remark to him, "Before a rooster crows twice, you will deny Me three times." And he began to weep.

A shipwreck is a unfortunate sight even when no lives are lost. It is sad to think of the destruction of property and disappointment of hopes which generally attend it. It is painful to see the suffering and hardship which the ship's crew often have to undergo in their struggle to escape from drowning. Yet no shipwreck is half so sad a sight as the backsliding and fall of a true Christian. Though raised again by God's mercy and finally saved from hell, he loses much by his fall. Such a sight we have brought before our minds in the verses we have now read. We are there told that most painful and instructive story of how Peter denied his Lord.

Let us learn, in the first place from these verses, *how far and how shamefully a great saint may fall*. We know that Simon Peter was an eminent apostle of Jesus Christ. He was one who had received special commendation from our Lord's lips after a noble confession of His messiahship. *"Blessed are you, Simon Barjona." "I will give you the keys of the kingdom of heaven"* (Matthew 16:17, 19). He was one who had enjoyed special privileges and had special mercies shown to him. Yet here we see this same Simon Peter so entirely overcome by fear that he actually denies his Lord. He declares that he knows not Him whom he had accompanied and lived with for three years! He declares that he knows not Him who had healed his own mother-in-law, taken him up into the Mount of Transfiguration, and saved him from drowning in the Sea of Galilee! And he not only denies his Master once, but does it three times! And he not only denies Him simply, but also begins *to curse and swear* as he is denying Him! And above all, he does all this in the face of the plainest warnings and in spite of his own loud protestation that he would do nothing of the kind, but would rather die!

These things are written to show the church of Christ what human nature is even in the best of men. They are intended to teach us that even after conversion and renewal by the Holy Spirit, believers are compassed with infirmity and liable to fall. They are meant to impress upon us the immense importance of daily watchfulness, prayerfulness, and humility so long as we are in the body. *Therefore let him who thinks he stands take heed that he does not fall* (1 Corinthians 10:12).

Let us carefully remember that Simon Peter's case does not stand alone. The Word of God contains many other examples of the infirmity of true believers which we shall do well to observe. The histories of Noah, Abraham, David, and Hezekiah will supply us with mournful proof that the infection of sin remains even in the regenerate, and that no man is so strong as to be beyond the danger of falling. Let us not forget this. Let us walk humbly with our God. *How blessed is the man who fears always* (Proverbs 28:14).

Let us learn, in the second place from these verses, *how small a temptation may cause a saint to have a great fall.* The beginning of Peter's trial was nothing more than the simple remark of *one of the servant-girls of the high priest. "You also were with Jesus the Nazarene."* There is nothing to show that these words were spoken with any hostile purpose. For anything we can see, they might fairly mean that this servant-girl remembered that Peter used to be a companion of our Lord. But this simple remark was enough to overthrow the faith of an eminent apostle and to make him begin to deny his Master. The chief and foremost of our Lord's chosen disciples is cast down, not by the threats of armed men but by the saying of one weak woman!

There is something deeply instructive in this fact. It ought to teach us that no temptation is too small and trifling to overcome us, except we watch and pray to be held up. If God be for us, we may remove mountains and get the victory over a host of foes. *I can do all things,* says Paul, *through Him who strengthens me* (Philippians 4:13). If God withdraws His grace and leaves us to ourselves, we are like a city without gates and walls, a prey to the first enemy, however weak and contemptible.

Let us beware of making light of temptations because they seem little and insignificant. There is nothing little that concerns our souls. A little leaven leavens the whole lump. A little spark may kindle a great fire. A little leak may sink a great ship. A little provocation may bring out from our hearts great corruption and end in bringing our souls into great trouble.

Finally, let us learn from these verses *that backsliding brings saints into great sorrow.* The conclusion of the passage is very affecting. *Peter remembered how Jesus had made the remark to him, "Before a rooster crows twice, you will deny Me three times."* Who can pretend to describe the feelings that must have flashed across the apostle's mind? Who can conceive the shame, and confusion, and self-reproach, and bitter remorse which must have overwhelmed his soul? To have fallen so foully! To have fallen so repeatedly! To have fallen in the face of such plain warnings! All these must have been cutting thoughts. The iron must indeed have entered into his soul. There is deep and solemn meaning in the one single expression used about him: *Peter remembered how Jesus had made the remark to him . . . And he began to weep.*

The experience of Peter is only the experience of all God's servants who have yielded to temptation. Lot, and Samson, and David, and Jehoshaphat in Bible history – Cranmer and Jewell in the records of our own English church – have all left evidence, like Peter, that *the backslider in heart will have his fill of his own ways* (Proverbs 14:14). Like Peter, they erred grievously. Like Peter, they repented truly. But like Peter, they found that they reaped a bitter harvest in this world. Like Peter, they were freely pardoned and forgiven. But like Peter, they shed many tears.

Let us leave the passage with the settled conviction that *sin is sure to lead to sorrow, and that the way of most holiness is always the way of most happiness.* The Lord Jesus has mercifully provided that it shall never profit His servants to walk carelessly and to give way to temptation. If we turn our backs on Him, we shall be sure to hurt for it. Though He forgives us, He will make us feel the folly of our own ways. Those who follow the Lord most fully shall always follow Him most comfortably. *The sorrows of those who have bartered for another god will be multiplied* (Psalm 16:4).

Mark Chapter 15

Mark 15:1-15

Early in the morning the chief priests with the elders and scribes and the whole Council, immediately held a consultation; and binding Jesus, they led Him away and delivered Him to Pilate. Pilate questioned Him, "Are You the King of the Jews?" And He answered him, "It is as you say." The chief priests began to accuse Him harshly. Then Pilate questioned Him again, saying, "Do You not answer? See how many charges they bring against You!" But Jesus made no further answer; so Pilate was amazed. Now at the feast he used to release for them any one prisoner whom they requested. The man named Barabbas had been imprisoned with the insurrectionists who had committed murder in the insurrection. The crowd went up and began asking him to do as he had been accustomed to do for them. Pilate answered them, saying, "Do you want me to release for you the King of the Jews?" For he was aware that the chief priests had handed Him over because of envy. But the chief priests stirred up the crowd to ask him to release Barabbas for them instead. Answering again, Pilate said to them, "Then what shall I do with Him whom you call the King of the Jews?" They shouted back, "Crucify Him!" But Pilate said to them, "Why, what evil has He done?" But they shouted all the more, "Crucify Him!" Wishing to satisfy the crowd, Pilate released Barabbas for them, and after having Jesus scourged, he handed Him over to be crucified.

THESE VERSES BEGIN the chapter in which Mark describes the slaying of *the Lamb of God who takes away the sin of the world* (John 1:29). It is a part of the gospel history which should always be read with peculiar reverence. We should call to mind that Christ was cut off not for Himself but for us (Daniel 9:26). We should remember that His death is the life of our souls, and that unless His blood had been shed, we would have perished miserably in our sins.

Let us observe in these verses *what a striking proof the Jewish rulers gave to their own nation that the times of Messiah had come.*

The chapter opens with the fact that the chief priests bound Jesus *and delivered Him to Pilate*, the Roman governor. Why did they do so? Because they had no longer the power of putting anyone to death and were under the dominion of the Romans. By this one act and deed, they declared that the prophecy of Jacob was fulfilled: *The scepter shall not depart from Judah, nor the ruler's staff from between his feet, until Shiloh [the Messiah] comes,* whom God had promised to send (Genesis 49:10). Yet there is nothing whatsoever to show that they remembered this prophecy. Their eyes were blinded. They either could not or would not see what they were doing.

Let us never forget that wicked men are often fulfilling God's predictions to their own ruin and yet know it not. In the very height of their madness, folly, and unbelief, they are often unconsciously supplying fresh evidence that the Bible is true. The unhappy scoffers who make a jest of all serious religion and can scarcely talk of Christianity without ridicule and scorn would do well to remember that their conduct was long ago foreseen and foretold. *In the last days mockers will come with their mocking, following after their own lusts* (2 Peter 3:3).

Let us observe secondly in these verses *the meekness and lowliness of our Lord Jesus Christ.* When He stood before Pilate's bar and Pilate said to Him, *"See how many charges they bring against You!"* He answered nothing. Though the charges against Him were false and He knew no sin, He was content to endure the contradiction of sinners against Himself, not answering again (Hebrews 12:3). Though He was innocent of any transgression, He submitted to bear groundless accusations made against Him without a murmur. Great is the contrast between the second Adam and the first! Our first father Adam was guilty and yet tried to excuse himself. The second Adam was guiltless and yet made no defense at all. *Like a sheep that is silent before its shearers, so He did not open His mouth* (Isaiah 53:7).

Let us learn a practical lesson from our Savior's example. Let us learn to suffer patiently and not to complain, whatever God may think fit to lay upon us. Let us take heed to our ways that we offend not in our tongues in the hour of temptation (Psalm 39:1). Let us beware of giving way to irritation and ill temper, however provoking and undeserved our trials may seem to be. Nothing in the Christian character glorifies God so much as patient suffering. *If when you do what is right and suffer for it you patiently endure it, this finds favor with God. For you have been called for this purpose, since Christ also suffered for you, leaving you an example for you to follow in His steps* (1 Peter 2:20-21).

Let us observe thirdly in these verses *the wavering and undecided conduct of Pilate.*

It is clear from the passage before us that Pilate was convinced of our Lord's innocence. *He was aware that the chief priests had handed Him over because of envy.* We see him feebly struggling for a time to obtain our Lord's acquittal and to satisfy his own conscience. At last he yields to the importunity of the Jews and *wishing to satisfy the crowd,* he delivered Jesus to be crucified – to the eternal disgrace and ruin of his own soul.

A man in high place without religious principles is one of the most pitiable sights in the world. He is like a large ship tossed to and fro on the sea without compass or rudder. His very greatness surrounds him with temptations and snares. It gives him power for good or evil which, if he knows not how to use it aright, is sure to bring him into difficulties and to make him unhappy. Let us pray much for great men. They need great grace to keep them from the devil. High places are slippery places. No wonder that Paul recommends intercession *for kings and all who are in authority* (1 Timothy 2:2). Let us not envy great men. They have many and peculiar temptations. How hard it is for a rich man to enter the kingdom of God. *Are you seeking great things for yourself? Do not seek them* (Jeremiah 45:5).

Let us observe fourthly in these verses *the exceeding guilt of the Jews in the matter of the death of Christ.* At the eleventh hour the chief priests had an opportunity of repenting if they would have taken it. They had the choice given them whether Jesus or Barabbas should be let go free. Coolly and deliberately they persevered in their bloody work. They chose to have a murderer let go free. They chose to have the Prince of Life put to death. The *power* of putting our Lord to death was no longer theirs. The *responsibility* of His death they publicly took upon themselves. *"Then what shall I do with Him whom you call the King of the Jews?"* was Pilate's question. *"Crucify Him!"* was the dreadful answer. The agents in our Lord's death were undoubtedly Gentiles. But the guilt of our Lord's death must always rest chiefly upon the Jews.

We marvel at the wickedness of the Jews at this part of our Lord's history – and no wonder. To reject Christ and choose Barabbas was indeed an astounding act! It seems as if blindness, madness, and folly could go no further. But let us take heed that we do not unwittingly follow their example. Let us beware that we are not found at last to have chosen Barabbas and rejected Christ. The service of sin and the service of God are continually before us. The friendship of the world and the friendship of Christ are continually pressed upon our notice. Are we making the right choice? Are we cleaving to the right Friend? These are solemn questions. Happy is he who can give them a satisfactory answer.

Let us observe finally in these verses *what a striking type the release of Barabbas affords of the gospel plan of salvation.* The guilty is set free and the innocent is put to death. The great sinner is delivered and the sinless one remains bound. Barabbas is spared and Christ is crucified.

We have in this striking fact a vivid emblem of the manner in which God pardons and justifies the ungodly. He does it because Christ has suffered in their stead, the just for the unjust. They deserve punishment, but a mighty Substitute has suffered for them. They deserve eternal death, but a glorious Surety has died for them. We are all by nature in the position of Barabbas. We are guilty, wicked, and worthy of condemnation. But when we were without hope, Christ the innocent died for the ungodly (Ephesians 2:12). And now God for Christ's sake can be just and yet *the justifier of the one who has faith in Jesus* (Romans 3:26).

Let us bless God that we have such a glorious salvation set before us. Our plea must ever be not that we are deserving of acquittal, but that Christ has died for us. Let us take heed that having so great a salvation we really make use of it for our own souls. May we never rest until we can say by faith, "Christ is mine. I deserve hell. But Christ has died for me, and believing in Him I have a hope of heaven."

Mark 15:16-32

The soldiers took Him away into the palace (that is, the Praetorium), and they called together the whole Roman cohort. They dressed Him up in purple, and after twisting a crown of thorns, they put it on Him; and they began to acclaim Him, "Hail, King of the Jews!" They kept beating His head with a reed, and spitting on Him, and kneeling and bowing before Him. After they had mocked Him, they took the purple robe off Him and put His own garments on Him. And they led Him out to crucify Him. They pressed into service a passer-by coming from the country, Simon of Cyrene (the father of Alexander and Rufus), to bear His cross. Then they brought Him to the place Golgotha, which is translated, Place of a Skull. They tried to give Him wine mixed with myrrh; but He did not take it. And they crucified Him, and divided up His garments among themselves, casting lots for them to decide what each man should take. It was the third hour when they crucified Him. The inscription of the charge against Him read, "THE KING OF THE JEWS." They crucified two robbers with Him, one on His right and one His left. [And the Scripture was fulfilled which says, "And He was numbered with transgressors."] Those passing by were hurling abuse at Him, wagging their heads, and saying, "Ha! You who are going to destroy the temple and rebuild it in three days, save Yourself, and come down from the cross!" In the same way the chief priests also, along with the scribes, were mocking Him among themselves and saying "He saved others; He cannot save Himself. Let this Christ, the King of Israel, now come down from the cross, so that we may see and believe!" Those who were crucified with Him were also insulting Him.

The passage we have now read is one of those which show us the infinite love of Christ toward sinners. The sufferings described in it would fill our minds with mingled horror and compassion if they had been inflicted on one who was only a man like ourselves. But when we reflect that the sufferer was the eternal Son of God, we are lost in wonder and amazement. And when we reflect further that these sufferings were voluntarily endured to deliver sinful men and women like ourselves from hell, we may see something of Paul's meaning when he says, *The love of Christ . . . surpasses knowledge* (Ephesians 3:19). *God demonstrates His own love toward us, in that while we were yet sinners, Christ died for us* (Romans 5:8).

We shall find it useful to examine separately the several parts of our Lord's passion. Let us follow Him step by step from the moment of His condemnation by Pilate to His last hour upon the cross. There is a deep meaning in every jot and tittle of His sorrows. All were striking emblems of spiritual truths. And let us not forget as we dwell on the wondrous story that we and our sins were the cause of all these sufferings. *Christ also died for sins once for all, the just for the unjust, so that He might bring us to God* (1 Peter 3:18). It is the death of our own Surety and Substitute of which we are reading.

First of all, we see Jesus delivered into the hands of the Roman soldiers as a criminal condemned to death. He before whom the whole world will one day stand and be judged allowed Himself to be sentenced unjustly and given over into the hands of wicked men.

And why was this? It was that we, the poor sinful children of men, believing on Him, might be delivered from the pit of destruction and the torment of the prison of hell. It was that we might be set free from every charge in the day of judgment and be presented faultless before God the Father with exceeding joy.

Secondly, we see Jesus insulted and made a laughingstock by the Roman soldiers. They *dressed Him up in purple* in derision and put *a crown of thorns* on His head in mockery of His kingdom. *They kept beating His head with a reed, and spitting on Him,* as one utterly contemptible and no better than *the scum of the world* (1 Corinthians 4:13).

And why was this? It was that we, vile as we are, might have glory, honor, and eternal life through faith in Christ's atonement. It was done that we might be received into God's kingdom with triumph at the last day and receive the crown of glory that fades not away.

Thirdly, we see Jesus stripped of His garments and crucified naked before His enemies. The soldiers who led Him away *divided up His garments among themselves, casting lots for them.*

And why was this? It was that we, who have no righteousness of our own, might be clothed in the perfect righteousness that Christ has wrought out for us and not stand naked before God at the last day. It was done that we, who are all defiled with sin, might have a wedding garment wherein we may sit down by the side of angels and not be ashamed.

Fourthly, we see Jesus suffering the most ignominious and humiliating of all deaths, even the death of the cross. It was the punishment reserved for the worst of malefactors. The man on whom it was inflicted was counted accursed. It is written, *Cursed is everyone who hangs on a tree* (Galatians 3:13).

And why was this? It was that we, who are born in sin and are children of wrath, might be counted blessed for Christ's sake. It was done to remove the curse which we all deserve because of sin by laying it on Christ. *Christ redeemed us from the curse of the Law, having become a curse for us* (Galatians 3:13).

Fifthly, we see Jesus reckoned a transgressor and a sinner. *They crucified two robbers with Him.* He who had done no sin, and in whom there was no deceit, *was numbered with transgressors.*

And why was this? It was that we, who are miserable transgressors both by nature and practice, may be reckoned innocent for Christ's sake. It was done that we, who are worthy of nothing but condemnation, may be counted worthy to escape God's judgment and be pronounced not guilty before the assembled world.

Lastly, we see Jesus mocked when dying, as one who was an impostor and unable to save Himself.

And why was this? It was that we, in our last hours, through faith in Christ may have strong consolation. It all came to pass that we may enjoy a strong assurance, may know whom we have believed, and may go down the valley of the shadow of death fearing no evil.

Let us leave the passage with a deep sense of the enormous debt which all believers owe to Christ. All that they have, and are, and hope for may be traced to the doing and dying of the Son of God. Through His condemnation, they have acquittal; through His sufferings, they have peace; through His shame, they have glory; and through His death, they have life. Their sins were imputed to Him. His righteousness is imputed to them. No wonder that Paul says, *Thanks be to God for His indescribable gift!* (2 Corinthians 9:15).

Finally, let us leave the passage with the deepest sense of Christ's unutterable love for our souls. Let us remember what we are – corrupt, evil, and miserable sinners. Let us remember who the Lord Jesus is – the eternal Son of God, the maker of all things. And then let us remember that for our sakes Jesus voluntarily endured the most painful, horrible, and disgraceful death. Surely the thought of this love should constrain us daily to live not unto ourselves but unto Christ. It should make us ready and willing to present our bodies a living sacrifice to Him who lived and died for us (2 Corinthians 5:4; Romans 12:1). Let the cross of Christ be often before our minds. Rightly understood, no object in all Christianity is so likely to have a sanctifying as well as a comforting effect on our souls.

Mark 15:33-38

When the sixth hour came, darkness fell over the whole land until the ninth hour. At the ninth hour Jesus cried out with a loud voice, "Eloi, Eloi, lama sabachthani?" which is translated, "My God, My God, why have You forsaken Me?" When some of the bystanders heard it, they began saying, "Behold, He is calling for Elijah." Someone ran and filled a sponge with sour wine, put it on a reed, and gave Him a drink, saying, "Let us see whether Elijah will come to take Him down." And Jesus uttered a loud cry, and breathed His last. And the veil of the temple was torn in two from top to bottom.

We have in these verses the death of our Lord Jesus Christ. All deaths are solemn events. Nothing in the whole history of a man is so important as his end. But never was there a death of such solemn import as that which is now before us. In the instant that our Lord drew His last breath, the work of atonement for the world's sin was accomplished. The ransom for sinners was at length paid. The kingdom of heaven was thrown fully open to all believers. All the solid hope that mortal men enjoy about their souls may be traced to the giving up of the spirit on the cross.

Let us observe in these verses *the visible signs and wonders which accompanied our Lord's death.* Mark mentions two in particular which demand our attention. One is the darkening of the sun for the space of three hours. The other is the tearing of the veil which divided the holy of holies from the Holy Place in the temple. Both were miraculous events. Both had, no doubt, a deep meaning about them. Both were calculated to arrest the attention of the whole multitude assembled at Jerusalem. The darkness would strike even thoughtless Gentiles like Pilate and the Roman soldiers. The torn veil would strike even Annas and Caiaphas and their unbelieving companions. There were probably few houses in Jerusalem that evening in which men would not say, "We have heard and seen unusual things today."

What did the miraculous darkness teach? It taught the wickedness of the Jewish nation. They were actually crucifying their own Messiah and slaying their own King. The sun itself hid its face at the sight. It taught the exceeding sinfulness of sin in the eyes of God. The Son of God Himself must needs be left without the cheering light of day when He became sin for us and carried our transgressions.

What did the miraculous tearing of the veil mean? It meant the abolition and termination of the whole Jewish law of ceremonies. It meant that the way into the holiest of all was now thrown open to all mankind by Christ's death (Hebrews 9:8). It meant that Gentiles as well as Jews might now draw near to God with boldness through Jesus the one High Priest, and that all barriers between man and God were forever cast down.

May we never forget the practical lesson of the torn veil! To attempt to revive the Jewish ceremonial in the church of Christ by returning to altars, sacrifices, and a priesthood is nothing better than closing up again the torn veil and lighting a candle at noonday.

May we never forget the practical lesson of the miraculous darkness! It should lead our minds on to that blackness of darkness which is reserved for all obstinate unbelievers (Jude v. 13). The darkness endured by our blessed Surety on the cross was only for three hours. The chains of darkness which shall bind all who reject His atonement and die in sin shall be forevermore.

Let us observe secondly in these verses *how truly and really our Lord Jesus Christ was made a curse for us and bore our sins.* We see it strikingly brought out in those marvelous words which He used at the ninth hour: *"My God, My God, why have You forsaken Me?"*

It would be useless to pretend to fathom all the depth of meaning which these words contain. They imply an amount of mental suffering such as we are unable to conceive. The agony of some of God's holiest servants has been occasionally very great under an impression of God's favor being withdrawn from them. What then may we suppose was the agony of the holy Son of God when all the sin of all the world was laid upon His head, when He felt Himself reckoned guilty though without sin, and when He felt His Father's countenance turned away from Him? The agony of that season must have been something past understanding. It is a high thing. We cannot attain to a comprehension of it. We may believe it, but we cannot explain and find it out to perfection.

One thing, however, is very plain, and that is the impossibility of explaining these words at all, except we receive the doctrine of Christ's atonement and substitution for sinners. To suppose, as some dare to do, that Jesus was nothing more than a man, or that His death was only a great example of self-sacrifice, makes this dying cry of His utterly unintelligible. It makes Him appear less patient and calm in a dying hour than many a martyr or even than some heathen philosophers.

One explanation alone is satisfactory. That explanation is the mighty scriptural doctrine of Christ's vicarious sacrifice and substitution for us on the cross. He uttered His dying cry under the heavy pressure of the world's sin laid upon Him and imputed to Him.

Let us observe lastly in these verses that *it is possible to be forsaken by God for a time and yet to be loved by Him*. We need not doubt this when we read our Lord's dying words on the cross. We hear Him saying to His Father, *"Why have You forsaken Me?"* and yet addressing Him as *My God*. We know too that our Lord was only forsaken for a season, and that even when forsaken, He was the beloved Son in whom, both in His suffering and doing, the Father was *well-pleased*.

There is deep experimental instruction in this which deserves the notice of all true Christians. No doubt there is a sense in which our Lord's feeling of being *forsaken* was peculiar to Himself, since He was suffering for our sins and not for His own. But still after making this allowance, there remains the great fact that Jesus was for a time forsaken by the Father, and yet for all that was the Father's *beloved Son*. As it was with the great head of the church, so it may be in a modified sense with His members. They too, though chosen and beloved of the Father, may sometimes feel God's face turned away from them. They too, sometimes from illness of body, sometimes from peculiar affliction, sometimes from carelessness of walk, sometimes from God's sovereign will to draw them nearer to Himself, may be constrained to cry, "My God, my God, why have You forsaken me?"

It becomes believers who feel *forsaken* to learn from our Lord's experience not to give way to despair. No doubt they ought not to be content with their position. They ought to search their own hearts and see whether there is not some secret thing there which causes their consolations to be small (Job 15:11). But let them not write bitter things against themselves and hastily conclude that they are cast off forever, or are self-deceivers and have no grace at all. Let them still wait on the Lord and say with Job, *"Though He slay me, I will hope in Him"* (Job 13:15). Let them remember the words of Isaiah and David: *Who is among you that fears the* LORD, . . . *that walks in darkness and has no light? Let him trust in the name of the* LORD *and rely on his God* (Isaiah 50:10). *Why are you in despair, O my soul? And why have you become disturbed within me? Hope in God, for I shall yet praise Him* (Psalm 42:11).

Mark 15:39-47

When the centurion, who was standing right in front of Him, saw the way He breathed His last, he said, "Truly this man was the Son of God!" There were also some women looking on from a distance, among whom were Mary Magdalene, and Mary the mother of James the Less and Joses, and Salome. When He was in Galilee, they used to follow Him and minister to Him; and there were many other women who came up with Him to Jerusalem. When evening had already come, because it was the preparation day, that is, the day before the Sabbath, Joseph of Arimathea came, a prominent member of the Council, who himself was waiting for the kingdom of God, and he gathered up courage and went in before Pilate, and asked for the body of Jesus. Pilate wondered if He was dead by this time, and summoning the centurion, he questioned him as to whether He was already dead. And ascertaining this from the centurion, he granted the body to Joseph. Joseph bought a linen cloth, took Him down, wrapped Him in the linen cloth and laid Him in a tomb which had been hewn out in the rock; and he rolled a stone against the entrance of the tomb. Mary Magdalene and Mary the mother of Joses were looking on to see where He was laid.

The death of our Lord Jesus Christ is the most important fact in Christianity. On it depend the hopes of all saved sinners both for time and eternity. We need not therefore be surprised to find the reality of His death carefully placed beyond dispute. Three kinds of witnesses to the fact are brought before us in the verses we have now read. The Roman centurion, who stood near the cross – the women, who followed our Lord from Galilee to Jerusalem – the disciples, who buried Him were all witnesses that Jesus really died. Their united evidence is above suspicion. They could not be deceived. What they saw was no swoon, or trance, or temporary insensibility. They saw that same Jesus who was crucified, laid down His life, and became obedient even unto death. Let this be established in our minds. Our Savior really and truly died.

Let us notice, for one thing in this passage, *what honorable mention is here made of women.* We are specially told that when our Lord gave up the spirit, *there were also some women looking on from a distance.* The names of some of them are recorded. We are also told that they were the same who had followed our Lord in Galilee and ministered unto Him, and that *there were many other women who came up with Him to Jerusalem.*

We would hardly have expected to have read such things. We might well have supposed that when all the disciples but one had forsaken our Lord and fled, the weaker and more timid sex would not have dared to show themselves His friends. It only shows us what grace can do. God sometimes chooses the weak things of the world to confound the things that are mighty. The last are sometimes first and the first last. The faith of women sometimes stands upright when the faith of men fails and gives way.

But it is interesting to observe throughout the New Testament how often we find the grace of God glorified in women, and how much benefit God has been pleased to confer through them on the church and on the world. In the Old Testament, we see sin and death brought in by the woman's transgression. In the New, we see Jesus born of a woman, and life and immortality brought to light by that miraculous birth. In the Old Testament, we often see woman proving a hindrance and a snare to man. The women before the flood, the histories of Sarah, Rebekah, Rachel, Delilah, Bathsheba, and Jezebel are all painful examples. In the New Testament, we generally see women mentioned as a help and assistance to the cause of true religion. Elizabeth, Mary, Martha, Dorcas, Lydia, and the women named by Paul to the Romans are all cases in point. The contrast is striking, and we need not doubt intentional. It is one of the many proofs that grace is more abundant under the gospel than under the law. It seems meant to teach us that women have an important place in the church of Christ, one that ought to be assigned to them and one that they ought to fill. There is a great work that women can do for God's glory without being public teachers. Happy is that congregation in which women know this and act upon it!

Let us notice for another thing in this passage that *Jesus has friends of whom little is known*. We cannot conceive a more remarkable proof of this than the person who is here mentioned for the first time, Joseph of Arimathea. We know nothing of this man's history. We know not how he had learned to love Christ and to desire to do Him honor. We know nothing of his subsequent history after our Lord left the world. All we know is the touching collection of facts before us. We are told that he *was waiting for the kingdom of God*, and that at a time when our Lord's disciples had all forsaken Him, he *gathered up courage and went in before Pilate, and asked for the body of Jesus*, and buried it honorably in his own tomb. Others had honored and confessed our Lord when they saw Him working miracles, but Joseph honored Him and confessed himself a disciple when he saw Him a cold, blood-sprinkled corpse. Others had shown love to Jesus while He was speaking and living, but Joseph showed love when He was silent and dead.

Let us take comfort in the thought that there are true Christians on earth of whom we know nothing and in places where we would not expect to find them. No doubt the faithful are always few. But we must not hastily conclude that there is no grace in a family or in a parish because our eyes may not see it. We know in part and see only in part outside the circle in which our own lot is cast. The Lord has many "hidden ones" in the church who, unless brought forward by special circumstances, will never be known until the last day. The words of God to Elijah should not be forgotten: *"Yet I will leave 7,000 in Israel"* (1 Kings 19:18).

Let us notice lastly in this passage *what honor our Lord Jesus Christ has placed on the grave by allowing Himself to be laid in it*. We read that Joseph laid Him *in a tomb which had been hewn out in the rock; and he rolled a stone against the entrance of the tomb*.

This is a fact that in a dying world we should always remember. It is appointed unto men once to die. We are all going to one place, and we naturally shrink from it. The coffin and the funeral, the worm and corruption are all painful subjects. They chill us, sadden us, and fill our minds with heaviness. It is not in flesh and blood to regard them without solemn feelings. One thing, however, ought to comfort believers, and that is the thought that the grave is *the place where He was laying.* As surely as He rose again victorious from the tomb, so surely shall all who believe in Him rise gloriously in the day of His appearing. Remembering this, they may look down with calmness into *the house of meeting for all living* (Job 30:23). They may recollect that Jesus Himself was once there on their behalf and has robbed death of its sting. They may say to themselves, *The sting of death is sin, and the power of sin is the law; but thanks be to God, who gives us the victory through our Lord Jesus Christ* (1 Corinthians 15:56-57).

The great matter that concerns us all is to make sure that we are spiritually buried with Christ while we are yet alive. We must be joined to Him by faith and conformed to His image. With Him we must die to sin and be buried by baptism into His death (Romans 6:4). With Him we must rise again and be quickened by His Spirit. Unless we know these things, Christ's death and burial will profit us nothing at all.

Mark Chapter 16

Mark 16:1-8

When the Sabbath was over, Mary Magdalene, and Mary the mother of James, and Salome, bought spices, so that they might come and anoint Him. Very early on the first day of the week, they came to the tomb when the sun had risen. They were saying to one another, "Who will roll away the stone for us from the entrance of the tomb?" Looking up, they saw that the stone had been rolled away, although it was extremely large. Entering the tomb, they saw a young man sitting at the right, wearing a white robe; and they were amazed. And he said to them, "Do not be amazed; you are looking for Jesus the Nazarene, who has been crucified. He has risen; He is not here; behold, here is the place where they laid Him. But go, tell His disciples and Peter, 'He is going ahead of you to Galilee; there you will see Him, just as He told you.'" They went out and fled from the tomb, for trembling and astonishment had gripped them; and they said nothing to anyone, for they were afraid.

LET US OBSERVE IN THIS PASSAGE *the power of strong love for Christ.* We have a forcible illustration of this in the conduct of Mary Magdalene and the other Mary which Mark here records. He tells us that they had *bought spices* to anoint our Lord and that *very early on the first day of the week, they came to the tomb when the sun had risen.*

We may well believe that it required great courage to do this. To visit the grave in the dim twilight of an eastern daybreak would try most women under any circumstances. But to visit the grave of one who had been put to death as a common malefactor and to rise early to show honor to one whom their nation had despised, this was a mighty boldness indeed. Yet these are the kinds of acts which show the difference between weak faith and strong faith – between weak feeling and strong feeling towards Christ. These holy women had tasted of our Lord's pardoning mercies. Their hearts were full of gratitude to Him for light, and hope, and comfort, and peace. They were willing to risk all consequences in testifying to their affection for their Savior. So true are the words of Solomon: *"Love is as strong as death . . . Many waters cannot quench love, nor will rivers overflow it"* (Song of Solomon 8:6-7).

Why is it that we see so little of this strong love for Jesus among Christians of the present day? How is it that we so seldom meet with saints who will face any danger and go through fire and water for Christ's sake? There is only one answer. It is the weak faith and the low sense of obligation to Christ which so widely prevail. A low and feeble sense of sin will always produce a low and feeble sense of the value of salvation. A slight sense of our debt to God will always be attended by a slight sense of what we owe for our redemption. It is the man who feels much forgiven who loves much. *"He who is forgiven little, loves little"* (Luke 7:47).

Let us observe secondly in this passage *how the difficulties which Christians fear will sometimes disappear as they approach them.* These holy women, as they walked to our Lord's tomb, were full of fears about the stone at the entrance. *They were saying to one another, "Who will roll away the stone for us from the entrance of the tomb?"* But their fears were needless. Their expected trouble was found not to exist. *Looking up, they saw that the stone had been rolled away.*

What a striking emblem we have in this simple narrative of the experience of many Christians! How often believers are oppressed and cast down by anticipation of evils, and yet, in the time of need, find the thing they feared removed and the "stone rolled away." A large proportion of a saint's anxieties arise from things which never really happen. We look ahead to all the possibilities of the journey towards heaven. We conjure up in our imagination all kinds of crosses and obstacles. We mentally carry tomorrow's troubles as well as today's. And often, very often, we find at the end that our doubts and alarms were groundless, and that the thing we dreaded most has never come to pass at all. Let us pray for more practical faith. Let us believe that in the path of duty, we shall never be entirely forsaken. Let us go forward boldly, and we shall often find that the lion in the way is chained, and what appears to be a hedge of thorns is only a shadow.

Let us observe thirdly in this passage *that the friends of Christ have no cause to be amazed by angels.* We are told that when Mary Magdalene and her companion saw an angel sitting in the tomb, *they were amazed.* But they were at once reassured by his words, *"Do not be amazed; you are looking for Jesus the Nazarene, who has been crucified. He has risen; He is not here."*

The lesson at first sight may seem of little importance. We see no visions of angels in the present day. We do not expect to see them. But the lesson is one which we may find useful at some future time. The day is drawing near when the Lord Jesus shall come again to judge the world with all the angels around Him. The angels in that day shall gather together His elect from the four winds. The angels shall gather the tares into bundles to burn them. The angels shall gather the wheat of God into His barn. Those whom the angels take they shall carry to glory, honor, and immortality. Those whom they leave behind shall be left to shame and everlasting contempt.

Let us strive so to live that when we die we may be carried by angels into Abraham's bosom. Let us endeavor to be known by angels as those who seek Jesus, and love Him in this world, and so are heirs of salvation. Let us give diligence to make our repentance sure and so to cause joy in the presence of the angels of God. Then, whether we wake or sleep, when the archangel's voice is heard, we shall have no cause to be amazed. We shall rise from our grave and see in the angels our friends and fellow servants in whose company we shall spend a blessed eternity.

Let us observe lastly in this passage *the exceeding kindness of God towards His backsliding servants.* The message which the angel conveys is a striking illustration of this truth. Mary Magdalene and the other Mary were bidden to tell the disciples that *"He is going ahead of you to Galilee; there you will see Him."* But the message is not directed generally to the eleven apostles. This alone, after their late desertion of their Master, would have been a most gracious action. Yet Peter, who had denied his Lord three times, is specially mentioned by name. Peter, who had sinned particularly, is singled out and noticed particularly. There were to be no exceptions in the deed of grace. All were to be pardoned. All were to be restored to favor – and Peter as well as the rest.

We may well say when we read words like these, "This is not the manner of man." On no point perhaps are our views of religion so narrow, low, and contracted as on the point of God's exceeding willingness to pardon penitent sinners. We think of Him as such a one as ourselves. We forget that *He delights in unchanging love* (Micah 7:18).

Let us leave the passage with a determination to open the door of mercy very wide to sinners in all our speaking and teaching about religion. Not least, let us leave it with a resolution never to be unforgiving towards our fellow men. If Christ is so ready to forgive us, we ought to be very ready to forgive others.

Mark 16:9-14

Now after He had risen early on the first day of the week, He first appeared to Mary Magdalene, from whom He had cast out seven demons. She went and reported to those who had been with Him, while they were mourning and weeping. When they heard that He was alive and had been seen by her, they refused to believe it. After that, He appeared in a different form to two of them while they were walking along on their way to the country. They went away and reported it to the others, but they did not believe them either. Afterward He appeared to the eleven themselves as they were reclining at the table; and He reproached them for their unbelief and hardness of heart, because they had not believed those who had seen Him after He had risen.

Let us observe in these verses *what abundant proof we have that our Lord Jesus Christ really rose again from the dead.* In this one passage

Mark records no less than three distinct occasions on which He was seen after His resurrection. First, he tells us our Lord appeared to one witness, Mary Magdalene – then to two witnesses, two disciples walking into the country – and lastly to eleven witnesses, the eleven apostles all assembled together. Let us remember, in addition to this, that other appearances of our Lord are described by other writers in the New Testament besides those mentioned by Mark. And then let us not hesitate to believe that of all the facts of our Lord's history, there is none more thoroughly established than the fact that He rose from the dead.

There is great mercy in this. The resurrection of Christ is one of the foundation stones of Christianity. It was the seal of the great work that He came on earth to do. It was the crowning proof that the ransom He paid for sinners was accepted, the atonement for sin accomplished, the head of him who had the power of death bruised, and the victory won. It is well to observe how often the resurrection of Christ is referred to by the apostles. *He who was delivered over because of our transgressions,* says Paul, *was raised because of our justification* (Romans 4:25). He *has caused us to be born again to a living hope,* says Peter, *through the resurrection of Jesus Christ from the dead* (1 Peter 1:3).

We ought to thank God that the fact of the resurrection is so clearly established. The Jew, the Gentile, the priests, the Roman guard, the women who went to the tomb, and the disciples who were so hesitant to believe are all witnesses whose testimony cannot be refuted. Christ has not only died for us but has also risen again. To deny it shows far greater credulity than to believe it. To deny it a man must put credit in monstrous and ridiculous improbabilities. To believe it a man has only to appeal to simple, undeniable facts.

Let us observe secondly in these verses *our Lord Jesus Christ's singular kindness to Mary Magdalene.* We are told that *after He had risen early on the first day of the week, He first appeared to Mary Magdalene, from whom He had cast out seven demons.* To her before all others of Adam's children was granted the privilege of being first to behold a risen Savior. Mary, the mother of our Lord, was yet alive. John, the beloved disciple, was yet upon earth. Yet both were passed over on this occasion in favor of Mary Magdalene. A woman who at one time had probably been chief of sinners, a woman who at one time had been possessed by seven demons was the first to whom Jesus showed Himself alive when He rose victorious from the tomb. The fact is remarkable and full of instruction.

We need not doubt, for one thing, that by appearing first to Mary Magdalene our Lord meant to show us how much He values love and faithfulness. Last at the cross and first at the tomb, last to confess her Master while living and first to honor Him when dead, this warmhearted disciple was allowed to be the first to see Him when the victory was won. It was intended to be a perpetual memorial to the church that those who honor Christ He will honor, and that those who do much for Him upon earth shall find Him even upon earth doing much for them. May we never forget this. May we ever remember that for those who forsake all for Christ's sake, they *will receive a hundred times as much now in the present age.*

We need not doubt for another thing that our Lord's appearing first to Mary Magdalene was intended to comfort all who have become penitent believers after having run into great excesses of sin. It was meant to show us that however far we may have fallen, we are raised to entire peace with God if we repent and believe the gospel. Though before far off, we are now made near. Though before enemies, we are now made dear children. Old things are passed away, and all things are become new (2 Corinthians 5:17). The blood of Christ makes us completely clean in God's sight. We may have begun like Augustine and John Newton and been ringleaders in every kind of iniquity. But once brought to Christ, we need not doubt that all is forgiven. We may draw near with boldness and have access with confidence. Our sins and iniquities, like those of Mary Magdalene, are remembered no more.

Let us observe lastly in these verses *how much weakness there is sometimes in the faith of the best Christians.* Three times in this very passage we find Mark describing the unbelief of the eleven apostles. Once when Mary Magdalene told them that our Lord had risen, *they refused to believe it.* Again, when our Lord had appeared to two of them as they walked, we read of the others to whom these two reported it, that *they did not believe them either.* Finally, when our Lord Himself appeared to them *as they were reclining at the table,* we are told that *He reproached them for their unbelief and hardness of heart.* Never, perhaps, was there so striking an example of man's unwillingness to believe that which runs counter to his early prejudices. Never was there so remarkable a proof of man's forgetfulness of plain teaching. These eleven men had been told repeatedly by our Lord that He would rise again. And yet, when the time came, all was forgotten, and they were found unbelieving. Let us, however, see in the doubts of these good men the overruling hand of an all-wise God. If they were convinced at last, who were so unbelieving at first, how strong is the proof supplied us that Christ rose indeed. It is the glory of God to bring good out of evil. The very doubts of the eleven apostles are the confirmation of our faith in these latter days.

Let us learn from the unbelief of the apostles a useful practical lesson for ourselves. Let us cease to feel surprise when we feel doubts arising in our own heart. Let us cease to expect perfection of faith in other believers. We are yet in the body. We are men of like passions with the apostles. We must count it no strange thing if our experience is sometimes like theirs, and if our faith, like theirs, sometimes gives way. Let us resist unbelief manfully. Let us watch, and pray, and strive to be delivered from its power. But let us not conclude that we have no grace because we are sometimes harassed with doubts, nor suppose that we have no part or lot with the apostles because at seasons we feel unbelieving.

Let us not fail to ask ourselves, as we leave this passage, whether we have risen with Christ and been made partakers spiritually of His resurrection. This, after all, is the one thing needful. To know the facts of Christianity with the head and to be able to argue for them with the tongue will not save our souls. We must yield ourselves to God as those alive from the dead (Romans 6:13). We must be raised from the death of sin and walk in newness of life. This and this only is saving Christianity.

Mark 16:15-18

And He said to them, "Go into all the world and preach the gos-
pel to all creation. He who has believed and has been baptized
shall be saved; but he who has disbelieved shall be condemned.
These signs will accompany those who have believed: in My name
they will cast out demons, they will speak with new tongues;
they will pick up serpents, and if they drink any deadly poison, it
will not hurt them; they will lay hands on the sick, and they will
recover."

We ought to notice firstly in these verses *the parting commission which our Lord gives to His apostles.* He is addressing them for the last time. He observes out their work until He comes again in words of wide and deep significance. *"Go into all the world and preach the gospel to all creation."*

The Lord Jesus would have us know that all the world needs the gospel. In every quarter of the globe, man is the same – sinful, cor-rupt, and alienated from God. Civilized or uncivilized, in China or in Africa, he is by nature everywhere the same – without knowledge, without holiness, without faith, and without love. Wherever we see a child of Adam, whatever be his color, we see one whose heart is wicked and who needs the blood of Christ, the renewing of the Holy Spirit, and reconciliation with God.

The Lord Jesus would have us know that the salvation of the gos-pel is to be offered freely to all mankind. The glad tidings that *God so loved the world, that He gave His only begotten Son* (John 3:16) and that *Christ died for the ungodly* (Romans 5:6) is to be proclaimed freely *to all creation.* We are not justified in making any exception in the proc-lamation. We have no warrant for limiting the offer to the elect. We come short of the fullness of Christ's words and take away from the breadth of His sayings if we shrink from telling anyone, "God is full of love for you; Christ is willing to save you." *Let the one who wishes take the water of life without cost* (Revelation 22:17).

Let us see in these words of Christ the strongest argument in favor of missionary work, both at home and abroad. Remembering these words, let us be unwearied in trying to do good to the souls of all mankind. If we cannot go to the heathen in China and India, let us seek to enlighten the darkness which we shall easily find within reach of our own door. Let us labor on, unmoved by the sneers and taunts of those who disapprove of missionary operations and hold them up to scorn. We may well pity such people. They only show their ignorance both of Scripture and of Christ's will. They understand neither what they say nor what they affirm.

We ought to notice secondly in these verses *the terms which our Lord tells us should be offered to all who hear the gospel. "He who has believed and has been baptized shall be saved; but he who has disbelieved shall be condemned."* Every word in that sentence is of deep importance. Every expression in it deserves to be carefully weighed.

We are taught here the importance of baptism. It is an ordinance generally necessary to salvation, where it can be obtained. Not *he who has believed* simply, but he *who has believed and has been baptized shall be saved.* Thousands no doubt receive not the slightest benefit from their baptism. Thousands are washed in sacramental water who are never washed in the blood of Christ. But it does not follow therefore that baptism is to be despised and neglected. It is an ordinance appointed by Christ Himself, and when used reverently, intelligently, and prayerfully, is doubtless accompanied by a special blessing. The baptismal water itself conveys no grace. We must look far beyond the mere outward element to Him who commanded it to be used. But the public confession of Christ, which is implied in the use of that water, is a sacramental act which our Master Himself has commanded, and when the ordinance is rightly used, we may confidently believe that He seals it by His blessing.

We are taught here, furthermore, the absolute necessity of faith in Christ for salvation. This is the one thing needful. *He who has disbelieved* is the man that shall be lost forevermore. He may have been baptized and made a member of the visible church. He may be a regular participant at the Lord's Table. He may even believe intellectually all the leading articles of the creed. But all shall profit him nothing if he lacks saving faith in Christ. Have we this faith? This is the great question that concerns us all. Except we feel our sins, and feeling them flee to Christ by faith and lay hold on Him, we shall find at length it would have been better never to have been born.

We are taught here, furthermore, the certainty of God's judgments on those who die unbelieving. *He who has disbelieved shall be condemned.* How dreadful the words sound! How fearful the thought that they came from the lips of Him who said, *"My words will not pass away."* Let no man deceive us with vain words. There is an eternal hell for all who will persist in their wickedness and depart out of this world without faith in Christ. The greater the mercy offered to us in the gospel, the greater will be the guilt of those who obstinately refuse to believe. *"Would that they were wise, . . . that they would discern their future!"* (Deuteronomy 32:29). He that died upon the cross has given us plain warning that there is a hell, and that unbelievers shall be damned. Let us take heed that His warning is not given to us in vain!

We ought to notice lastly in these verses *the gracious promises of special help which our Lord holds out in His parting words to His apostles.* He knew well the enormous difficulties of the work which He had just commissioned them to do. He knew the mighty battle they would have to fight with heathenism, the world, and the devil. He therefore cheers them by telling them that miracles shall help forward their work. *"These signs will accompany those who have believed: in My name they will cast out demons, they will speak with new tongues; they will pick up serpents, and if they drink any deadly poison, it will not hurt them; they will lay their hands on the sick, and they will recover."* The fulfillment of most of these promises is to be found in the Acts of the Apostles.

The age of miracles no doubt is long past. They were never meant to continue beyond the first establishment of the church. It is only when plants are first planted that they need daily watering and support. The whole analogy of God's dealings with His church forbids us to expect that miracles would always continue. In fact, miracles would cease to be miracles if they happened regularly without cessation or intermission. It is well to remember this. The remembrance may save us much perplexity.

But though the age of physical miracles is past, we may take comfort in the thought that the church of Christ shall never lack Christ's special aid in its seasons of special need. The great Head in heaven will never forsake His believing members. His eye is continually upon them. He will always time His help wisely and come to their support in the day that He is needed. *He will come like a rushing stream which the wind of the* LORD *drives* (Isaiah 59:19).

Finally, let us never forget that Christ's believing church in the world is of itself a standing miracle. The conversion and perseverance in grace of every member of that church is a sign and wonder as great as the raising of Lazarus from the dead. The renewal of every saint is as great a marvel as the casting out of a demon, or the healing of a sick man, or the speaking with a new tongue. Let us thank God for this and take courage. The age of spiritual miracles is not yet past. Happy are they who have learned this by experience and can say, "I was dead, but am alive again; I was blind, but I see."

Mark 16:19-20

So then, when the Lord Jesus had spoken to them, He was received up into heaven and sat down at the right hand of God. And they went out and preached everywhere, while the Lord worked with them, and confirmed the word by the signs that followed.

These words form the conclusion of Mark's Gospel. Short as the passage is, it is a singularly suitable conclusion to the history of our Lord Jesus Christ's earthly ministry. It tells us where our Lord went when He left this world and ascended up on high. It tells us what His disciples experienced after their Master left them and what all true Christians may expect until He appears again.

Let us observe in these verses *the place to which our Lord went when He had finished His work on earth and the place where He is at this present time.* We are told that *He was received up into heaven and sat down at the right hand of God.* He returned to that glory which He had with

269

the Father before He came into the world. He received, as our victorious Mediator and Redeemer, the highest position of dignity and power in heaven which our minds can conceive. There He sits, not idle, but carrying on the same blessed work for which He died on the cross. There He lives, ever making intercession for all who come unto God by Him and so *is able also to save [them] forever* (Hebrews 7:25).

There is strong consolation here for all true Christians. We live in an evil world. We are often anxious and troubled about many things and are severely cast down by our own weakness and infirmities. We live in a dying world. We feel our bodies gradually failing and giving way. We have before us the dreadful prospect of soon launching forth into a world unknown. What then shall comfort us? We must lean back on the thought of our Savior in heaven, never slumbering, never sleeping, and always ready to help. We must remember that though we sleep, Jesus is awake; though we faint, Jesus is never weary; though we are weak, Jesus is almighty; and though we die, Jesus lives forevermore. Blessed indeed is this thought! Our Savior, though unseen, is an actually living person. We travel on toward a dwelling where our best Friend has gone before to prepare a place for us (John 14:2). The Forerunner has entered in and made all things ready. No wonder that Paul exclaims, *Who is the one who condemns? Christ Jesus is He who died, yes, rather who was raised, who is at the right hand of God, who also intercedes for us* (Romans 8:34).

Let us observe, for another thing in these verses, *the blessing which our Lord Jesus Christ bestows on all who work faithfully for Him.* We are told that when the disciples went forth and preached, *the Lord worked with them, and confirmed the word by the signs that followed.*

We know well from the Acts of the Apostles and from the pages of church history the manner in which these words have been proved true. We know that bonds and afflictions, persecution and opposition were the first fruits that were reaped by the laborers in Christ's harvest. But we know also that in spite of every effort of Satan, the word of truth was not preached in vain. Believers from time to time were scattered out into the world. Churches of saints were founded in city after city and country after country. The little seed of Christianity grew gradually into a great tree. Christ Himself worked with His own workmen, and in spite of every obstacle, His work went on. The good seed was never entirely thrown away. Sooner or later there were *signs that followed.*

Let us not doubt that these things were written for our encouragement, on whom the latter ends of the world are come. Let us believe that no one shall ever work faithfully for Christ and find at last that his work has been altogether without profit. Let us labor on patiently, each in our own position. Let us preach, and teach, and speak, and write, and warn, and testify, and rest assured that our labor is not in vain. We may die ourselves and see no result from our work. But the last day will assuredly prove that the Lord Jesus always works with those who work for Him and that there were *signs that followed*, though it was not given to the workmen to see them. Let us then *be steadfast, immovable, always abounding in the work of the Lord* (1 Corinthians 15:58). We may go on our way heavily and sow with many tears, but if we sow Christ's precious seed, we shall *come again with a shout of joy, bringing [our] sheaves with [us]* (Psalm 126:6).

And now let us close the pages of Mark's Gospel with self-inquiry and self-examination. Let it not content us to have seen with our eyes and heard with our ears the things here written for our learning about Jesus Christ. Let us ask ourselves whether we know anything of Christ *dwell[ing] in [our] hearts through faith.* Does the Spirit testify with our spirit (Romans 8:16) that Christ is ours and we are His? Can we really say that we are living *by faith in the son of God* and that we have found by experience that Christ is precious to our own souls? These are solemn questions. They demand serious consideration. May we never rest until we can give them satisfactory answers! *He who has the Son has the life; he who does not have the Son of God does not have the life* (1 John 5:12).

J. C. Ryle – A Brief Biography

JOHN CHARLES RYLE was born into a wealthy, affluent, socially elite family on May 10, 1816 – the firstborn son of John Ryle, a banker, and his wife Susanna (Wirksworth) Ryle. As the firstborn, John lived a privileged life and was set to inherit all of his father's estate and pursue a career in Parliament. His future promised to be planned and comfortable with no material needs.

J. C. Ryle attended a private school and then earned academic scholarships to Eton (1828) and the University of Oxford (1834), but he excelled in sports. He particularly made his mark in rowing and cricket. Though his pursuit of sports was short lived, he claimed that they gave him leadership gifts. "It gave me a power of commanding, managing, organizing and directing, seeing through men's capabilities and using every man in the post to which he was best suited, bearing and forbearing, keeping men around me in good temper, which I have found of infinite use on lots of occasions in life, though in very different matters."

In 1837, before graduation, Ryle contracted a serious chest infection, which caused him to turn to the Bible and prayer for the first time in over fourteen years. One Sunday he entered church late as Ephesians 2:8 was being read – slowly, phrase by phrase. John felt the Lord was speaking to him personally, and he claims to have been converted at that moment through the Word without any commentary or sermon.

His biographer wrote, "He came under conviction, was converted, and from that moment to the last recorded syllable of this life, no doubt ever lingered in John's mind that the Word of God was living and powerful, sharper than any two-edged sword."

After graduation from Oxford, John went to London to study law for his career in politics, but in 1841, his father's bank crashed. That was the end of the career in politics, for he had no funding to continue.

In later years, John wrote, "We got up one summer's morning with all the world before us as usual, and went to bed that same night completely and entirely ruined. The immediate consequences were bitter and painful in the extreme, and humiliating to the utmost degree."

And at another time, he said, "The plain fact was there was no one of the family whom it touched more than it did me. My father and mother were no longer young and in the downhill of life; my brothers and sisters, of course, never expected to live at Henbury (the family home) and naturally never thought of it as their house after a certain time. I, on the contrary, as the eldest son, twenty-five, with all the world before me, lost everything, and saw the whole future of my life turned upside down and thrown into confusion."

After this financial ruin from abundance, Ryle was a commoner – all in a day. For the first time in his life, he needed a job. His education qualified him for the clergy, so with his Oxford degree, he was ordained and entered the ministry of the Church of England. He proceeded in a totally different direction with his first assignment in the ministry at Exbury in Hampshire, but it was a rural area riddled with disease. His recurring lung infection made a difficult couple of years until he was transferred to St. Thomas in Winchester. With his commanding presence, passionately held principles, and warm disposition, John's congregation grew so large and strong it needed different accommodations.

Ryle accepted a position at that time in Helmington, Suffolk, where he had much time to read theologians like Wesley, Bunyan, Knox, Calvin, and Luther. He was a contemporary of Charles Spurgeon, Dwight Moody, George Mueller, and Hudson Taylor. He lived in the age of Dickens, Darwin, and the American Civil War. All of these influenced Ryle's understanding and theology.

His writing career began from the tragedy of the Great Yarmouth suspension bridge. On May 9, 1845, a large crowd gathered for the official grand opening festivities, but the bridge collapsed and more than a hundred people plunged into the water and drowned. The incident shocked the whole country but it led Ryle to write his first tract. He spoke of life's uncertainties and God's sure provision of salvation through Jesus Christ. Thousands of copies were sold.

That same year, he married Matilda Plumptre, but she died after only two years, leaving him with an infant daughter. In 1850, he married Jessie Walker, but she had a lingering sickness, which caused Ryle to care for her and their growing family (three sons and another daughter) for ten years until she died. In 1861, he was transferred to Stradbroke, Suffolk, where he married Henrietta Clowes.

Stradbroke, Suffolk, was Ryle's last parish, and he gained a reputation for his straightforward preaching and evangelism. Besides his travelling and preaching, he spent time writing. He wrote more than 300 pamphlets, tracts, and books. His books include *Expository Thoughts on the Gospels* (7 Volumes, 1856-1869), *Principles for Churchmen* (1884), *Home Truths, Knots Untied, Old Paths,* and *Holiness.*

His *Christian Leaders of the Eighteenth Century* (1869) is described as having "short, pithy sentences, compelling logic and penetrating insight into spiritual power." This seems to be the case with most of his writing as he preached and wrote with five main guidelines: (1) Have a clear view of the subject, (2) Use simple words, (3) Use a simple style of composition, (4) Be direct, and (5) Use plenty of anecdotes and illustrations.

In all of his success with writing, he used the royalties to pay his father's debts. He may have felt indebted to that financial ruin, for he said, "I have not the least doubts, it was all for the best. If I had not been ruined, I should never have been a clergyman, never preached a sermon, or written a tract or book."

In spite of all of the trials that Ryle experienced – financial ruin, loss of three wives, his own poor health – he learned several life lessons. First, care and tend to your own family. Second, swim against the tide when you need to. He was evangelical before it was popular and he held to principles of Scripture: justification by faith alone, substitutionary atonement, the Trinity, and preaching. Third, model Christian attitudes toward your opponents. Fourth, learn and understand church history. Important benefits come from past generations. Fifth, serve in old age; "die in the harness." And, sixth, persevere through your trials.

These were life principles that Ryle learned as he lived his life, as he preached, as he wrote, and as he spread the gospel. He was forever a supporter of evangelism and a critic of ritualism.

J. C. Ryle was recommended by Prime Minister Benjamin Disraeli to be Bishop of Liverpool in 1880 where he then worked to build churches and mission halls to reach the whole city. He retired in 1900 at the age of 83 and died later that year. His successor described him as "a man of granite with a heart of a child."

G. C. B. Davies said "a commanding presence and fearless advocacy of his principles were combined with a kind and understanding attitude in his personal relationships."[14]

14   Sources:
William P. Farley, "J. C. Ryle: A 19th-century Evangelical," *Enrichment Journal,* http://enrichmentjournal.ag.org/200604/200604_120_jcryle.cfm.
"J. C. Ryle," *The Banner of Truth,* https://banneroftruth.org/us/about/banner-authors/j-c-ryle/.
"J. C. Ryle," *Theopedia,* https://www.theopedia.com/john-charles-ryle.
David Holloway, "J. C. Ryle – The Man, The Minister and The Missionary," *Bible Bulletin Board,* http://www.biblebb.com/files/ryle/j_c_ryle.htm.

Other Similar Titles

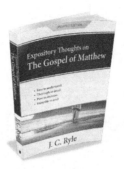

Expository Thoughts on the Gospel of Matthew,
by J. C. Ryle

A Commentary

Therefore everyone who hears these words of Mine and acts on them, may be compared to a wise man who built his house on the rock. – Matthew 7:24

Wisdom, encouragement, and exhortation is contained in these pages. Not because of the author's brilliance, but because of the words of truth contained in the gospel of John. And just as the Apostle John didn't draw any attention to himself, so also J. C. Ryle clearly and wonder-fully directs his words and our thoughts towards the inspired words of scripture. If we truly love God, we will love His word; and the more study His word, the more we will love God.

Available where books are sold.

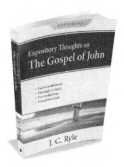

Expository Thoughts on the Gospel of John,
by J. C. Ryle

A Commentary

In the beginning was the Word, and the Word was with God, and the Word was God. – John 1:1

Wisdom, encouragement, and exhortation is contained in these pages. Not because of the author's brilliance, but because of the words of truth contained in the gospel of John. And just as the Apostle John didn't draw any attention to himself, so also J. C. Ryle clearly and wonderfully directs his words and our thoughts towards the inspired words of scripture. If we truly love God, we will love His word; and the more study His word, the more we will love God.

Available where books are sold.

Holiness
by J. C. Ryle

A thorough study of sin, salvation by faith, and the Christian's journey of sanctification.

He who wants a correct understanding of holiness must first begin by examining the vast and solemn subject of sin. He must dig down very deep if he wants to build high. Wrong views about holiness are generally traceable to wrong views about human corruption.

Practical holiness and entire self-consecration to God are not given adequate attention by modern Christians. The unsaved sometimes rightly complain that Christians are not as kind and unselfish and good-natured as those who make no profession of faith. Far too many Christians make a verbal proclamation of faith, yet remain unchanged in heart and lifestyle. But Scripture makes it clear that holiness, in its place and proportion, is quite as important as justification. Holiness, without which no one shall see the Lord (Hebrews 12:14). It is imperative that Christians are biblically and truly holy.

The aim of this book is to instruct you, equip you, and encourage you in the pursuit of holiness.

Available where books are sold.

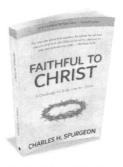

Faithful to Christ,
by Charles H. Spurgeon

If there is a true faith, there must be a declaration of it. If you are a candle, and God has lit you, then let your light so shine before men that they may see your good works and glorify your Father who is in the heavens (Matthew 5:16). Soldiers of Christ must, like soldiers of our nation, wear their uniforms; and if they are ashamed of their uniforms, they ought to be drummed out of the army.

I believe that many Christians get into a lot of trouble by not being honest in their convictions. For instance, if a person goes into a workshop, or a soldier into a barracks, and if he does not fly his flag from the beginning, it will be very difficult for him to run it up afterwards. But if he immediately and boldly lets them know, "I am a Christian, and there are certain things that I cannot do to please you, and certain other things that I cannot help doing even though they might displease you" – when that is clearly understood, after a while the peculiarity of the thing will be gone, and the person will be let alone.

– Charles H. Spurgeon

Available where books are sold.

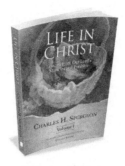

Life in Christ,
by Charles H. Spurgeon

Volume 1

Men who were led by the hand or groped their way along the wall to reach Jesus were touched by his finger and went home without a guide, rejoicing that Jesus Christ had opened their eyes. Jesus is still able to perform such miracles. And, with the power of the Holy Spirit, his Word will be expounded and we'll watch for the signs to follow, expecting to see them at once. Why shouldn't those who read this be blessed with the light of heaven? This is my heart's inmost desire.

I can't put fine words together. I've never studied speech. In fact, my heart loathes the very thought of intentionally speaking with fine words when souls are in danger of eternal separation from God. No, I work to speak straight to your hearts and consciences, and if there is anyone with faith to receive, God will bless them with fresh revelation.

– Charles H. Spurgeon

Available where books are sold.

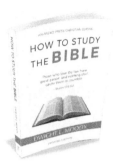

How to Study the Bible,
by Dwight L. Moody

There is no situation in life for which you cannot find some word of consolation in Scripture. If you are in affliction, if you are in adversity and trial, there is a promise for you. In joy and sorrow, in health and in sickness, in poverty and in riches, in every condition of life, God has a promise stored up in His Word for you.

This classic book by Dwight L. Moody brings to light the necessity of studying the Scriptures, presents methods which help stimulate excitement for the Scriptures, and offers tools to help you comprehend the difficult passages in the Scriptures. To live a victorious Christian life, you must read and understand what God is saying to you. Moody is a master of using stories to illustrate what he is saying, and you will be both inspired and convicted to pursue truth from the pages of God's Word.

Available where books are sold.

Absolute Surrender,
by Andrew Murray

God waits to bless us in a way beyond what we expect. From the beginning, ear has not heard, neither has the eye seen, what God has prepared for those who wait for Him (Isaiah 64:4). God has prepared unheard of things, things you never can think of, blessings much more wonderful than you can imagine and mightier than you can conceive. They are divine blessings. Oh, come at once and say, "I give myself absolutely to God, to His will, to do only what God wants." God will enable you to carry out the surrender necessary, if you come to Him with a sincere heart.

Available where books are sold.

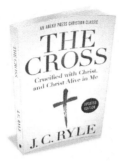

The Cross,
by J. C. Ryle

I want to tell you what perhaps the greatest Christian who ever lived (the Apostle Paul) thought of the cross of Christ. Believe me, the cross is of deepest importance. This is no mere question of controversy; this is not one of those points on which men may agree to differ and feel that differences will not shut them out of heaven. A man must be right on this subject, or he is lost forever. Heaven or hell, happiness or misery, life or death, blessing or cursing in the last day – all hinges on the answer to this question: "What do you think about the cross of Christ?"

Available where books are sold.